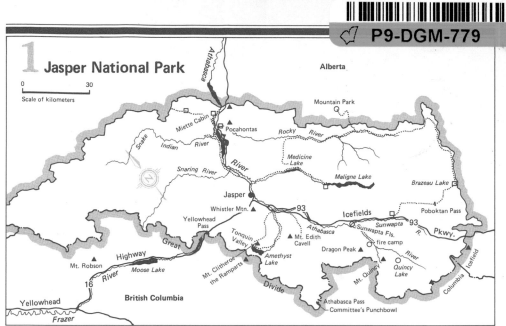

1 Jasper National Park

Scale of kilometers
0   30

Alberta

British Columbia

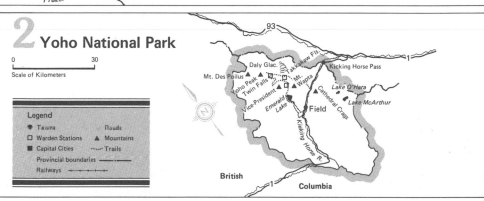

2 Yoho National Park

Scale of Kilometers
0   30

Legend

- ● Towns
- □ Warden Stations
- ■ Capital Cities
- Provincial boundaries
- Railways

Roads
▲ Mountains
······ Trails

British

Columbia

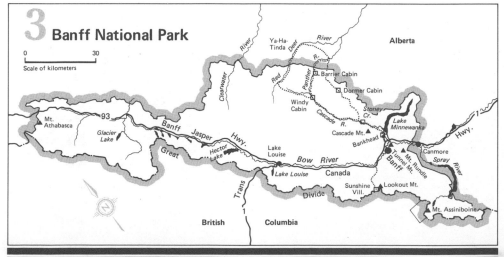

3 Banff National Park

Scale of kilometers
0   30

Alberta

British   Columbia

Men for the Mountains

Men For The Mountains

Sid Marty

The Vanguard Press, Inc.

917.1

Library of Congress Catalogue Card Number: 78-71651

ISBN: 0-8149-0812-8

1 2 3 4 5 6 7 8 9

To the men and women of the national parks'
Warden Service, past, present, and future.

To my sons Paul and Nathan, for showing
patience far beyond their tender years, and most
of all to Myrna, first editor and only muse, whose
love makes all things possible.

Acknowledgements

I would like to thank the following individuals and agencies for their support and assistance during the last three years:

Mary Alice Stewart, former Head Archivist, and E.J. Hart, present Head Archivist, of the Archives of the Canadian Rockies in Banff, who, along with their staff, helped immeasurably in researching this book; thanks to the Ontario Arts Council for a grant when it was needed most; and to the Banff Centre for providing space in which to write.

I am grateful to Mac Elder and Jim Sime of Parks Canada for putting me in touch with some of the old timers; a special thanks to the old timers themselves; to former wardens Frank Wells, George Camp, Malcolm McNab, Frank Burstrom, the late J.C. "Bo" Holroyd, and former guide and outfitter, James Boyce, for sharing their experiences with me. Thanks also to Mona Matheson, Shirley Klettl, and Julie Winkler, for their accounts of the life of a warden's wife in the backcountry.

Lines from "Inflation" and "Sentences" taken from *Emergency Poems* by Nicanor Parra, translation by Miller Williams. Copyright© 1972 by Miller Williams and Nicanor Parra. Reprinted by permission of New Directions Publishing Corporation, New York, and Marion Boyars Publishers Ltd., London.

"The Parks are hereby dedicated to the people of Canada for their benefit, education and enjoyment ... and such Parks shall be maintained and made use of so as to leave them unimpaired for the enjoyment of future generations."
—National Parks Act, 1930

Invocation

It was a windy, moonlit night with the teeth of winter in its breath, and a skiff of new snow glowed under the lunar sky. I had mixed a hot rum toddy and drank it in front of the fire before turning in.

I was alone; that is to say, there was no human company. But I have never really been alone in the mountains; in fact, it's impossible to be alone there. Whole species crawl on the back of a horse. Turn up a stone and constellations of life flash and speed away in orbits under the earth. A moose comes down in two days from the high country and runs my horses out of the meadow. Two days later he's gone, and a black bear runt is scratching on the cabin door of nights, reappearing every two weeks to steal oats from the box under the porch.

For the mice who temporarily share the mattress, for the bear and other predators, the cabin is a landmark to be sought out on their rounds of habit. It is enough of man's presence to arouse their curiosity and remind them to be afraid when they leave the safety of the park valleys and cross the boundary where the settlements and the hunters' guns are waiting.

For company that night I had my two horses feeding in the meadows and a herd of elk, watched over by an old bull, which chased me back to the cabin when, while counting heads, I ventured too close to his harem.

7

The faint murmur of the creek had lulled me to sleep. Around midnight I was startled awake. It was dead quiet for a moment, then there came a shrill, whistling cry that modulated effortlessly down the scales between the timbre of a flute and a clarinet, haunting and wild.

A young bull elk was standing a few feet away from the cabin. I could hear him raking the earth with his forefeet, bugling a challenge to the harem master, the old bull. I heard the drumming of hooves and the clack of antlers as they met in the moonlight. I pulled the sleeping bag closer around my neck. It was the right place to be on a cold night, and the herd was conveniently close for watching over, in case a poacher slipped into my demesne to spoil the mating ritual with his rifle. I heard the reassuring cling of the bell on Cathy, my white mare. Through my two windows I could see the silver outline of mountains leaning over the cabin. A log crackled in the heater; my world was in order.

Then the wind picked up in a sighing gust and a shutter bumped against the wall. I had the habit of leaving the door partly ajar to let in fresh air and now I heard it swing open with a bang. Moonlight flooded into the room, along with a sheaf of poplar leaves, mixed with fine snow. I got out of bed, shivering in the sudden cold, and went to the door to close it. Outside, I saw the moonlight shining on their antlers, as the two powerful bulls pushed back and forth over the snowy meadow.

Suddenly, a human voice shattered my solitude.

"Can't a man get a cup of coffee in this shack?" it said from the darkness behind me.

My hair stood up and I spun around to stare into the dimly-lit room. Three figures sat around the Herald heater. There was a movement from one of them toward the wood box, then the heater door opened with a squeal of iron hinges and there came a clunk as a log was tossed inside. The flames flared up.

I edged back toward the door, frightened, ready to run for it. It seemed that the weeks I had spent without the sound of another human voice had preyed on my mind after all. "Must be bushed," I said to myself, "hearing things, seeing things," and I reached for the doorknob.

"I wouldn't go out there buck naked if I was you, pilgrim," the voice warned me. "It's colder than a mother-in-law's kiss out there."

"You call this cold?" said the first voice, scoffing. "Why

8

hell's bells, man. You young bush apes don't know what cold means. I've seen it so cold in these mountains here that the gawdamn whiskey-jacks had to pull the friggin' squirrels to get 'em started."

The third man laughed. I shook my head and blinked, but the apparition persisted. Deciding to go along with whatever was happening, I edged by the three of them, got my jeans and wool shirt and put them on.

The moon picked out the features of my uninvited guests. Dressed in antique stetsons, with high, round crowns, they sat regarding me, while the ruddy light of the open heater danced and flickered on their weathered faces. One wore a tattered buckskin jacket and his rifle leaned against the wall within easy reach. The others wore thick wool mackinaws, and the biggest man had a heavy revolver holstered on one hip. The firelight glinted on a badge, worn on the buckskin coat, and I could see the insignia: "Fire and Game Warden, RMP."

RMP could only mean Rocky Mountains Park, the name by which Banff had once been known. But badges like that hadn't been issued for over thirty years.

"What the hell?" I muttered fearfully.

"Who the hell, you mean," said the big man, amiably. "Just leave that contraption alone. No sense in wasting fuel," he added, stopping me in the act of reaching for the Coleman lantern.

I had thought that some manufactured light would dispel the apparition. I saw his friendly smile. "Is this some kind of joke?" I demanded.

"Well, I guess I'd better introduce the delegation," he said, as if he hadn't heard me. He cocked his wide-brimmed hat back with the front of one hand, and cleared his throat. "On my right is Bill Peyto, from Rocky Mountains Park. This gloomy-looking galoot is Bill Neish, also from Rocky, and I'm George Busby, from the Jasper outfit."

"Very funny," I ventured.

Busby drew his hat down over his forehead and held his hands out to the flames. "Funny?" he said quietly. "What's funny about it? I call it funny that I catch you campin' in my shack here without my permission," he said, his voice taking on an edge of menace as he stared into the flames.

I met the appraising eyes of the other two, who sat silently in the shadows. Their reputations were well-known in the Warden Service. Bill Peyto's eyes glittered like the play of

9

blue water over granite. He was noted for a variety of eccentricities, such as silencing alarm clocks permanently with one shot from his revolver, or snowshoeing down Banff Avenue, on one of his brief forays into town, while eating a raw and bloody steak, alarming the tourists.

Bill Neish's eyes were even harder to meet. He had once shot it out with two fugitives who had gunned down four policemen. Neish called on them to surrender, but they opened fire on him instead, a fatal mistake. Neish was a man of action, not words. In his warden diary that day he made one terse entry: "Oct. 7th. Shot two bandits."

When the Director of National Parks in Ottawa telegraphed, demanding a more detailed report, he wrote back: "Oct. 7th. Shot two bandits. Snowing like hell."

I turned back to Busby. "Did you say your cabin?"

"Damn right. I built her by hand with nothing but an axe, every log of her. Skidded 'em down with old Ned, finest old packhorse these hills ever saw." He looked around, proudly. "An' she's still tight and snug. Lookit the fit of them corners."

I looked at him. The shack was a frame building, the walls of shiplap, built on the old cabin site. The eyes of the other two watched my reaction, daring me to contradict the old timer.

"How about that coffee, pilgrim?" said Peyto. "Call yourself a warden, and you don't offer a man a cup of coffee on a cold night like this?"

"Sorry." I got out the cups and handed them around. They helped themselves from the pot that was simmering on the back of the heater. "Cream and sugar?" The words echoed hollowly in the room.

"Cream and sugar, my ass," said Neish. He pulled out a bottle of rum from his coat. "I've got the snakebite oil right here."

"And I brought a sack of snakes," said Peyto, still watching me suspiciously as Neish proffered the bottle. I declined, but Peyto cautioned, "I don't trust a man who won't drink with me."

I took a slug and flinched as the molten liquor burned right down to my toes. My veins bristled, as if shot with electricity. It was a brew I had never tasted before. Neish grinned for the first time, and the corners of Peyto's drooping moustache lifted slightly.

"Ain't that a piss-cutter?" Busby chuckled. The wind moaned in answer outside, and the three stirred uneasily.

"Better get on with it, George," Neish said.

10

"All right. It's about this here story book yer writin' on, kid. Seems to me this here book of yours has "eye" trouble. I done this and I done that—what about the rest of us? We figger we should be in there too somewheres."

I thought, "So that's the reason for this visitation." Busby had put his finger on something that had been bothering me for a long time.

"Yeah," Peyto growled, "'stead of blowin' your own horn all the time. Here, have another snort. Looks like you could use it."

I took another shot, feeling braver by the moment. "Well, the trouble is with subjective non-fiction like this, it has to be first person, and . . . "

"The hell you say! That's another thing, all them big words. What's a body to make of it all? Here. Have another shot."

I drank it, almost eagerly, and felt the spirits taking me over. "All right. I'll get you in there somewhere."

"That's right," Busby said emphatically. "Just kinda throw some in, buckshee like."

The bottle went around the circle. "Another thing," he went on, "tell about the women. Them that was tough enough to live out here in the high lonesome with us. Now there's a real story."

"Women!" Peyto interjected. "To hell with that. One of them tried to poison me once. Leave 'em out."

"Bullshit," said Neish quietly. He and Peyto glared at each other.

"Hell's bells, Peyto," said Busby, "are you sure it wasn't herself she was tryin' to poison, after livin' with you . . .? No kid, you get the women in there somewheres. Nobody ever gave them credit for nothin'."

"Okay."

They sat quietly for a moment, staring into the fire. Busby took out a tin of snoose and tucked a bite into his lower lip. "Well now, kid, one thing we'd like to know. How you gonna treat them bureau-craps and windbags in yer story? You gonna tell the truth about them?"

"How do you mean?"

"You know. Them with the shiny-assed breeches and the soft hands. Always figurin' and schemin' how to build another road into the high country. Them that always smiles with a closed mouth so a man can't see their forked tongue."

"Well," I ventured uneasily, "that's been bothering me.

11

Frankly, I don't know if this book is the place to engage in polemics. It's basically a story . . . "

"There he goes again!" said Neish angrily, "spoutin' them jaw-breaker words. You talk to him, Peyto. Yer the one's got the schoolin'."

Peyto fixed me with his glittering eyes, freezing me as I sat by the hot stove. "Now you listen well. There's a special place on the far side of the mountains for bureaucrats, and right beside it is the place for writers that lie."

"What kind of place?" I asked anxiously.

"I'll tell you this much. There ain't no mountains there, there ain't no big rivers boilin' down between the spruce. There ain't no grizzlies prowlin' through the slides, makin' a man's blood tingle, makin' him thank God to be alive. No panthers, no wapiti buglin' outside the cabin. Nothin' living. She's flat there and she's *safe*. Flat as a pool table, white as paper. The sun is God's eye, and there ain't no shadows for a liar to hide in."

He sat back in his chair, still watching me.

"All right. I'll tell both sides of the story, the good and the bad."

"Let's seal the bargain," said Busby. "Kill the bottle."

As I drank, the door blew open again. I set the bottle down and went to close it. "While you boys are here, why don't you tell me a bit about yourselves. All I really know about you is what's been handed down by word of mouth."

In the open doorway I felt the cold night air pressing in and heard the clack of antler on antler, saw the light shining still on the wicked horns, as the two bulls fought back and forth, tearing up the ground. The old bull was weakening but the battle wasn't over quite yet.

"Some other time," Busby answered.

I turned around but they were gone. There was a bottle on the table and three cups. I picked one up, and found the coffee was ice cold. On the floor was a skiff of snow, and a sheaf of yellow poplar leaves.

The bottle was empty. I lit the lantern, got out paper and pencil and started writing.

1

A Little Knowledge
Can Be Dangerous

"The ability to laugh at one's self can
be the beginning of a lifetime of comedy."

Brian H. Coulter

Lowlying clouds streamed restlessly between the peaks like runaway horses in a high wind, their tails floating out behind them. Last night's rain glistened on the earth, and along the gnarled branches of the spruce. It shone on the log bars of the corral, outlining them against the dark blue wedge of Mount Rundle, which towers over the town of Banff, its white crest rising above the battered stetson of the horse guide as he sat on a top rail, his tobacco pouch lying on the leather thigh of his chaps. Behind him, the horses stuck their noses enquiringly between the bars, breath steaming out in the cold dawn, smelling dude. The guide licked his cigarette paper and looked at me again as he rolled the white cylinder, considering.

Waves of cool earth smells washed up from the ground on that May morning, and the tang of wet spruce forest rode the wind along with another smell, powerful and acrid as the gardens of my prairie childhood, rank with decay and with the promise of green things stirring amid the dead cells of the old. The smell persisted. It was emanating, I discovered, following the cowboy's curious gaze, from a pile of still steaming crap that I had stepped in, which was caked like chocolate dough between the treads of my Vibram-soled climbing boots. Picking up a stick, I went to work scraping it out, determined not to flinch from the mission that had brought me to Martin's Corrals. The stuff was like glue. I swore quietly.

"Horseshit is right," said the cowboy, seconding my diagnosis. "You said a mouthful, Slim." He zipped up his down vest and slid off his perch, the cigarette bobbing from the corner of his mouth. "But what the hell. From what you tell me, you're gonna need all the help you can get. If you want to rent a horse, I'll show you a few things."

I slid between the bars and followed him to the barn. It was the beginning of my apprenticeship to the horse business. I'd just returned west from Sir George Williams University in Montreal to find a letter waiting for me at my parents' home in Calgary. It was a job offer from the Chief Warden of Yoho National Park, B.C., which lies about forty-five miles west of Banff, on the west side of the Great Divide. I'd worked there two summers between university terms as an assistant warden at Lake O'Hara, and had been looking forward to returning there all through the long Quebec winter. O'Hara is a high alpine area where many of the trails are little more than mountaineering routes, and where the assistant warden, unlike in most other districts, did his patrols and his trail maintenance on foot. However, bureaucracy moves in strange ways, and is inordinately suspicious of any employee who is happy at his work. A Chief Warden is, by definition, someone who is convinced that somehow, somewhere, somebody in the park is having a good time. The letter informed me that I'd been transferred to Takakkaw Falls where I would be issued two horses, one to ride and one on which to pack my equipment. The letter darkly hinted that the length of my job might well depend on how well I got along with the horses.

Most of the veteran wardens had been raised with horses or had learned that part of the trade working as guides or outfitters before they joined the service. Since I had neither ridden nor packed, and since the alternative to working for the Warden Service was likely to be swinging a pick on the chain gang (park trail crew), I was worried.

But not for nothing had I spent four winters in university, poring over the printed word in classroom and library. My education had prepared me to deal with all of life's problems—or so I chose to believe, as would anyone who had gotten as far in debt as I had to pay for it. So when a problem reared its warty brow, I did the logical, educated thing—I bought a book about it. It was in my duffle, a learned tome entitled *Everything You Need to Know About Horses*. I had had enough experience in the real world to suspect that not quite everything can be learned from books, so now I stopped in Banff to get some practical instruction to illustrate my text. I had bribed the cowboy to show me how to dress a horse. On the hoof.

"It's all in the sashay, Slim," my professor explained, "and that's the whole shiteree. You've got to run a bluff on these ponies."

"Not to mention the Chief Warden," I thought to myself.

We ambled into the hay and dung smell of the barn. A string of horses trotted in behind us and went to their stalls for their morning feeding. Sets of leather tack, looking somewhat different from the pictures in my book, were hung from wooden pegs on one wall. I grabbed a saddle as confidently as if it were a briefcase, and suddenly found myself lying in the dirt with the horn sticking me in the gut. Those things are heavy.

"That goes on the horse, not the rider," said the cowboy. "Jest grab the saddle under the horn, and sashay up to yer plug this a-way," he directed, hoisting the saddle casually up by one hand. Dragging the stirrups in the dust and displaying a pair of legs set wide enough to straddle a small elephant, he sauntered arrogantly up to a nearby horse. I tottered along behind him, walking on the sides of my boots to try and emulate his simian-like grace, but it was hopeless. My legs were straight and set in their ways, thanks to a mother who had gone without luxuries to make sure I had plenty of milk as a boy. The lesson continued.

"Stand up to the horse's shoulder, Slim," the cowboy ordered. "That way he can't strike at you with his forefeet. If he's a real wildie, you can always sink yer teeth in his ear; it's an old trick that gentles 'em down in a hurry."

The horse in question seemed to be asleep. "Them warden horses ain't tame like these dude ponies," he said, sensing my disbelief. "They get fat and sassy from eatin' good grain, just like the folks that ride 'em."

I grunted knowingly, as if ear biting was a long-mastered art with me, and tried the edge of my canines with my tongue. They definitely needed stropping, preferably on a thick, juicy steak. I hadn't had a square meal in the last eight months at university.

He showed me how to bridle the horse, how to get it to open its mouth by gingerly inserting the middle finger between its back molars. "Shove it in there, Slim. Jesus. You're as nervous as a bridegroom on his wedding night." Then I practised tying

15

the cinch knot, keeping a weather eye peeled for a rain of flying hooves.

After an hour's practice with the tack, and a lesson on boarding and disembarking, along with a few tips on how the angle of the ears was a reliable semaphore that might preface the sudden elevating of the hindquarters, followed by the violent ejection of the pilot, my teacher said, "Well, that's about five bucks' worth. In my experience, too much-knowledge can be fatal to yer average greenhorn." We hung the tack back on the wall. "There is one other thing, though," he added. "If you intend to ride in those climbing boots, better make sure the Chief Warden knows where to ship the ree-mains."

"Dangerous, eh?"

"Deadly. They could slip through the stirrup if your horse bucked, and you'd get dragged to death."

I winced at the thought. "Thanks. I was planning to buy riding boots and a hat. Anything else you figure I'll need?"

"Yeah," he said with a tight smile. "Buy yourself a rosary. And before you step on yer first shitter, go once around the beads."

"Hell. You could at least wish me luck."

"Kid," he said, "where you're going, luck ain't got nothin' to do with it."

Undeterred, I sashayed downtown to buy some saddle duds. I bought a pair of suede riding boots, the cheapest available, paying about five bucks more for the privilege of buying them in Banff than they would have cost back in Stampede City. Then I picked out a ten-gallon hat, which cost about two dollars per gallon. Actually, that rag wouldn't have held even a pint of water. After the first heavy rainstorm, it surrendered its high, lonesome look and collapsed around my ears into a soggy felt toque, which served as a wick for letting off the head of steam I worked up, cursing the manufacturer.

All duded up in my Rexall regalia, I got the Volks reined around and headed west for Yoho Park, the new hat being slowly hammered down around my ears by the low roof every time we hit a bump in the road.

I wasn't too enthusiastic about the horse business, it must be admitted, and the talk of kicking and ear biting didn't help. My first horsey-back ride at age ten had been my last. It ended with me getting bucked off into a dense bed of prickly-pear cactus. As a climber and a hiker, I shared the prejudices of my fellow heel-peelers when these centred on horses. Legend had it that they turned the trails into mud holes, and that their dung spoiled the look of one's nifty sixty-dollar climbing boots. After all, how can you impress the girls in the Varsity Outdoor Club, walking through the student lounge with horse-shit trailing out of your waffle-stompers? To my generation, dressing like a hick was *de rigueur*; smelling like one was quite another thing. After all, we had been raised in the age of television, where the popular image dictates that we must spend half our lives sniffing our armpits for telltale odours.

All in all, I seldom thought of horses without a feeling of trepidation, remembering that painful hour bent over my mother's knee, while she plucked those long spines of cactus out of my blushing behind. You might say that the very thought of horses gave me a pain in the ass. Yet my dark mood could not last long on such a fine spring day. Even though there was still snow near the summit of the Great Divide at 5,332 feet, it could not last long. Spring was promised by the homely resurrection of last winter's beer bottles, slowly lifting their necks from the thawing ditches to salute a platoon of empty Kentucky Fried Chicken buckets that some clown had thrown out on the road. There was even a robin, resting on the black limb of a spruce, regarding the deep drifts that hid the frozen worm of its desire.

The battered Volkswagen rolled up the last incline of the Kicking Horse Pass and over the summit of the Great Divide with a weary cough and a triumphant blast of the horn. It was downhill all the way to the town of Field, headquarters of Yoho Park, on the Trans-Canada Highway. The park was named with an Indian word that is a shout of joy, kind of a cross between "Godalmighty!" and "hot damn!" and I hollered something like it myself as the blaze of ice and snow poured in through the dirt-stained windows of the car, reflected off the ice-capped ridges of Cathedral Crags and Mount Stephen above me. A small ocean of ice beamed down on the pass, poised in elegant imminence high above the toothpick scale of avalanche sheds on the CPR main line, which parallels the highway through the Rockies. It was good to be back in the mountains.

Far below, the silver run of the Kicking Horse River yawned open in its jagged canyon. There was that name again, spoiling the festive mood with its ominous image. Sir James Hector of the Palliser expedition had named it. The idea came to him suddenly one day in 1858, when a crusty pack pony teed off on him, knocking him senseless. His Canadian guides, tired of making history on empty stomachs, were not prone to grieve overlong. They'd already begun to bury the gent, when he inconveniently came to, and finding himself speechless, managed to wink one eye to show them he wasn't dead, or perhaps to show he could take a joke. At any rate, the pass got its colourful name.

Down the hill I clattered, mufflerless, and in a few minutes drove into Field, where the park headquarters is overlooked by ten and eleven thousand foot mountains. Neil Woledge, the Chief Warden, welcomed me back for the season, and ordered me to get my hair cut.

"I just got it cut," I protested.

"Get it cut again," Neil ordered. "You look like one of them goo-roos."

Genialities concluded, I looked up my boss, Gord Rutherford. Takakkaw Falls was part of his district. Gordon gave me a friendlier reception, and took me over to the park stores where I mortgaged a set of khaki uniforms bearing national parks badges. They had two sizes: too big and too small—if it fits, you're abnormal. Gord told me to drive up to the falls and get moved in, and he'd be up to see me in a day or two. I stashed the jackets, shirts, and two useless green ties in the back seat of Hitler's Revenge, and headed for the local grocery where I bought all that my remaining cash would allow; four cans of tomato soup and a loaf of bread. Then I drove back down the highway to the junction with the Takakkaw Falls road.

———

The Yoho River is a brawling froth of a stream, white with glacial silt, which flows down into the quieter run of the Kicking Horse below the Big Hill east of Field. The road swings north from the Trans-Canada Highway, following the Yoho River for a few miles to the mouth of its canyon. Then it winds up a couple of switchbacks tight enough to kink a snake. These switchbacks have reduced more than one bus driver to tears, and put ten years on a certain warden I know when the loose wheel nuts on his truck suddenly sent a tire flying out into space like an ugly, black frisbee. A guard-rail at that place helps to keep the hapless from zooming yoho into eternity.

The road winds up around the side of Mount Wapta and across the remains of two avalanches. On this May day, walls of dirty snow still rose twenty feet above the car. Then,

18

through a rift in the timber, I saw the big silver mane of Tak-akkaw Falls streaming out into thin air. Takakkaw, a Stoney word, means "it is wonderful."

Up above that 1,200 foot drop the long tongue of the Daly Glacier reaches down from several hundred square miles of ice that stretch north to the Columbia Icefield in Jasper National Park. At its apex, the ice is up to three thousand feet thick. Studded with sharply-defined mountain peaks, this ice mass is the source of river systems that empty into three oceans. These rivers start as meltwater, percolating down through cracks in the ice under the magnified glare of the spring sun. Under the mill of gravity, the water collects at the toe of the glaciers, a million strands join into one current, sometimes white with rock flour, ground up by the slow-moving ice. At Takakkaw, a hard band of rock forces it into a narrow cleft at the brink of the falls. Tons and tons of water, set completely free of the rock, fall and then smash on the long, black wall of the cliffs.

In a way, the big waterworks belonged to me now, since I was the resident Mayor, Police Chief, and Water Inspector. Looking at the falls, I hoped the plumbing didn't expect any macroscopic adjustments from my microscopic capabilities.

I pulled up in front of the log warden cabin and got out of the car. Here was the centre of operations for seventy square miles of mountains, rivers, glaciers, and streams, all bounded by the drainage of the Yoho River, all mine to oversee until September, provided I could get along with the horses. The scent of moss and the wet smell of marine life wafted up from the river below my cabin, cleansing my head of engine fumes and stale air. I breathed in deeply, exulting in the fragrance, like a man welcomed back to his lover's perfumed arms after a long absence.

The cabin was well-chinked and sound-looking, painted in the dark brown colour that was in favour with the National Parks Service at that time. A huge mound of firewood overflowed from the porch, and two cords of unsplit butts, some of it still covered with lingering snow, were piled in the yard. The last patrolman had been a lonely young German with limitless ambitions and inexhaustible energy. I might starve to death up here, might even get a little bushed, but I sure as hell wouldn't freeze for lack of firewood.

I opened the shutters, kept locked to discourage bears, wolverines, and two-footed vandals from breaking in, and opened the door with my warden passkey. Inside, it smelled of warm spruce logs, soap, and fresh oil cloth. I stood for a minute letting my eyes adjust to the darker light of the room, and then looked around. An enamelled floor, done in the government's battleship grey, gleamed from the scrubbing given it by the last owner. Mattresses and piles of red Hudson's Bay blankets hung from wires, safely out of the reach of pack rats or mice, which could work their way in through a loose chink. A Quebec heater, well-used by the look of it, dominated the centre of the room with friendly iron ugliness. In one corner stood a white enamelled wood-stove bearing a heraldic trademark with the word "Enterprise" worked into the door in brass. It stood near the door, under a wall hung with polished cook pots.

Like all district wardens, the last man had been a stickler for cleanliness. There was a time when the Warden Service used to believe that the dingiest shack was still public property, which must serve as an office where people could come for advice or help. Therefore, it had to be kept in top shape.

The cabin contained a VHF radio, powered by a six-volt battery mounted on one wall, a cupboard, a white kitchen table, and two chairs carved out of a massive fir stump by a chainsaw, polished by years of use. A closet and two iron bunks completed the furnishings. It was built for utility and spartan bachelorhood, but some brightly checked red curtains on the four windows broke the severity of the place. I walked into the room, looking happily around, and was just putting my duffle-bag down, when a rattling and banging in the heater suddenly startled the quiet of the cabin. A stove lid raised up slightly and settled with a clang. The place appeared to have a resident poltergeist. I walked over and cautiously pried open the iron door with a poker. Nothing happened, so I bent over to peer into the dark interior.

With a rush of wings and an explosion of ashes, phoenix-like, a sparrow hawk fluttered around the room, leaving a cloud of soot and a few feathers in his wake. Then he caught sight of the open door and was gone, leaving black dust settling on the clean floor. I looked outside and saw him sitting in the top of a spruce, preening the dirt out of his pinions. The chimney cap was missing, and I could see how he'd fallen down the stove-pipe a few days before, to find himself trapped in the stove, with no escape until he heard my footsteps on the cabin floor. I grabbed the broom, clucking away like an old bachelor warden at the mess he had left for me to clean up. I was home.

The falls thundered its welcome and the pots on the stove trembled and tinkled along in sympathetic harmonies. I cooked myself a brief supper and sat on the front porch looking up at the cliffs.

Two summers before, I had climbed the left-hand side of the waterfall, something that hadn't previously been done.

A friend of mine, one of the better rock climbers in this country, once came up with the following definition of a modern rock-jock: "He is," he said, "a lunatic who has to think he's about to die in order to feel he's still alive."

Rather an unflattering description. But it suited me to a tee that day in 1966, as mountain guide Bernie Schiesser led the first pitches on that crumbling wall.

With most accessible peaks in the Rockies already climbed, many mountaineers have turned to scaling the most difficult new routes they can find up previously climbed mountains. Since Bernie and I made our first ascent up the falls, other men, even more desperate for adventure, have taken to climbing the falls in winter, when it turns into a 1,248 foot icicle. They climb with crampons strapped on their boots to keep them from taking the long drop. Anyway, we were the first, at least as far as I know.

Bernie had led the climb up that slippery face on June 20, my birthday, which seemed like a bad omen at the time, especially when I heard the threatening roar of the falls just a few yards to our right. Hear it? Hell, we could feel the rock vibrating under our hands and feet. I had belayed Bernie from below, unable to help him in any way, until he pounded in a piton a hundred feet above me, snapped in a carabiner, and passed the perlon rope through the biner for a sky hook. Hopefully he wouldn't fall too far past that pin if he slipped, with me belaying him, as long as the pin didn't pull out, that is.

Bernie went over a bulge and out of sight to me as I played out the rope. I shouted out the length of rope remaining, but the rumble of the falls drowned out my voice. Then the umbilical cord of the rope pulled tight on my chest harness and I felt three sharp tugs. I went up, fingers searching over the rock for a hold.

Oh, the delicate peregrinations of those ten sensitive fingers, scuttling across the rocks in desperate Braille. The trembling

21

in the knees. The hard hat, which fitted like a beer cap on a bowling ball, kept sliding cockeyed. You never knew when it might come in handy as a buffer between a boulder and your *medulla oblongata.* Bernie said it was mind over matter. "If you don't mind, it don't matter."

In two fast leads, we gained a narrow ledge 300 feet above the river, and a few yards from the water's edge, which sprayed us with an icy mist when the wind veered our way. Thirsty from the work, we edged across to the falls, and stretched out our red climbing helmets to catch a drink of thunder water.

With a length of sling, I tied on to a pinnacle of limestone that stands out from the wall at that point and played the rope out as Bernie climbed up, looking for a route. Peering straight down between the toes of my climbing boots, I could see the tourists far below.

Bernie led around a corner and up a slab that weighed half a ton, but still shifted slightly under his weight, the way such things often do in the crumbling cliffs. The slab had cracked off the face a few millenniums ago but caught its base on a ledge a few inches below the fracture plane.

The rope jerked for me to climb. Holding my breath, I moved tenderly across the slab. Above it was a pitch of eroded stone, with holes as big as salad bowls. It felt like a staircase compared to the scant pickings below. My nose came suddenly even with Bernie's boot toes. He was standing on a platform just wide enough for our feet, anchored by a piton driven into a crack. He was grinning down at me.

"C'mon up. It's bombproof," he said.

There was a small cirque beginning just above his head but he had run out of rope. Moving with shortened rope together on a scrambling pitch, high above the beetling cars, we climbed this natural bowl. A horn blared occasionally to let us know, should it be necessary for us to be hospitalized, possibly in the looney-bin, there were solid citizens waiting to say "I told you so."

What we faced then was a horrendous overhang, a chilling sight, which meant we might have to rappel all the way back down the face. We traversed towards the right-hand corner where the water bisected it, hoping to find a pitch that was less convex.

Behind a slab in the corner, we found an alcove that at least offered a good belay point. But, in the bottom of this, we found one of those rare and beautiful gifts that few men are given in such desolate terrain. A cave.

The black entrance hole was about three feet across. We were slightly screened in the corner from the roar of the falls but, when we bent down to the hole, the noise was suddenly amplified again as if this was the mouth of some natural trumpet.

"Let's try it," Bernie said.

We crawled in. The sandy-floored tunnel led in about fifty feet. It was good going at first. Then we came to a constriction in the roof that forced us to wriggle through on our stomachs. It was like being in the belly of a whale, reaching out blindly in the darkness, not knowing what terrible pit might suddenly open on us, what depths might lie below.

Then, like a cliché, we saw a faint light, a promise of day. The tube levelled off, beginning to climb for the blue porthole, which was partially blocked by a large chockstone. We wedged out underneath this and found ourselves standing in a smooth-walled collecting basin, open to the sky.

I looked over the edge and was washed in a cold wind from the lip of the falls. I was looking straight down 1,200 feet, down the waterfall. The dark green wave of the water stretched across the lip in front of me. Below was the road and the red roof of the warden cabin, which would one day be a home to me. Above us was a fifty-foot section of falling water and a cliff we had yet to climb.

Across the valley to the west·was the green plateau of the Yoho Pass, a low point between Wapta Mountain and the President Range that led down to Emerald Lake. At 6,030 feet, the pass was only five or six hundred feet higher than where we stood. Bernie checked it on the topo map.

After this, we crossed the stream above the last fall, traversed across the cliff to the south, and descended in a series of airy rappels to the forest below.

We were elated with the climb and our discovery of the cave. We knew that Takakkaw had not always held that single banner of spray out to the sun. There was a time, aeons ago, when an even more spectacular twin falls had shone over the valley. Then the water had worn deeper in that band of rock to the south and the other falls had disappeared.

Now, sitting on the porch of that same red-roofed warden cabin, I watched the single plume of the waterfall, stained red by the setting sun. When it was dark, I went inside and made

23

up a bedroll of thick woollen blankets. The muted tintinnabulation of falling water was a lullaby into quick sleep.

I was goosed awake at 5:30 by the icy fingers of a mountain
morning, creeping through an opening in the covers. Something hovered in a cloud of steam in front of my face. Rubbing
my eyes, I discovered it was my breath. I had forgotten how
cold it could be at this altitude in June. Jumping out of bed, I
gasped as my feet hit the enamelled floor. It was colder than
the surface of a skating rink and just as slippery.

I scuttled around the room, crab-fashion, finding flashlight
and matches. A robin was cheeping away above the roar of
the falls, trying to convince itself that this was indeed spring. I
congratulated myself on having left a pile of squaw sticks on
the stove. These are little pieces of split pine, whittled with a
sharp knife into little bushes of shavings. These you pile in the
firebox, strike a match with numb fingers (easier, if not as
aesthetically pleasing as rubbing two Boy Scouts together),
and heap on some pieces of fir to get a quick fire.

There was no point standing around waiting for things to
heat up; that would take half an hour. Once dressed in chilly
cotton uniform shirt and blue-jeans, I forced my feet into the
stiff new boots and, taking the bucket, I stepped out into the
morning.

Sheer cliffs rose up to the clouds on both sides of the narrow valley. Crossing the road, I came to where the Yoho River
flowed milk-white with the flour of glacial silt. From the river
bank, just above this heavy-looking fluid, there issues a miraculously clear spring. It bubbles up inside a small fir box, set
into the gravel by a warden many years ago.

A weak sun forced its tentative beams through the low
clouds. To the south, the falls swept a crimson plume through
the red dawn high above the river. The spring bubbled out
slowly, in no hurry to join the brawling meeting of waters below.

I broke the thin skiff of ice that had formed during the night
and the shards tinkled merrily against the sides of the box. A
tiny water-shrew swam out from behind the moss-covered
box and made a circle in the half-submerged pail before
swimming out the open end. Now that the water had been
blessed, it could be drunk.

As I straightened up with a full pail, a white cloud floated
over, low enough to reach up and touch. Fragrant smoke from
the cabin chimney spiralled up to meet it above the steep-

24

pitched red roof with its overhanging eaves. That spring water made coffee of medicinal virtue. I went inside to get it started.

Making coffee is a ritual very important in the mountains and may not be lightly assigned to novices. Coffee, rum, tea, and tobacco are the big medicines of the outdoors, sacrosanct from the meddlings of greenhorns and the nay-saying of a new generation of macrobiotic fanatics. To hell with their tiresome good health, I say. After pouring ice-water into a gallon coffee pot, until it was half full, I pried the lid off the stove and placed the pot over the open flame. The stove had been designed, some fifty years ago, with just such an enamel pot in mind. In the mountains, we boil our coffee. Percolators and the people that use them are regarded with suspicion.

Taking a can of Edward's coffee, and surrendering to the grace of the ritual, I sprinkled in just the right amount without the benefit of measurement—either you have the knack or you don't. Then I made breakfast, which in this case was a dollop of mush from a package of oatmeal, left in the cupboard the summer before by a wealthier man than I. When this gorp was ready to choke down, the coffee came to a slow, sure boil, filling the cabin with an enticing aroma that steamed the edge off the cold morning.

I sat back with a cupful, awaiting the day's events. They were not long in unfolding.

Yoho National Park is a relatively small park, about 507 square miles as compared with the 2,564 square miles of neighbouring Banff. Not being able to command the budget of the bigger national parks, it is usually a trifle short of manpower, especially that summer when the number of park visitors reached 857,000 and the warden staff consisted of five full-time men and two patrolmen.

I was only mildly surprised, then, that the Chief Warden himself should arrive that first morning, driving the horse truck with my two cayuses peering suspiciously over the front stock racks. This kind of slumming is unheard of in a big park like Banff where the chief stays in his office, ensconced in godlike omniscience for the duration, venturing out into the backcountry only on the odd foray, fishing rod in hand.

But this Chief Warden had been sitting in the saddle of horses and the seats of horse-trucks since he was a boy. He used to jump at the chance to escape the piles of paper in his office back in Field and ride out into the bush to see if he could catch us slacking off.

25

Neil backed the two-ton truck expertly up to the unloading ramp and jumped out to give me a hand lifting the battered tailgates. He handed me a halter rope and I backed nervously down the ramp as if I had a wild dog on a leash. After we tied the horses to the hitching post in the corral, we unloaded the saddles from a box over the cab.

"You'll find a chainsaw rig in the barn, Marty," Neil told me, and he glanced at his watch. "Best saddle up and take off. There's plenty of deadfall to clear. From here clean up to the Little Yoho."

What means "chainsaw rig?" I wondered, but was afraid to ask too many questions.

"Ever been up here before?" he asked, noticing my uncertainty.

I toed a horse ball with my new boots and reluctantly admitted that I hadn't been further than the falls.

"Well, the horses know this country pretty well," he said amiably. "They'll show you where everything is."

Neil gave me some advice on feeding and watering the horses and handed me a jar of cinch ointment for doctoring cuts and blisters–on the horses. He caught sight of my new riding boots.

"Suede, eh?"

"Yeah."

"You done any ridin' before, kid?"

"Not much," I allowed, trying to make it sound like that was still quite a bit.

Neil looked at me doubtfully. "Well, I guess you'll have to learn in a hurry. We don't have time to give any lessons right now. Too busy down below, chasin' bears and whatnot."

"I'll make out."

"Sure, kid. Like I say, the horses'll show you everything."

He went into the barn to check on the hay supply. I headed for the cabin to check something out in the warden manual I'd discovered there. The tone of Neil's voice on the word "everything" had reminded me of it.

Leafing through the pages, I came to the heading "Horsemanship." "The art of riding horseback is not something that can be learned from a book . . . ." I passed over that pretty quickly and read on. "1. Strange horses should be handled as though dangerous. 2. When acquiring an animal, it is good practice to obtain a record of its bad or dangerous traits or habits, together with information concerning any previous injuries." This was reassuring news.

26

Outside, the engine of the truck coughed and started. I went out the door, book in hand, and ran down the road after the truck, shouting "Stop!" Suddenly, I had questions to ask, manifold and various.

Neil slammed on the brakes and I ran up alongside.

"Hey, chief, how about telling me a bit more about those two horses. It says here they might be dan ... "

"Oh yeah, I meant to tell yuh," Neil interrupted me. "You can ride or pack both of 'em. Either way. You might try packing that gelding," he said, a smile curling around the corners of his eyes, betraying the serious set of his mouth. "Travel light, kid, hold on tight."

His face was framed in the side-view mirror as he drove away. He was grinning to himself at some private joke that I didn't catch.

I looked at the book suspiciously. "Strange horses should be handled as though dangerous," it told me again. Under that sentence, for those who might not get the point, someone had left a bloody finger print, and one pencilled word: "Amen."

It's always a big moment in the warden outfit when the horses arrive from their winter range on the Ya-Ha-Tinda Ranch, west of Sundre, Alberta. Their arrival signals the end of the long mountain winter, of patrolling by ski or snowshoe through deep snow, or wrestling with ungainly oversnow vehicles that have a habit of breaking down forty miles from nowhere.

Horses were destined to become an integral part of my outdoor world, a link between man and environment. But, by the time that first day of initiation was over, I couldn't have imagined ever wanting to climb aboard such an abominable creature again.

I had inherited two old but honourable equines that went with the district, like the cabins, the packsack, and the old .308 rifle, which was a repeater– "load on Sunday, shoot all week." In a very real sense, the horses would show me around the country about which they knew much more than I. As they stood dejectedly in the corral staring at the ground, they reminded me of two old retainers who suddenly found that their estate had been sold to a member of the nouveau riche.

Shawn, the dark brown gelding, looked away first, curling his lower lip in contempt at the sight of my boots, which seemed to offend his sense of propriety. He was long in the tooth and short-tempered from more than a decade of mountain service. I soon discovered that he had the temperament and tractability of a jackass, combined with the speed and killer instinct of a rattlesnake. He was an ex-RCMP gelding, with an unfortunate dose of thoroughbred blood and a steely determination to "get his man."

Too many years in the Mounties' famed musical ride had turned Shawn into an exhibitionist with a love for the sound of applause. His dark colouring, more black than brown, combined with his thin flanks, gave him the look of an aging racehorse, which he was not. He came equipped with an old stock saddle so high in the pommel and cantle that I imagined the original owner of it must have ridden a charger carrying a shield and broadsword. Shawn loathed me from the first, though he granted me a grudging respect for perseverance after a few weeks. He was a horse with principles–a fool killer.

Bess, the bay mare, would prove to be my only friend at the falls. Her ample swayback was easy to ride. Sitting on that comfortable rocking chair, I would sometimes dare to think myself a skilled horseman. She was patient too, refusing to panic when halter ropes broke, when bears jumped out of the scenery to introduce themselves, or when Shawn did his rodeo number, crow-hopping around like a senile version of Midnight, the famous bucking horse.

The sound of the Chief Warden's truck faded down the valley, and I was alone with my two horses. "Might as well get acquainted," I thought. If I had known what lay in store for me, I might well have packed up the Volkswagen and left right then. Being unfamiliar with the delight that cowboys get in seeing a dude come unglued, I had accepted Neil's advice on the gelding at face value, and decided to pack him. It was a disastrous mistake, for Shawn was a saddle horse of the kind that turned up its nose at any kind of a pack outfit. Whatever his reasons, the traces of his aristocratic blood flared up at the sight. In short, he took offence and he took it the moment I picked up the pack saddle and turned in his direction.

Looking back at that callow youth, edging fearfully toward his adversary, looking back at myself with the hindsight of seven years' experience, I can see the problem clearly and it lay in my unconscionable scuffle. I had forgotten the sashay, and the existential importance of this manoeuvre cannot be overemphasized. This arrogant ambulation is to horses what the contemptuous shrug of the Prime Minister is to the House of Commons. It implies mastery. So it was that Shawn, that fine morning at Takakkaw Falls, took one look at my hesitant footwork and knew me for the greenhorn that I was.

Laying the chainsaw down beside him, I regarded the pack saddle with anxious eyes. It was the first time I'd ever seen one. The iron hames on the old cavalry saddle were confusing. Which was the front, which the back? I wondered. Lack of this knowledge turned out to be the least of my troubles.

Shawn stood there, trembling with rage, head bowed—a sign which I unfortunately took for obeisance. Gaining confidence, I strode up to his shoulder with my best "let's get down to business" manner. Shawn jumped sideways, shocked at this familiarity.

"Nice horsey," I crooned, and tried again. This time I succeeded in flopping the felt saddle pad on his back. The gelding waited until it was nicely smoothed out, then turned his long neck, grabbed a corner of it with his teeth and flipped it off onto the ground. This reminded me that the grey saddle blanket was supposed to go on first.

A jet plane went over us, a silver glint high in the heavens, an incongruity reminding me that I was starting my cowboy career a little late in the century.

With the blankets sorted out, I picked up the pack saddle. It smelled of Neat's Foot Oil and horseflesh. The gelding froze in disgust as I eased it on. It looked all right to me, except for one of the two cinches, which was hung up under the saddle skirt on the off-side. His legs trembled as I crawled underneath to free it.

"Don't worry, old fellah," I said soothingly, "I won't hurt you."

I wondered what was causing this nervousness. "Probably just impatient to get back to work," I reassured myself, as I reached for the strap. A ground-squirrel poked its head up a few inches from my nose and crash dived again in a string of fading squeaks. I must have given it a terrible shock, as I groped around Shawn's loins. I was blissfully unaware of the fact that my head might get kicked off at any moment for daring to thus fidget near the gelding's personal particulars—or what was left of them. But the horse must have decided that would have been too quick a death for me. He was waiting for something more satisfyingly prolonged.

He waited while I knotted the cinches, struggling with the stiff latigo leather. He waited while I hung the chainsaw box from the metal hooks on top of the saddle. He waited as I stepped out in front of him to pick up the fuel box, my back turned, calculating as I bent over to pick it up.

Then he made his move. With no warning snort or whinny, he thrust his nose between my legs and, moving at a run, butted me forward into the corral logs. I went between the middle two like a snake, nearly knocking myself out on a log as I scraped through.

Holding my bleeding head, I watched wide-eyed as Shawn came apart, bucking and kicking, snorting and farting. He threw the saw box into the dust, whirled and stomped it into kindling with his steel-shod forefeet. I winced at the impact, realizing that it could have been my head. After a few minutes of furious demolition, he took a run towards me as I staggered upright, kicking up his heels in defiance. Then, tiring of this sport, he trotted over to the trough to have a drink and grin at his reflection in the water.

The mare was still tied up, gazing stolidly at nothing.

I stifled my obscenities, as a car screeched to a halt. Studiously ignoring it, I regarded the dark blood on my hands. It wasn't arterial at least. A cloud of dust billowed in behind the car and settled on me like fine cement.

"That horse sure doesn't like you," the driver chirped gleefully.

I smiled sweetly at him, imagining how pleasurable it would be to have my hands wrapped around his windpipe. "Just a friendly little altercation," I told him, not adding that I would have settled it cheerfully with the old .308 rifle in the heat of the moment.

The driver guffawed in reply. I choked back a comment on his mental obtuseness and the possibly illicit nature of his conception.

It was embarrassing. There were quite a few people at the falls view point by this time. Sensing that more blood might soon be spilt, these were now moving in for the kill. The click of their 35mm cameras rattled in the air like bears' teeth.

"Hey, buddy. Can you do that again? I didn't have my camera loaded."

"Are you gonna try him again, mister?" a young voice trilled excitedly.

It was the last thing on my mind. But what could I do? The reputation of the Warden Service was at stake, so was my job, not to mention my neck. So I dusted myself off with as much aplomb as I could muster, undented my sombrero, which was in danger of being pissed on by the mare, and turned to square off with my opponent.

Inspired by the audience, Shawn minced delicately around the corral, head held high, feinting to the left and right like a prize fighter, as I tried to grab the end of the broken halter rope. By now I figured there must be some connection between the pack saddle and the gelding's display of temper. I decided I would try and ride him instead.

In the barn, I got a can of oats and the riding saddle and went back out. Smelling the oats, the gelding settled down and let me catch him.

By this time, I had quite a gallery of spectators leaning on the corral bars and offering all kinds of useless advice. It was getting late, well past high noon already. My stomach was growling, but I decided to forego eating in order to get some miles on the horses that day, while I still had a modicum of rage to keep me going because the next morning I was expecting an attack of debilitating horrors at the prospect of having to start all over again.

Shawn stood quietly while I threw the saddle on and took the bit without undue complaint. I put the pack saddle on Bess and lashed on the remains of the chainsaw rig as best I could. I would have to repair it later. Then I took her halter rope, grabbed a handful of reins and a handful of mane and, lurching fearfully up into the seat, poked my boots around trying to find the stirrups. To my relief, the gelding stood stock still. This was fortunate because the halter rope had gotten wrapped around my neck.

I straightened everything out and tried to look as western as possible under the circumstances. Unfortunately, the dramatic effect was somewhat marred by the shortness of my stirrups. The last owner of the saddle must have been a dwarf, I decided. I found myself sitting with my knees far above the gelding's withers. The crowd, getting restless at the lack of violent action, was turning hostile.

"Mommy," some little cretin whined, "that cowboy looks like a jockey." There were titters of amusement, disappointed mutterings. I had to get out of there.

Somebody opened the corral gate to a round of cynical applause. The gelding perked his ears up momentarily, then subsided. Crimson-faced with embarrassment, I managed a sick grin and muttered grimly to the horse, "Mush, you sonofabitch," nudging him with a booted toe—but gently.

31

Shawn turned his head for a moment and eyed me with disbelief. He stretched his neck down against the slack reins to nibble at the grass.

"Go on, get up, willya?" I pleaded. I hauled up on the reins then, much too hard it seems. Shawn reared up on his hind legs like a poor man's Trigger. I clung desperately to the saddlehorn with the left hand, and grabbed my hat brim just as it fell off with the other. The crowd gasped in admiration. They thought I was deliberately stunting for them.

Just when it was certain that Shawn was going to fall over backwards and waffle me into the turf, Bess must have jerked her head up to catch the show because the bight of her halter rope, which was still clutched in my right hand, swivelled underneath the gelding's tail. Now, that is the most sensitive part of a horse's—or anybody else's—anatomy.

The gelding snorted hard, came down onto his front feet and leaped forward in one explosive lunge toward the open gate. I grabbed for leather as the halter rope went taut on the mare, who had yet to move, and jerked me half out of the saddle. She jumped forward and we were gone out of that hated circle and galloping down the road, where cars pulled quickly out of our way to avoid collisions. Shawn had the bit in his teeth. I looked down and saw the gravel flying by with sickening speed. All I could do was hang on tight, keeping a low profile as overhanging tree limbs swept across my back.

We barrelled past the youth hostel, where hostile youths stared blankly at us and thundered through the campground, scattering campers and dogs amid bleats and barks of fear.

Out in the open flats at last, I pulled back hard at the reins with one hand, the other welded to the saddlehorn as I clung and cried. "Whoa! Whoa, you sonofa . . . WHOA!!"

But that plug had a mouth like a lion. At length we came to the first stream crossing in the open gravel flats north of the falls. Shawn slowed down at the sight of the slippery boulders on the wide alluvial fan. I breathed a little easier, managing to get his head up at last and check him with the bit.

The people were far behind us now, probably well satisfied with the entertainment. We splashed and lurched across the creek, my spine jolting at every step and my legs numb from gripping the saddle. I rode, as they say in the outfit, "like a sack of crap." After half a mile my buttocks felt like two gigantic bunions being pulverized in a meat grinder.

We followed the river toward its headwaters in the Yoho

Glacier, some six miles upstream. The trail entered the spruce forest, which sweeps up the steep-sided mountains on either side of the narrow valley. Ahead of us was the high ridge of the Whaleback with Twin Falls Chalet at its foot. I would try and cut our way as far as the chalet in what was left of the day.

We splashed across another creek and I consoled myself with knowing that my feet might stay dry this summer at least. Also, I wouldn't have the heavy, greasy chainsaw on my back like I had the other two summers. It rattled up and down on the mare. To her it appeared to have no weight at all.

I looked back to where she trudged behind us, friendly as an old milk cow, her nose stuck enquiringly in Shawn's skinny croup. There she was serenaded by a flatulent bagpipe of awesome volume and melodic range. This seemed to pass as music to her ears, which pricked up at nuances in the delivery. Shawn proved to be a master, sounding his heavy calibre instrument in both basso and soprano motifs—depending on the weather, his mood, and how much green feed he had crammed down the night before.

Thus we clanked and trumpeted *fortissimo* toward the lowering sun. The gelding had settled down a little and I was almost lulled into a pained sense of well-being. Soon, the winding trail zagged slightly east, then straightened out to run right along the river bank, giving me some unenviable views into the whirling green depths. Shivering, I tightened my grip on the reins. We were still a mile from where the first windfalls of last winter's storms were blocking the trail.

I wasn't looking forward to getting off my steed to unbolster that saw because I frankly dreaded the prospect of having to shinny back on again. Old westerns replayed themselves in my head, as I tried to remember how Wayne or Cooper would have handled the situation. But they would not have deigned to carry so much as a saddle axe through their marvellously unobstructed vistas. Anyway, the problem was about to solve itself.

There is a strange sensation in the point of balance when a saddle starts to fall off, and the body lists slowly to the right in a kind of impromptu Immelman turn. Strange because the numbed synapses in my butt and knees were temporarily out of service, so my brain was short on stimulus-response-type information.

The eyes telegraphed what they were seeing: "Aiee! Ground getting close."

And the brain replied: "Am taking evasive action." But it came too late. I found myself sliding crazily under the gelding's belly to land with a crash on the ground.

The old stud hopped sideways and pulled on the end of his lines which were still clutched in my left hand. The saddle and blankets had slid halfway down his ribs. Since I had dropped the halter rope, I looked anxiously for the mare who stood patiently biting the grass beside the trail, eyes politely averted from the humiliating spectacle.

Shawn, I learned later, had been "holding out on me," a favourite trick of greedy junkies and cinch-wise horses. He'd sucked himself full of hot air back in the corral when I cinched him up and then he'd let it out later. There were two good inches of slack between the woven cinch band and the gelding's breastbone.

I tidied it all up and tightened the cinch again, ignoring the gelding's protestations that it was too tight. He was one of those phony plugs that moaned and groaned as soon as you touched the latigo, hoping he could con you into leaving it loose. Since then, I've seen a few old cowboys let the wind out of this kind of scam with a sudden boot in the guts. I was lucky not to know that trick because when it came to kicking, Shawn definitely had me outclassed.

With the cinch tight, I stepped on and started to swing my right leg up. But I had committed the sin of the slack rein, which is otherwise known as the Big Step, the Lift-off, or the Cemetery Leap. With the left rein slack, the gelding was able to bog his head, that is, get it down low enough to obtain the leverage he needed to really sock it to me. One fast buck was enough to make sure I never found my seat. It helped to magnify the slight arc begun when I threw the right leg up. He put a little top on me, I was airborne without a parachute.

A big dome-shaped boulder came up like a howdydoo and I landed on it, chest first. The wind went out of me and I remember thinking that it wasn't coming back in this world. The lights blinked on and off and shuffled into a wild kaleidoscope. The pain was severe.

How long I lay there, coiled into a foetal ball, I don't know. But the cold shadows of the spruce were stretching across me and the sun was halfway down the big wall of the Vice-President before I even dreamed of getting up.

Earlier, I had seen a bear sign on the trail, so the cold lick of a long wet tongue on my neck almost finished the pain with a terminal heart attack. I eased slowly around after a minute and came eye to eyeball with the mare, towering above me. Her ears lifted with mild interest to see that I wasn't yet a corpse.

It doesn't do to get hurt when alone in the mountains, several miles from the nearest radio or road. The temperature at night can drop to near freezing and, without extra clothing or a fire, an injured man could lapse into hypothermia. I thought that they'd find me in a day or two with clothes ripped off in my delerium and a nasty grimace on my face. Perhaps I would leave them a little note telling them where they could shove their horses.

These unpleasant thoughts, coupled with the fading warmth of the sun, inspired me to try my bruised limbs. There was a tender area on my chest which was swelling into a lemon-sized lump, but all the hinges worked, and there didn't seem to be any spokes poking inconveniently into any lungs.

My reluctant charger pawed impatiently at the ground. His reins had tangled in a deadfall and stopped him from galloping home in riderless triumph. The red haze in front of my eyes made it difficult to focus on the gelding, as I hauled myself carefully towards him by the branches of a handy spruce. Sensing my frame of mind, he danced warily backwards into the shadows, teeth and eyeballs flashing. I lunged forward and grabbed the lines. Shawn went up over me, striking the air with his forefeet. No longer caring, I laughed a malicious chuckle.

"Gotcha, you slippery sonofabitch," I cried. "Now I'm gonna give you your lumps."

Crazed notion. Hundred-and-eighty-pound greenhorn versus 1,000-pound hammerhead. I punched wildly as he came down, hitting him a glancing blow on his rock-hard jaw that nearly broke my wrist. The shooting pain that went up my arm would have popped my skull off had I not already flipped my lid. Shawn snorted and tap-danced on the rocky trail, while I hopped and hollered my frustrated pain and rage. It was the fear that I suddenly noticed in the mare's eye that snapped me out of it. If I was reduced to sparring with my horse this early in the game, I might as well pack the whole job in tomorrow.

Full of real despair, I sat down and calmed my nerves with a bowl of tobacco and thought it over. It was pretty obvious that up until now the gelding had mastered me and, if I wanted the

35

job, I would have to master him, starting immediately. I couldn't outmuscle him so I'd have to outsmart him. Somehow.

Shawn and I had a little talk about far pastures and dog food factories while I lengthened the stirrups, and with threats dire, hauled myself painfully into the saddle. His only response was to roll his sensuous old lip over his yellow teeth, breaking into a trot for home, and nearly unsaddling me again as Bess took up the slack. Not that I needed the halter. Both nags could smell hay at least four miles upwind. As long as the direction was home, they needed no prompting from me.

In the months that followed, Shawn was absolutely merciless. Whenever I stepped behind him, he would show me the white of his eye, depress his ears, and cock one back foot for a kick that never quite came. I guess he aimed to wear me out with suspense. But he taught me a lot. He taught me never to take anything for granted, to keep my eyes peeled for trouble, speaking softly and moving slowly. He taught me how to survive.

I couldn't afford to quit that job. As a bankrupt candidate for marriage that fall, I needed every cent. So I consoled myself with a comparison, drawn from my expensive and, up until now, useless education, a quote from Geoff Chaucer about another poor student who lived many centuries ago.

"As leene was his horse as is a rake," I told Shawn, in my best Middle English.

And he was nat right fat, I undertake
But he looked holwe, and thereto sobrely . . .
But al be that he was a philosophre
Yet hadde he but litel gold in cofre . . .

And needed some soon, to get himself a square meal. To keep up his strength for busting senile broncos.

———————

A week later I ran into Fred Dixon, one of the best horsemen in the outfit.

"I hear you had a little go-round with Shawn," Fred said casually.

I answered with a string of unrepeatables.

Fred cocked his hat back to let his hair uncurl. "I kinda wondered why you'd want to pack that Shawn horse," he replied.

"Why do you say that?"

"Well, I may be wrong, but I don't believe anyone packs that horse. He's pretty well just a saddle horse."

Then he strolled off to let me chew over the implications of the Warden Service's rough sense of humour, which builds good-natured camaraderie in those fortunate enough to survive it.

2

Euclid Never Threw the Diamond

"Reloading the packs at the cabin,
tied with diamond hitches,
his only conversation was,
'Whoa there, you sons a bitches.'"

Timberline Jim Deegan

When they first come to the Rockies city folk are prone to babble enthusiastically about the beauties of every vista. This is understandable, but there is one comment heard more than any other: "It's so quiet here," they exclaim rapturously, "so peaceful, so still."

I'd cock an ear towards whatever it was they weren't listening to but all I heard were mountain sounds. Finally I tried it with a finger stuck in each ear. Nothing. Perhaps the strident wail of the city's permanent traffic jam has overwhelmed their auditory sense, causing an invisible tuner in the head to switch the hearing off. The psychologists used to call this phenomenon "cognitive dissonance," which is their bafflegab for mental self-defence. For without this mutiny in the medulla, the cerebral cortex would soon burst like a barbequed sausage under the sensory overload of city noise.

Only the loudest sounds, those that indicate a real threat to the organism–like the warning horn of a braking car–are allowed to penetrate that coarse filter, the modern ear, an ear that seems destined to turn into a vestigial organ. The songbird's voice is caught in the metallic purr of the air-conditioner; the guitar, descended from the lyre of an ancient poet, has been amplified beyond distortion, to pierce the auditory veil, to bridge the abyss in the synapses. Pity our jangled genes.

If you listen long enough to the megawatt lament of a guitar, you may still detect in it one quieter echo now and again that can stretch the imagination back in time, back to a solitary hunter hidden at the forest edge, idly plucking his finger across a taut bow-string as he waits for a meal to walk out into the meadow. As he listens to the liquid "plonk" of the deer sinew echoing in the clearing, perhaps an idea forms between sound and sensation. He was the first artist: one of a long line of those creators who are always seeking a road that leads through death and beyond, seeking the medium that will carry their spirits into the future. It is a human voice that speaks through those strings, transformed by vibrations of rosewood and catgut. But the arrow of such indeterminate desire, aimed down the years to us, falls short. Who can hear that subtle flight against the roar of the jet engine?

If the modern ear is an auditory appendix, there is still hope of restoration, but first the jammed switches have to be freed. There's only one way to do this. You have to dunk the head in a bucket of icy mountain water, drawn from as close to the toe of a glacier as possible, just before sunrise. The war-whoop emitted when you try this will create the back pressure needed to clear those smog-bound circuits.

Listen.

The head, vibrated like a gong these many months by the jackhammers of progress, now seems amazingly still, and the world is miraculously silent. This is a temporary deception. The landscape has a pulse that beats with or without our perception of it and only on a dead world is there no sound. To the moth caught in a web over the cabin door, the feet of the approaching spider strike these strands with the force of piano hammers on stretched wire.

This new sensation takes some getting used to, this feeling that the ears have suddenly taken wing, have turned into flying microphones hovering over the grass to interview crickets, record the ululations of a leaf, and relay messages from the earth to an amazed listener. The ears will have their fling— hearing is a gift; we take what's given gratefully.

In my case, what was given was pounding, pulsating Takak- kaw, whose gushing trajectory kept my bladder overactive both day and night, especially night, and whose plunging pandemonium made the stony earth quiver as if it was jello, so that the cabin always seemed like a ship adrift in a stormy sea.

A visiting couple, friends from the city, came up to spend

39

the night with me, raving, as usual, about the marvellous peace and quiet.

"I beg your pardon?" I shouted.

"I say it's so peaceful here."

"I'm sorry. You'll have to speak up," I yelled. "I can't hear you over the noise of the falls."

They smiled politely, no doubt thinking I'd grown a little eccentric from living alone.

That night I had a nightmare about drowning. In the morning I awoke, gratefully, only to find that my iron cot had jiggled across the floor a few inches during the night. This gave me the heebie-jeebies anew because in my dream the bed had taken me on a slow journey across the room, out the door, over the road and whoosh, down the bank into the river, setting sail. I awoke to the sound of breakers—it was only the falls.

Thrilled into a cold sweat, I got out of bed and started the fire. Breakfast for my friends would be hotcakes à la Bernie Schiesser, since the syrup was made from a recipe devised by him one cold morning at Lake O'Hara. The ingredients are mapeline extract, brown sugar, boiling water and 100 overproof rum. Since my hotcakes were invariably heavy as lead, the syrup was mandatory for the melting of said lead into digestible form. I hauled a bag of pancake mix out of the cupboard, which bore on it the heraldic trademark of a coyote in full cry, the design devious, the motto hilarious. "Coyote Pancake Batter, It's A Howling Success!" The falls rumbled, the knives and forks jingled merrily in their drawer beneath the table, as I mixed the stuff with milk in a bowl. A hunk of oakum chose that moment to vibrate loose from the chinking tamped between two logs and fell with a plop into the batter. I fished it out with my spoon, cursed it roundly, and consigned it to hell in the stove.

My friend and his wife finished dressing in their corner of the cabin, then sat down, smiling at each other, and hinting aloud that the vibrations of the place had a salutary effect, aphrodisiac in nature.

Distracted by this salaciousness, I managed to burn the "howling success" to a smouldering crisp. Myself being celibate, though not by choice, slept at night like a consecrated log, and during the day, worked like a dog.

My friends left after breakfast and I went to work outside.

The Hi-Line Trail above the cabin was still partially blocked by a spring avalanche which had buried a hundred yards of it under a pile of rock and trees, welded together with hard-packed snow. Since the place was close by, about a half-hour's walk, I decided to let the horses lard up for a few days while I developed a bit of muscle tone for the next encounter. Actually, I was still licking my wounds from the first jackpot and I needed a few days to get ready for the next one, both physically and psychologically.

I loaded a Trapper Nelson Packboard with chainsaw, gas, grubhoe, and axe, and started up the trail east of the cabin. The roar of the falls, muted by dense stands of spruce and fir, soon faded behind me as I walked up the steep switchbacks with the heavy load, taking short, slow steps, breathing in rhythm with the gait. In this terrain, gravity enforces its own slow speed limits on the body.

The Hi-Line Trail drops over Yoho Pass on its way from Emerald Lake and swings north below the wall of Vice-President Mountain, 1,400 feet above the valley. The first white man in the Takakkaw Falls area was Ralph Edwards, a guide from Field, who made the trip back in 1897. He found acres of downed timber and moss belly-high on his horses. So rough was the terrain that it took him eight days to travel a distance of twelve miles from the town of Field. That's why trails are needed.

I climbed up toward the junction with the Hi-Line, working up a good sweat, and cooled down quickly by dew-laden branches of alder and willow that swabbed my wet arms and legs. The early morning chill kept the mosquitoes and bulldog flies in a torpor, for which I gave thanks. Soon I was up to the last switchback, where the Hi-Line takes off across the avalanche slopes and alpine meadows below the Emerald Glacier, headed for Little Yoho Valley. There's an Alpine Club chalet in there and a small line cabin for the wardens.

I took off my pack to rest, hanging it on the handy splinter of what had once been a two-foot-thick spruce. It had been snapped off by a winter snow slide as easily as a man snaps a matchstick between his fingers. Sitting down on a flat-topped rock, I overlooked my protectorate.

Behind me was the stair-like ridge of Michael Peak, stepping south into Yoho Pass. To the left, the walls of the Vice-President stretched north until they bent in to form the cirque of the Emerald Glacier. In the distance, the humped plateau of Whaleback Peak marked the entrance to Little Yoho Valley.

41

Above it, a red dawn swept colour over the dome of the Wapta Icefield, stretching up the flanks of sharp-spined mountains. I rolled their names on my tongue, invoking them like deities: Des Poilus, Yoho, Trolltinder.

To the east, rays of sunlight pierced the predatory clouds. There was wind up there on the summits, a jet stream of air clearing the dark hosts from the towering square of Balfour, the patriarch of this chain. Above the falls, the Daly Glacier shimmered and darkened in the unsteady light like a long sheet of glass. Then the crest of the sun rose over the eastern ridges, embossing the ice with golden details. Down below, the river valley was still a dark pit, lit only by brief flashes of light on Takakkaw, refracted through prisms of morning rainbow on the brink, that spun colours down to the depths.

The day welled over my senses. An upslope breeze washed me in warm air, displacing the cold that billowed down over the falls from the ice above and bringing the clean scent of wet limestone and spruce needles, the punkiness of willow leaves and wet earth.

The mountains were waking up, feeling the hot tongue of the sun probing their frigid crevices. A crack like artillery fire boomed over the icefields. High up on Balfour, a whole mountainside of snow, weakened by meltwater, had sheared away from the rock to go crashing down on the glacier below. A rock-rabbit squeaked at me from a pile of boulders. The wind stopped, and in the hiatus of quiet, a cone dropped in a spruce, clicking down from limb to limb to land with a rattle in a pile of cones below. The squirrel that had cut it loose scolded and toe-nailed the bark, spiralling up the trunk. A patter of dead needles fell in its wake in a minute displacement of energies.

I was sitting in the centre of a small universe of interrelated lives and events. The sun blessed me as indifferently as it did the rest. To me it was a warm hand caressing my lonely wrist. To the earth it was life that stirred the very mud awake at my feet. A toad, freed from its winter hibernation in the trail mud, moved feebly against the wall of my boot, going on an existential errand of its own that my feet had interrupted. I picked it up, feeling the coldness of it. It struggled briefly, then settled quietly in the warm oven of my palm. The pulse stirred in its iridescent throat, the eyes regarded me as implacably as two gold coins, the small heart beat against my flesh, not questioning the outcome of the uncontrollable moment. I put it down

42

on the sun-washed rock to finish thawing, and picked up the grubhoe.

Meltwater had torn a section of the tread apart and washed the earth down to the morainal rocks beneath. I would have to chop out a new tread with the hoe.

Lift, breathe, and swing. Down it goes through the world's thin skin, through three inches of living dirt. The heavy iron sliced a window to the roots, lighting the secret tunnel of a red-backed mouse and decapitating a wriggling white grub. It showed the nerve ends of a thousand roots, thin as hairs, that bind the stippled shade to the mute stone.

I stepped up the new tread and slammed the blade home. It whanged off an unseen boulder and jarred my arms with high voltages of pain. The mountain spoke to me and it told me not to be fooled by the transitory green of plants and trees. *That's all lace and pigment. Rock is what I'm of and about. Plenty of rock, and more forming in my molten centre, to thrust a stone iceberg up into another mountain.*

Lunchtime came and went. The afternoon air was livid with mosquitoes and I was their meat. I slapped away between swings.

The new tread was a wound in the mountain a hundred feet long, three feet wide, and a few inches deep. But it was a carefully made wound, designed to drain itself by means of water bars, and stitch itself in place with rip-rap made of rocks and wooden debris. I stepped up the wet grade and swung against the pull of gravity, walking on the nerve ends of the universe, which begins and ends where anybody says it does.

I chopped and levelled my way to the edge of the slide, and sat down to sharpen the chainsaw with a file. One knuckle dripped red on the wet snow, and a whiskey-jack came up to peck at it, interested. The first time I'd seen one of those little grey and white bandits, it had been hanging upside down on a tree limb at Lake O'Hara, squawking and beating its wings. The garbage bins were underneath, and by one of them was a broken liquor bottle, with some whiskey still in it. The bird was dead drunk and for a long time after that I thought that a love of whiskey accounted for the peculiar name. But the incident only illustrated the cast iron gizzard of *wisagat chak*, the grey jay, whose Indian name got anglicized along the way.

The bird's ready acceptance of my presence reminded me that I wasn't the first warden to work this trail, or lay claim to the district. Other men had faced these piles of widowmakers, green trees bent over by the avalanche, their crown caught in a tangle of debris but holding a terrible force in their bent trunks; they were catapults, ready to fly up with a force that could crush a man like a bug if he cut through them in the wrong place. But after I'd sawed an alley through this giant "pick-up-sticks" of entangled trees, after I'd dodged the sixth widow-maker that flew at my head when I cut the counterbalance of snow off its crown, this, with other things, made me feel like I owned the place. Like a farmer or a rancher, like anyone who works with grass and flesh, I invested more than time and sweat in the territory that was mine to oversee. In the days ahead, I staked my claim in my own blood and in my love for the earth it watered.

Motivation, responsibility, enthusiasm, dedication–all the things that since those days a mammoth personnel department has laboured so mightily to instill, were instilled in me by one Chief Warden with a few simple words: "Well, this is your district, and here's your outfit. As long as you look after it, it's yours to run."

And that was what kept me busting my butt for the princely sum of $1.80 an hour. Hell, if they'd given me something to eat each day, I would have done it for nothing, as long as I could breathe the air, mark the movements of the game, climb those mountains, and fish those streams. And when I caught some sonofabitch in *flagrante delicto* spoiling my sheer paradise with fire, axe or garbage, I could collar him joyously, under the authority vested, and demand "Who and what the hell are you brewing, hewing or strewing, you serpent in the garden of Manitou ... ?"

Yes, they'd given it all to me. Later, they would take it all away, abolish the districts, and centralize the wardens into apartment buildings in the town sites where they would sit watching TV all evening or shoot a little pool, wondering what the hell had happened, what they had done so wrong to deserve this.

Goodbye motivation, farewell responsibility and enthusiasm. They all reside in the attachment of men to landscape and will never be found while riding herd in a swivel chair and sticking pins in a map–not for a warden who loves the outdoors, not for all the paper-shuffling bureaucrats in the federal public service.

But that was still a few years away, though the process itself, which had already failed miserably in the US was eagerly being examined by park bureaucrats in Calgary and Ottawa that very summer. Indeed, a carload of them in the guise of an efficiency team arrived that month at the falls and interviewed me for all of ten minutes to see what the job consisted of. On the basis of that interview, the position would be done away with the next summer as being unnecessary, only to be reinstated a year later, when experience showed the necessity of protecting such a valuable resource by having a patrolman constantly on duty in the area.

All this would come as a bitter lesson to me and other wardens. We would learn that love for the park and the job was not enough, that the real game was the cynical struggle for power and rank, the ascent up the greasy totem pole of advantage. In that game, idealism and dedication would become a definite handicap.

Right then, I had no sense of these limitations. It was a pleasure to breathe that pure ether of hot spruce and wet earth, clearing the head of the winter's perplexed theorems; to let the muscles stretch and push against a tangible obstacle; let the saw rip and roar through the flying yellow sawdust and stink of the cut spruce. Let the trees roll, jubilation loud, down the avalanche slopes, sending rocks crashing with the rolling timber, cracking open to release a whiff of brimstone formed in the shells of sea creatures just a few million years ago, only a wink in the eye of old Kosmos.

The ache in my back was a delight; the pangs in my biceps were caresses that urged me on, finding out how much they could stand, how much they could grow. I lived for the work, surveying my accomplishments with unabashed pride—the log culverts I made, the short-railed bridges over the streams. Anyone would have thought I'd designed another Lion's Gate Bridge the way I strutted around, admiring their brief angles, the fit of the notched logs.

I sat down that day and made a vice with one leg to hold the axe steady while I sharpened it, and was sitting there shaping a gleaming sickle with the flat file, when a most familiar and unpleasant sound insisted on my attention. The infernal blatting of horns. These good people to whom the park is also dedicated were the tourists, there, down in the sunlit valley, driving by the little box of my cabin and the toy horses in their corral. Clouds of dust billowed up to the cabin, as lines of cars and tour buses drove past the sign that says NO THROUGH ROAD, to the campground where they stopped, each in turn, to stare blankly at the end of the conquered world—a place where you actually cannot drive a motor vehicle.

I wonder what they imagined lay beyond that sweep of boulders and white water under the fangs of a glacier waiting to pounce on any mouse-sized contraptions bold enough to venture past road's end. Did they see it as a mere inconvenience, or were there some motorists secretly glad to imagine a mystical wilderness? To them at last, here was the unconquerable unknown, ruled by grizzly bears and, who knows, sasquatches and sabre-toothed tigers. The spirit could imagine a wild world there, if the flesh could not traverse it.

It's a place, I pray, where cars will never be allowed to go. Any moron who proposes to build a road into those sacred precincts should be sentenced to ten years' convalescence in Disneyland to reconsider. And speaking of cars, let's get something straight. I don't hate them for the usual reasons: their pollution of the air, their poor construction and design, or their corrupt function as phallic-status symbols—whoever dreamt that last one up anyway? That's not what cars are about at all. A car is a mouth. Like a miniature black hole in the universe, a car is an insatiable vacuum for eating up space. And as you may have noticed, the one thing in limited supply in this world of ours is space, especially in tiny Yoho Park.

A conservationist once stated that " . . . the size of a park is directly related to the manner in which you use it." Now many pilgrims like to use up the scenery at sixty or seventy miles per hour, sealed in their air-conditioned coffins, with one kid holding a movie camera up to the back window like a tail-gunner in a Flying Fortress. That way they can see where they weren't when they get back home. This is just fine by me. There are highways designed to speed these people on their way, and the sooner they get out of the park the better.

But there is a growing number of other people to whom the future of the parks belong. These are the hikers, riders, skiers, and canoeists, who leave their cars behind and take a day to travel eight miles, savouring every inch of the route they travel. Some of the more sensitive backcountry spots have already been loved to death by the human foot alone. Where there is hardly enough room for the pedestrians there is no room for the automobile.

To my way of thinking, the most far-sighted legislation in park history was enacted in 1905, when the automobile was banned altogether from Rocky Mountains Park (now Banff).

The park environment, scarred by roads and gravel pits in every corner, has gone downhill ever since that ban was lifted in 1911.

So with these sad thoughts and unrealistic hopes in mind, I stood up, hoisting my load, and planning to move to a less violated landscape before my ears sealed up again. Then I noticed my plugs.

They had collected quite a crowd down there. The two of them had their noses stretched out toward the fence, and were nibbling at sugar or apples held out to them by the kids. That was all right with me. It might have been the first time the tykes had been close to a real horse. Maybe some of them thought it was a moose they were feeding, which was all right too since it wasn't. But what irritated me was the way Shawn kept breaking away to trot up and down the corral, tossing his head from side to side like a parade horse.

The lump on my chest gave a painful twinge; likewise the scab on my head. A fat bulldog fly chose that moment to saw itself a steak out of the back of my neck. Dodging my slap, it flew up into a spruce to have lunch.

"Crowbait!" I shouted aloud, waving a fist at the tiny horse circling beyond hearing there below. The word echoed and rolled on the wall of the Vice-President.

Something caught my eye, and I let the next shout fade to a mutter, as a group of hikers came cautiously up the new tread.

"Morning."

"Hi." "Hello." Two couples from the youth hostel, smiling nervously as they edged by this obviously deranged lone ranger, axe in hand and a sheepish grin on his face. With the hiking season under way, I made a mental note to refrain from loud emotional displays and headed back down the trail to take corrective action on the plugs.

There was plenty for the horses to do, new trail signs to be hauled to the junctions, equipment and supplies to be freighted over to the Little Yoho, cans of paint, gas, oil—not to mention the chainsaw, from which a trickle of gas was then leaking down my neck. The cap would have to be replaced before Bess carried it again because gasoline can give a packhorse painful burns and render it unusable for weeks.

There was lots to pack; the trouble was, I didn't quite know how to pack it yet. The chainsaw rig was easy to figure out because the whole thing just strapped on the saddle with its own buckled cinch. But packing anything else horseback is a ticklish business, for various reasons.

Although some horses will carry a loose pack for a mile or two, inevitably there will come that moment when they suddenly lose patience with the strain caused by a slipping pack and the obtuseness of the packer that put it there. They'll charge the lead rider—just to get his attention. Once started in a tantrum, they'll ignore all supplicating whines and angry threats and buck the loose packs off into the worst shintangle they can find. They'll spread butter, paint, underwear, and eggs from hell to breakfast. If they don't tangle a leg in the trailing pack ropes and break their fool necks, they might just find a cliff and jump off in suicidal spite.

Of all the things that have to be learned, such as balancing both sides of the load for even weight, padding noisy items like rattling tin cans that might spook the horse, putting a nose net on horses that want to stop and feed, etc., the most important thing to know is the knot that keeps it all together. It's a knot that keeps the cinch tight and holds the load so it can't be scraped off on a tree, bucked off in a frenzy, or rolled off in a mud wallow.

The knot that prevents these catastrophes, used from Alaska to Texas in infinite variation, is the diamond hitch. Its four-sided shape puts an equal strain on all points of the load and it can be pulled off in a hurry if a horse gets hung up in the timber or bogged down on a ford. It's not an easy knot to learn but no mountain man can travel efficiently without it. Some men have paid as much as $200 to learn how to "throw the diamond."

Neil came up from Field one night to see if I was still alive and seemed politely pleased to discover I was. When I told him of my problems with horse packing (the duel with Shawn I kept tactfully to myself), he offered to show me the famous diamond—gratis. It was dark outside, so Neil demonstrated the knot by lamplight in the cabin. He used a match box for a pack outfit, and a piece of fishing string for a lash-rope.

It took some coaching, but eventually I tied a helluva scale model diamond hitch on that match box which did Neil proud. But the next day, confronting a full-size pack and packhorse, my mind just couldn't seem to make the Brobdingnagian leap in proportion between a match box and a horse's ass. We tried though. Bess stood patiently still for an hour while I threw squares, triangles, rectangles—practically everything in Euclid's repertoire, including one very racy looking parallelogram.

But no diamond.

48

Without a command of the diamond, the packhorse business can turn into a definite liability, life-wise. I was still flailing the air blue with half-hitches when Warden Bernard Engstrom came up from Field with the horse truck and five more horses. I tried to ignore him, hoping it was a mirage that would go away.

Bernie jumped down and came over to the corral. He stood watching for a moment, then gave a disgruntled sigh and got out his makings.

"He told me you could pack, kid," he said sadly.

"Who did?"

"Woledge. Said you threw a real foolproof diamond."

I snorted angrily. "He tell you what I threw it on?"

Bernie lifted his eyebrows quizzically. "On a horse, I would suppose. Unless you were practising on that 'beetle' of yours."

I decided to change the subject. "That Chief Warden has some sense of humour. I've got a lump per laugh so far."

Bernie gave a grim smile. "Could be you and me'll be getting a few more in the next two days. And I don't mean laughs."

The horses pawed restlessly at the wooden deck of the truck. "Give me a hand," said Bernie. "You and me got work to do."

There was a park trail crew camped above Twin Falls and the Chief Warden wanted them moved down to a new camp by the river, where they would construct a new piece of trail surveyed by Gordon Rutherford and me. Slim Hogan, the park Barn Boss and Packer, had freighted their gear up to Twin Falls two weeks before. They were building a wooden bridge to replace the "Eleven Day Wonder," which was a costly steel bridge erected by the park's General Works, after being flown to the site by helicopter. It was lowered into place across the steep cliffs of a small waterfall, and anchored to the rock by steel cables and bolts.

Now, every winter, tons of avalanching snow go roaring down the slopes of Whaleback Peak and collect in the bed of the creek below. Every spring the creek tears itself a tunnel through this barrier of névé and slowly erodes the white arches until some time in July or early August. This process has probably been going on, at a conservative guess, for at least 10,000 years.

So eleven days after the bridge was erected, that clock of water and snow chimed its 10,000th hour. Several hundred tons of ice and snow teetered solemnly into the creek. The creek backed up behind it, gathering power, and began to push that hill of ice downstream. It came sailing noisily around the bend, headed for the lip of the small falls, where the bridge spanned the few feet of space underneath. That ship of ice could never pass. With a twang, those steel cables parted like piano wire and the bridge went flying through the air like a cap popped off a beer bottle.

The ice carried that twenty foot Meccano set downstream and dumped it unceremoniously in the collecting basin at the brink of Twin Falls where you can still see it to this day, rusting expensively, a monument to the power of mountain water and the pride of the engineer.

Slim Hogan had fallen victim to the same kind of mentality that would contemplate putting a steel bridge 7,000 feet up in an alpine meadow, six miles from the nearest road. His position as Barn Boss had recently been done away with in a spirit of economy.

With several thousand precious dollars saved by getting rid of Slim's job, the park was without a practical veterinarian and blacksmith to look after the valuable horse herd, or a packer to supply the fire lookouts and trail crews with food and equipment. That was no problem, the wardens could do it in their spare time. All of this leads me to wonder whether the park paid out more in overtime for the wardens to do Slim's job than they would have paid him to stay in it. What you save on the peanuts, you lose on the bags.

Slim, an equestrian for forty years, found himself demoted to a pedestrian job as labourer on the trail crew. Swallowing his pride, he hung on with the government, or he would have lost his pension benefits, something to consider for a working man of fifty years. To soften the blow, the foreman made Slim Bull Cook for the crew. It was a ludicrous situation. As a friend of Slim's, I can reveal he never did care that much for cooking. I don't know whether he could cook eggs without burning them, but I know damn well I couldn't pack him the eggs without breaking them.

I felt badly about Slim's case. It reminded me of how small a cog each person is in the big wheel of the public service. But if a park warden were to feel grief at every twist and turn of the rack and pinion of bureaucracy, he'd spend his whole life in mourning.

We swung into our saddles and I soon forgot my sense of outrage, as I watched the antics of the packhorses.

Like any bunch of animals, human beings included, they spend their first hour together sorting out the social hierarchy. This one turned out to be a matriarchy, consisting of a grandam, cronies, social climbers, and scapegoat. Each horse took a place in the string and, once under way, they settled into the serious business of jockeying for position. As grandam, Bess showed a side of her personality that I hadn't seen before. Following close behind Shawn, and followed by her crony June, a big roan, she defended her privileged position with a vicious showing of teeth and hooves. Any nag that managed to intimidate June got its ribs drummed on like a tympanum by Bess, until it backed off.

Occasionally a determined social climber would leave the string and try to outrun us, siwashing through the trees to get out front. This produced much outraged snorting and fidgeting in our little queue, which surged forward to bar entry by the usurper. Failing in the attempt, or having run into a *cul-de-sac* of deadfalls, the horse would get mad and try to pull out, headed back down the trail for home. A string of curses and threats from Bernard, usually prefaced by the words "you hammerheaded sonofa . . . ," would turn the pony and send it flying back up to the string, snorting and farting with rage and fear. There it would try to crash its old place in line but this would now be occupied by a new incumbent, who would lash out wickedly. The defeated upstart, now reduced to the role of scapegoat, would find itself at the end of the line, bearing the blame for any dawdling further up the string.

"I'll cut a switch for you," Bernie would growl, "you hammerheaded, knock-kneed, clubfooted sonofabuck!"

By noon we arrived at the foot of Twin Falls and started up the goat's path that leads over a steep rockslide to the plateau of Whaleback, and the trail crew camp. After an hour's hard climb through the switchbacks and over rockslides at the foot of towering cliffs, we stepped off the horses and led them on foot up the last narrow scree slope that led to the notched lip of the plateau.

Below us was the long alley of the Yoho Valley winding south to Takakkaw. A wedge of thunder clouds was pouring through the mountains to the east and spreading out in scavenger squadrons over the wide arc of the icefield above us. The exposed deck of the plateau, lightly covered with small firs, was right in the path of the elements. The white tents of the trail crew, set among sprays of white anemones and green heather, rustled in the afternoon breeze like sails.

51

The men waved hello and went back to packing their personal stuff into rucksacks. One fellow I remembered from a month spent on the crew greeted me as usual by proffering a can of Copenhagen snoose.

"No thanks," I told him. "The last time I took a hit of that shit, I swallowed some of the juice. I did the green-apple quick-step for three days."

He chuckled and spat, dissolving a paintbrush flower with a shot of amber nectar. We tied up the ponies. Zony, the foreman, was struggling with a sleeping bag, trying to stuff it into a tote bag that seemed hopelessly small.

"She's made to be fit, boys," he said. "She's got to be go. Slim's got the coffee hot, down by the creek."

Slim unbent his long, winding frame, taking a second or two to straighten it all the way up, with what seemed an audible creak, the result of too many cold nights spent sleeping on the ground. He looked over our horses and rigging with a practised eye, but made no comment. We stood self-consciously holding the cups of steaming coffee he had offered.

"Cream and sugar?" he asked. The words hung between us for a moment, like a thin veil of poison. The wind picked up and cleared the air, slapping the canvas tent door heavily against the spruce frame.

"Weather comin' in, boys," Slim commented.

"Rain in half an hour," Bernie agreed.

The crew was already heading down, carrying only their hand tools and sleeping bags. We drank the coffee in hurried silence. Slim packed his rucksack and turned to follow the others. He'd stacked the boxes of canned goods, bread, and meat along with the rest of the twelve-man kitchen outfit inside the big cook tent. There were also the tents, a 160 pound rock drill, the sheet metal camp stove, stove-pipes, and odds and ends to pack up.

Slim turned back. "I'll help you fold up the tents," he said to no one in particular.

"Like hell you will," Bernie told him. "If they don't want to pay you for the work, then you don't do it. It just ain't right," he added angrily.

Slim looked at him then. "Just so you know it ain't my idea," he said, and he turned to follow the others.

We finished our coffee. The weather was socking in fast, an electrical storm by the look of the clouds and, by the size of them, it was going to be a gulley washer. Bernie figured it would take two trips to move all the gear down to the valley, so we would take just the essentials today. This included the gas-powered rock drill, broken down into two unevenly weighted sections. The crew had some blasting to do the next day and they needed the drill to make their shot holes.

"Let's fly at it," Bernie said.

We worked for an hour filling the canvas-covered boxes, checking each other's work occasionally to make sure each pair was balanced. There had been bear signs around the cook tent, so the talk centred on bear problems down along the highway.

Bernie cocked his hat back to let the air cool his thinning hair. "Last night I took the bear by the tail and looked him in the eye," he told me, with a wry grin.

"I got a call from the Kicking Horse Campground: tourist up a tree, bear in a car. When I got there, the guy was sitting up in a spruce, bawling like a baby. 'My car is ruined, it's ruined,' he says.

"I looked at the car, and see a big black bear peering over the steering wheel at me. The guy had left a pound of bacon and a pound of jam in the car to keep it safe from bears. Thing is, he left the driver's window open about half an inch. The bear comes along, gets wind of the grub, and chases the guy up a tree, when he tried to defend his car, one of those little sports cars with a convertible hard top.

"The bear looked her over for a minute, kinda figurin' what to do. Then he stood up, slipped a couple of claws into the crack of the window, and popped that hard top off just like peelin' a banana. He sure ruined the upholstery gettin' at the grub.

"I got out the tranquillizer gun, and darted him in the behind. He went up a tree faster than a cat and then passed out, lying across the branches.

"The only way to get him out of there was to climb up after him. Which I did. But when I pulled his tail, to make sure he was still out, I got it right in the eye and all over my bare head: a quart of it, green and slimy." Bernie spat disgustedly at the memory of it, as if he'd got a taste of that bear dung as well as an ear full.

"I hear that stuff will make hair grow," I told him.

"I don't know about that, kid," he said, "but it'll sure make it curl. Especially when your wife gets a whiff of you and hollers for you to get the hell out of the house.

"That anectine really relaxes the bear's sphincter. But stink! Whew! The smell would knock a fly off a gut wagon."

We chuckled over the story as we baled up the tents; then it was time to tighten the cinches.

Bernie checked the back cinches carefully. "Torque them up snug," he ordered. "Especially that roan potlicker."

He took the cinch and booted her in the gut. The air hissed out of her nostrils and her stomach deflated like a punctured tire. "Otherwise they'll be wearing those packs around their ears by the time we get down that cliff," he said.

We started packing then. When the loads are first hung on the saddles, they are held in place with a basket hitch tied in the quarter-inch line kept wound on the hooks of the saddles. The top pack, in this case a stove or a baled tent, is placed on the top of the saddle and tied in place with a rope-end from the basket ropes. The knots are always tied so they can be pulled out quick after one half hitch is taken out.

It takes time to set the loads up properly, making sure that they are hung evenly on the saddle, and that the bottom of the load is higher than the pony's stifle joint at the hip. The portable drill was the worst load. One side had to be packed six inches higher than the other to counterbalance its uneven weight. We were getting tired now, fingers sore from the thin ropes, which were getting wet and stretching in the falling rain.

A word now about the croon. The croon is a very necessary figure of speech to have at your command. Especially when easing a pack mantle over the top of a cook stove mounted on a horse's back in a high wind, as sheet lightning moves steadily closer in a creeping artillery barrage over the glaciers. The pack mantle is a big square of canvas which is unfolded very slowly, while the packer is crooning, and tucked around the pack boxes, to keep it from suddenly turning into a flying jib, say, or a spinnaker, launching your horse into outer space. It keeps the rain off your long-johns, teabags or whatever.

The manual had told me that "When working around horses the individual should keep from becoming excited." And I tried to keep this in mind when June settled her forefoot comfortably down on one of my soggy suede boots, inside of which were the ruins of my five pointed toes. "Move quietly, speak softly but firmly," my manual had enjoined. "Treat the animal kindly," it had added, ironically.

"Would you get off my foot, please," I requested kindly.

"WHAT?" yelled Bernie from the off-side.

"She's standing on my foot," I told him, somewhat strained.

"Well drive the hammerheaded sonofabuck between the horns," shouted Bernie unkindly. He was holding the full weight of the rock drill and had no time for niceness.

Niceness really is a necessity, however, as I have found out through bitter experience, because horses are very high-strung and unpredictable beings. One that will stand still and let you vault into the saddle, to stand on the seat repairing the district phone line while it moves from insulator to insulator on command without mishap, will suddenly panic at the sight of a butterfly, and walk all over you trying to get away.

This is not desirable, as so-called light horses can weigh in at 1,400 pounds. To discourage such picayune antics, the wise greenhorn employs the croon, a kind of unctuous politician's whine of endearment. Mine varied between the cajoling notes of "easy, boys, easy" to the steadily rising tones of "whoa ponies, WHOA ponies! WHOA PONIES!!" as the crisis approached. This was usually brought on by the sight of a hiker's fluorescent red pack, towering three feet above his head and hung with clangorous frying pans and tin cups, as he snorted and hacked his way up a perilously thin trail, ringing a bear bell and blowing a whistle at intervals, to announce his presence to any bears that happened to be deaf or blind. Horses hate hikers even more than hikers hate horses.

So still crooning like Bing Crosby, I eased the pack mantle over the horse in question and tucked it in tight. Bernie said we didn't want any loose ends, which are tricky to clear up while balanced on the side of a cliff. The rain picked up in volume and content, rivalling the roar of Twin Falls Creek which flowed a few feet below the sweep of heather and wet rock where we worked. It was time to deal the diamonds.

"You better watch this carefully, kid," Bernie shouted, the rain pouring off his stetson when he lifted his head, "'cause I ain't gonna show it to you but once."

I wiggled my hat for "okay," and directed a quart of rainwater down the back of my neck. Water flowed in rivulets down our yellow slickers. My blue-jeans had turned into blue sponge. The horses were standing in clouds of their own steam. It was getting dark.

The diamond is tied on a twenty-foot length of nylon or hemp rope, preferably an old one. The new ones are stiff and develop more kinks per foot than a chiropractor's waiting-room. One end of the lash-rope is spliced into the ring of a

wide canvas cinch. On the other end of the cinch is a hard-
wood hook, bound to the cinch by a leather thong.

I've thrown the diamond a couple of hundred times since
that afternoon at Twin Falls, so I know how Bernie did it. At
the time, though, it was like watching a hustler doing card
tricks: the eye always a split second behind the moving hand.

He laid the rope out in a loose pile on the ground, took the
free end, and flipped a length up on the middle of the pack,
the free end trailing down behind the horse until it touched
the ground. Doubling the cinch in one hand and checking the
slack in the piled rope, he tossed the cinch over the pack to the
off-side, bent, and caught the hook as it snapped under the
horse's belly into his waiting hand. "You have to be acquainted with your horse before you try that trick," he
warned.

He adjusted the pack-cinch so that it overlapped the sad-
dle-cinch and wouldn't pinch the horse's breast. Then he
passed the slack of the rope still held in his left hand through
the wooden hook and pulled up tight on the pack-cinch. As
the slack came out of the cinch, he brought the rope up parallel with the one thrown across the pack, and pushed a bight of
it under that rope at the top of the pack, which made one and
a half wraps around the horse. Simple so far, isn't it? Out of
the aforementioned bight he pulled a U-shaped length from
the rope he had first laid down, the one that tails to the
ground, and he threw this loop to one corner of the pack.

Keeping the rope that led from the cinch tight, which is absolutely essential, he passed under the horse's neck to the off-
side, and pulled it snug. I hauled up on it from my side and
went around behind the horse to see if I could help out.

"If you want to help, stay on your own side of the horse,
damn it," said my partner.

The horse eyed me speculatively. "Don't even think about
trying anything," Bernie growled at it.

Keeping the rope snug, he passed it around the rear of the
box, brought it up to the front corner, grabbed with his right
hand at one of the rat's nests of turns that lay jumbled on top
of the pack, pulled the slack out and handed it to me.

"Suck on that one, kid."

I pulled it out and snugged it around the box as he directed.
He moved to the rear of the horse and took the rope end he
had first laid down. I felt the slack go out of my hands as he
pulled it out evenly through the top of the bight. All the ten-

sion of the hitch could now be applied through that one rope end. Bernie told me to hold down on the front of the pack. "Don't ever try this, kid," he said, and he put his boot up on the horse's buttock to get leverage. The veteran packhorse braced itself to take the strain at the touch of his boot, and let out a plaintive sigh as it felt the weight of the 160 pound load settle in. I tried to comfort it with a pat on the head, and it shifted over and stood on my foot again, friendly like.

Bernie tied off the tail rope with a horseman's slip knot that can be yanked out in a hurry. Once the hook is set free, the whole diamond hitch can be pulled off fast in an emergency.

"So now you know how it's done," Bernie said. Rain and sweat ran together down his affable, round face.

"Well, I see that it's done," I told him unhappily. "Just how you done it, I'm not that clear on."

Bernie glanced at his watch. "Don't worry," he said, sounding worried, "by the time we get those other four packed, you'll know all about it that you'll need to know."

The sun went down in an opening of the clouds, leaving only two parenthetical rays to accentuate the twilight. Naturally, we hadn't bothered to bring a flashlight. I learned to tie the diamond hitch in the dark, and to this day, whenever I throw it, I have to close my eyes so as not to get crossed up by that snakelike welter of turns and coils.

The seven horses, tied to trees, were invisible in the black of a most miserable night. The only light came from the occasional flash of lightning, which showed them skittering back and forth on the edge of panic. The sight was so unnerving, that when I thought of trying to round up seven runaways in the blind night, I preferred the blackness to sight. We felt our way from rope to rope like deck hands on the hull of a storm-tossed wreck, our slickers slapping against our wet legs like tattered sails in the eye of the cold wind. Our leather gloves were wringing wet, and we had to beat our numbed hands together to make the fingers respond. It wasn't the lightning or the darkness that was worrying the horses, but the prospect of following that dangerous trail down the mountainside over the wet rocks.

Trail is a poor word to describe that goat path, a drift of unsteady boulders that slides over the edge of the plateau above the valley of the Yoho River. In the daylight we could have tied up their halter ropes and let the packhorses follow us down in single file. But in the darkness we had to travel tailed up: the halter rope of one horse tied to the tail of another, so we wouldn't lose them in the storm or be knocked off our mounts by a spooky charge in the darkness.

The old gelding was collected but quiet, eager to get out of there, as I swung up into the wet saddle. I felt the stiff bight of the mare's halter rope handed up to me out of the ink. "Just give him his head," Bernie shouted over the black pool of the wind. "He knows the way down. Keep your head down, and hang onto the horn." Then he moved back to the end of the string, leaving us alone in the night and the storm.

The gelding stepped off through the rain. I had no sense of direction or motion. He could have been going the wrong way for all I knew, and the thought occurred to me that at any moment we could step off the brink of Twin Falls, off the edge of the world. I could feel the heather under us, by the soft beat of the hooves. Then branches of trees brushed against my legs, that must have been the krummholz that grew near the edge of the cliffs. There were sudden sparks, shooting brilliantly out from the shod hooves, falling down the cliffs like miniature shooting stars. An updraft of air whistled in my ears.

We were at the edge of the plateau, but which edge? Only one narrow chute of scree would lead us safely down. I felt the gelding stiffen his gait, edging his feet forward over the edge of the drop. I sat back slightly, while his forefeet found the steep angle of descent. In confirmation, the luminous thread of the river shimmered far below us, as from the bottom of a well.

The horse moved jerkily down the steep mountainside, almost sitting down at times, letting his forefeet slide until they found a little purchase in the wet shale, which was underlaid by littered bands of rock to form crude steps. The gelding dropped both forefeet together as he moved from step to step, in a brief surrender to gravity that made the muscles tighten spasmodically at the back of my neck. I could feel the scythe of the Grim Reaper caressing my nape, as he hovered over us in the black wings of the storm. I leaned back and back in the stirrups, trying not to push the horse forward with my weight, travelling blind. But Bernie had said the horses could see things in the night, and from travelling on a trail just once, they remembered every twist and turn. To me, the night was one dark story; to the horses it was a poorly lit, but still readable, page.

There came then an ominous but familiar sensation: a tingling wave, a breath that swept over me and made the hair on my arms and head stand on end. I had felt it often enough to know what it was and I pressed down in the saddle, flattening my body against the horse as if I would cover myself under the quilt of his mane.

Suddenly it came. A bolt of lightning tore through the night in a brilliant flare that made the horses crowd together. At the shattering roar of the thunder, which followed immediately, they lunged back hard on the halters, pulling my arm back in one fierce twist of pain. The bolt was close enough to make my head spin, with the same jolt one gets from jumping off a four-foot-high fence and landing stiff-legged on the soles of the feet. An ozone and brimstone smell drifted up from the strike that had hit below us, which shattered the rocks like a shellburst. A muffled shout from the rear drove the horses forward again. I didn't want any more illumination after that brief glimpse of a mountain dropping away from under my left stirrup. The light had gleamed down the wet-streaked walls of rock to the water below in a terrible, beckoning vertigo that made my feet tighten convulsively in the stirrups.

A mountain horse always walks on the outside of the tread, to keep itself clear of obstacles on the bank that might catch in its rigging, and it does this even on the steepest mountainside, walking on the very edge of the drop, like a confident aerialist on a wire hung in space. Occasionally a loose stone could be heard above the rush of the wind, clattering in a flurry of sparks down the cliff bands. The noise made me ease my feet out of the stirrups, until only the edge of the boots were home, readying myself for a sudden ejection. A short prayer would be my only parachute into the jaws of eternity.

There was a softening in the density of the storm and the rawness of the wind was lessened. The horses were on softer ground. Branches popped and the heavy hand of a limb brushed over my hat. The gelding had moved in toward the bank to avoid hanging me in a big spruce limb that hung over the trail. I knew where we were at last. That limb could easily be avoided in daylight and it was obvious that the gelding was completely at home in the dark.

I was leaning forward to pat his neck in gratitude, when a light popped behind us like a flashbulb. Bernie had struck a match to light a smoke. There was a terrified whinny and the sound of packs bashing together, the thud of a hoof on flesh, and the splintering sound of smashed wood. Something struck

59

the gelding's hindquarters and he jumped forward. The halter rope was jerked from my hands and I pulled in the reins, whoaing him up.

Behind us, rocks rolled off the trail and went crashing through the trees down to the river, to land with a splash in the shallow water. A bolt of lightning showed the mare sideways on the muddy tread, the rest of the string crowded behind her, their wild eyes rolling back to the whites. I saw the flash of Bernie's slicker, then the light went out, leaving a brilliant dazzle before my eyes.

"What's up?" he yelled.

"I'll take a look," I shouted back, and slid off looking for the edge of the trail with one foot. But I came down on the butt-end of a wet log that was lying down the slope. My feet went out from under me, and I went down that log as if it was a slide, without even time to yell. The silver water was all I had time to see when I was stopped, as if on belay, by a sharp pull on the belt that knocked the wind out of me. A branch had hooked under the back of my chaps making a deep scratch in the small of my back, which was better than a broken neck. Feeling for holds on the fallen tree, I went back up the hill and found the edge of the trail with my hands.

The gelding was waiting; I could smell him in the dark. It was the mare he was waiting for: he whickered at her, entreating her to move. I found her in the darkness and ran my hands gently up her front legs and around the pack, trying to find the problem. It was June's halter, wrapped around her back legs, that had stopped her. The roan bitch had sat down and broken the halter rope. I was thankful it was the rope that had given and not the mare's spine. Her hocks trembled with fear as I got out my knife and sawed at the stiff rope, but she stood still, counting on me to free her feet and cut the hated rope off her tail.

"Where you been?"

Bernie's voice, suddenly close, made me jump. He had pushed forward in the press of animals to find out what was wrong.

"Hanging around," I told him shortly.

"So's this drill," he grunted. "But not for long."

"Better give me a hand."

I peered toward the voice and made out Bernie's chunky frame outlined against the glow of the water that hissed and rumbled below us. He had his shoulder under the stem of the

60

heavy drill. The wet cinches had stretched and let the uneven load slip until the two pieces were well over the roan's left side. I didn't know what Bernie was standing on, and didn't have time to ask. Squeezing myself between the rocky bank and the horse, crooning endearments, I reached cautiously up and caught the steel handle of the drill, letting my weight come down slowly on it as a counterbalance. I could hear Bernie's harsh breathing on the other side and see the red ember of his cigarette describing frantic exclamation marks in the pitch darkness.

Then the roan surged forward into the mare, carrying me with it, banging its jaw into the steel camp stove on her back, which rang like a gong. The roan stopped dead, momentarily stunned, while I hung on over her withers.

"You still there, partner?" I shouted fearfully.

The cigarette end moved forward for an answer. The roan shook itself like a dog and squealed with fear. As it started to rear up, I clawed wildly for the cheek strap, twisting the horse's neck around to where I could get my teeth into her right ear. There I hung like a terrier, tasting salt and horse flesh. The pony trembled and stood still, as if in a trance. My fingers were slipping one by one off the greasy handle of the drill.

"Wait'll I get my hands on those sonsabitches in Field," Bernie yelled irrelevantly. "Hey kid, where the hell are you?"

"Ahmumphfear," I told him, and I heard him moving along the edge of the trail, his progress marked by a volley of falling rocks and curses. He came up on the left side and took the weight off my arm. The roan calmed down a little, knowing the horseman was near her again. I let go of her ear, but reluctantly.

"What do you want me to do?" I asked.

"Just do your best, kid," he said, "that'll be rough enough."

Between the two of us, with Bess blocking the roan's escape, we got her latigoes tightened and the drill back into delicate balance. Then we hauled ourselves back into the sloppy saddles and splashed down the last dark mile to the valley. When the trail widened, we stopped and tied up the muddy halter ropes so they could move freely again. The mare kept them from getting by me in the dark, until we rode silently into the glow of the crew's bonfire in the dripping spruce forest near Laughing Falls.

The rain hissed and spluttered in the fire. "Well, put on my

61

life-vest and kiss me for luck," said Slim, rolling out from under a spruce. "We was just about to swim up the trail and see if you boys had grounded on a reef or somethin'."

"Come on in, boys," he shouted to the dismal crew, "the water's fine." The men staggered up out of their soggy sleeping bags, muttering and cursing.

"Great weather for ducks."

"Whattaya mean by that quack?"

We unpacked the horses and turned them loose to deadhead back to the falls ahead of us, while we rode soggily behind, teeth chattering in the cold when the rain stopped. It was 3:00 A.M. before Shawn's feet struck the gravel road near my cabin. The pack ponies whinnied from the corral, where they waited to be unsaddled and given their oats.

I made us a pot of coffee and fell asleep in a chair, waking up at about dawn to find the door wide open, and the fire out. There was blood and mud smeared together on the coffee cup, from my dirty, bleeding hands, hands still soft from a long winter of holding pens and books, things that don't move, or have minds of their own like horses or waterfalls. In an hour, Bernie would return and I would help him pack one more load.

Ah, yes, the horse business. There's so much to learn about things like colic, spavins, wind-puffs and poll-evil, about proud flesh, which in its advanced stages, "may have to be burned out with a red-hot iron." Horses have enough afflictions to turn a hypochondriac green with envy and a full list of their vices would make the devil swoon.

Each night I pored over my manual, and every day I watched anxiously for signs of stable vices like "cribbing: chewing on the manger bars and sucking in air; weaving: a horse's rhythmic swaying back and forth in the stall; and bolting: eating too rapidly, which can be cured by putting stones at least as big as baseballs in its feed box."

I checked my horses' feet to make sure there was no crossfiring, scalping, or pointing, and pried into their mouths, relieved to find no molars that needed floating, that is, "filing: a condition which is characterized by much slobbering while chewing food." By the time a week went by, I was a nervous wreck and the horses were as healthy as hogs. I fired my manual into the back of the closet and forgot about it.

3

The Trap

"In the cage there is food.
Not much, but there is food.
Outside are only great stretches of freedom."

Nicanor Parra

It was late summer. The bright days grew shorter, though my callouses were getting thicker. The flies were unbearable and the tourists were unbelievable but, unlike the flies, park visitors could not be swatted or ignored. Serene in unswatability, they intruded on my privacy at all hours of the day or night, days off included. One incident stands out in particular.

It was Saturday evening, my·official bath time. I built a roaring fire in the stove, filled the water reservoir built into its side, and let it heat up until after supper. Then I got the galvanized tub down from its hook behind the cabin, stripped down, lit up a cigar, and soaked luxuriously in the hot suds. That is to say, part of me soaked luxuriously. The tub was only big enough to sit in. Most of me overflowed into the chilly air of the cabin in a quivering topography of goose flesh.

I was thus engaged when the door, which had a latch string instead of a lock, flew open, and I let out a cry of bashful alarm, nearly inhaling my El Producto. I was looking at the barrel of a 35mm camera, wielded by what looked to be an overweight skeet-shooter, crouched behind his rangefinder, wearing a hunting jacket covered with decals, and chrome-plated sunglasses. I leaped out of the tub with a roar and kicked the door shut with my bare foot.

"Some pilgrims up here to shoot sunset on the falls," I muttered to myself, levering my wet legs into my jeans.

Touri Ignoramus seldom knocks when out of his urban habitat. If he tried the stunts in the city that he tries in the woods, he would either be brained by an outraged homeowner, or jailed six months for B. & E. Somewhere along the way, he gets hold of the myth of the old trapper cabin *à la* Jack London. He figures that any building in a rural area smaller than a split-level is supposed to be left open for his use. To discourage trespassing by these larcenous twits, warden cabins, which contain the warden's personal gear and government equipment, are kept locked.

A lock is no guarantee of security, however. On my first trip to the Little Yoho, I found that someone had smashed a window to gain entry to my line cabin. They'd burnt every piece of split wood, left every plate, dish, fork, and pot covered in caked or burnt food, and having tried to light a fire in the oven, instead of the firebox, had turned the interior of the place into a smoke-blackened cave. Failing to master the complexities of a wood-stove, these wilderness adventurers had tried to build a fire in the middle of the floor. Fortunately, they'd lacked the savvy to get it started or the place would have been burnt down. As a crowning touch, they'd defecated in the waterpails, being too lazy to walk twenty yards to the outhouse.

Unfortunately, after they left, a wolverine had followed them through the broken window and tore apart the cupboards to get at the food. There were canned vegetables, flour, and jam mixed with wolverine urine spread all over the log walls. Nailed to the door was a note. The text of it showed, incredibly enough, that whoever had broken in was probably quite well-educated. It read:

> To Whom It May Concern,
>
> Thank you for the use of this lovely hotel.
> We enjoyed our stay tremendously, and we think
> all these cabins should be open to the public who
> know how to appreciate them.
>
> > Signed,   ?

It was potlickers like this that old timer, Wild Bill Peyto, had in mind when he used to leave beartraps set in his cabins. Wild Bill patrolled in deep snow country, so he often built his cabins with the only door located in the roof. Bill would snowshoe up onto the eaves and pick some rocks out of a can he kept tied in an overhanging tree. He used to peg them into the cabin until he heard the trap clang shut, and then he'd jump down inside. Fortunately, Bill had a good memory and never fell into his own snares. Neither did anybody else mainly because Bill had a habit of materializing out of the woodwork with a gun in one hand and a bloodhound named Lightning straining at a length of chain held in the other. Any greenhorn who didn't look self-sufficient, soon found himself running for town with the bloodhound baying on his track.

And so that Saturday, caught with my pants down by the pilgrim on my doorstep, I thought of Bill. A bit extreme he was, no doubt, but basically he had the right idea.

"I wish I had his bloodhound here right now," I thought, as the door creaked open again, and this man's eyes, full of good-natured bovinity, finally focused on me in my lair of steam and spilt water.

His brow wrinkled deeply in perplexity. "One more wrinkle, mister," I thought, "and you could screw that hat on." I braced myself for The Question.

"How ya tunitoff?" he demanded.

The zipper of my fly seemed to have jammed. I tugged at it desperately, with as much dignity as I could manage. The thing was frozen open, and I could hear a woman's voice outside, getting closer.

"I beg your pardon, sir?" Must maintain dignity and civility at all times, I told myself officiously. But the damn thing wouldn't move.

"Thuh watuh. Doncha tunoff thuh watuh, innawintuh?"

Flustered, I gave up and covered myself with a plate. "We don't turn it off, sir. It turns itself off on Christmas Eve. Automatically."

He stood in the doorway, blotting out the sunset, and pondered for a minute the hydrodynamics of my explanation. My own personal waterworks were in danger of being permanently frozen.

Without warning, he suddenly bellowed at me, "MOMMY? HE SAYS THEY LEAVE IT ON AUTOMATIC."

I yelped with alarm as the pots rattled on the stove. The tourist grinned at me, and lifted the peak of his corrective hat. It had on it the design of a Canada goose, rampant on a field of raised shotguns.

"That's what I TOLD you, Daddy," a sour voice replied from the porch. "Didn't I JUST tell you that? But of course you never listen to anything I say, do you, Daddy?"

"Now Mommy . . . " the voices trailed off as he turned and I eased the door shut. I peered out cautiously from behind a curtain, hoping they'd left. Two escapees from an Edward Albee play, footing the porch boards at bath time, was more than my tender psyche could bear. It raised goose bumps on my neurons to rival those on my arms.

He stuck his head back in. "Shuh is a lotta watuh, mistuh rainjuh," he marvelled. Then he was gone.

I watched the elephantine hindquarters of their mobile home recede down the road and then I peeled off the wet jeans and settled back into the tub.

"Tomorrow," I told myself, "I'll install an iron bar to close that door from the inside."

I had just relit the cigar and begun to lather my chest, when the door flew open again and a woman stormed into the room, her long, dark hair flying. She caught sight of me and stopped.

"It's all right," she said airily. "I'm a doctor."

I took the cigar out of my mouth, noting that it was bitten nearly in half. "I am not ill, doctor," I told her coldly, "so I would appreciate it if you would get the hell out of my cabin."

"Don't be silly," she said. "This is an emergency. My friend has fainted on the trail above the road. We need your help. Phew!" she added, wrinkling her nose, an attractive gesture, since it showed her even, white teeth, "What a foul cigar."

I glared at her from behind the El Producto, took a deliberate drag on it, and exhaled a thick smoke screen, to shield me from her appraising eyes. "I'll be glad to help your friend," I told her, "if you would just wait outside while I get dressed." Despite the bluff demeanour, I was a shy youth.

She arched her eyebrows as if to imply that I didn't have anything she hadn't seen before.

A lewdly unprofessional remark came to mind, but male vanity precluded uttering it. After all, what if she was right? But the lady said she would turn her back while I put on my clothes so I thanked her sarcastically and climbed out of the tub.

Once dressed, I radioed the ambulance and got them started on their way from Field. The doctor told me that she and her friend had been hiking all day on empty stomachs and now her friend was suffering from an acute deficiency of sugar, and if I found her conscious, I was to give her some sweet-stuffs at once. I found a can of Coca-Cola and a Hershey bar, grabbed some blankets, and went to the corral where I caught and saddled the mare. The doctor stayed behind to wait for the ambulance while I galloped up the trail in the dark, Coca-Cola in hand, like an actor in some insane soft drink commercial, to rescue a damsel in distress.

Bess found her for me in the dark. A mile up the trail, the horse stopped suddenly and turned her neck to the right, as she caught wind of the victim, who had collapsed a few feet off the trail and was now trembling with shock. I gave her the can of Coke, the universal solvent, and she responded as if it had been a transfusion of plasma. She came around and thought she could ride the horse, so I wrapped her in blankets and, after lifting her into the saddle, I led the mare back down to the road.

The ambulance was waiting. The doctor bundled her friend inside, gave me a friendly smile and they were gone, leaving me with the mare as sole female company. I watched them go, somewhat confused at this sudden bonanza of women, which had now withdrawn again.

I turned the mare out and went back to the cabin, determined to finish my ablutions. I wedged the door shut with my ice axe, poured a hot kettle of water into the tub, and settled back in the foam.

I was inclined to feel lonely, but after a while, I had the distinct impression that I was being watched. There was a scuttling and rustling noise in the cupboard and the patter of tiny feet. It meant livestock, in the form of mice. Disgusted, I finished my bath, wrapped a towel around me and opened the cupboard doors to investigate. A mouse jumped out of a flour sack and dived down through a hole in the back of the cupboard. Raisins, oatmeal, and macaroni were scattered everywhere. The mice had walked in the butter, gnawed the cheese, and had spilt a jar of honey on the top shelf, which oozed down the inside of the doors in a sticky tide, studded with mouse droppings.

A trail of tiny tracks, outlined in flour, led me to the woodpile, where the burglars squeaked defiance under several hundred pounds of firewood. They must have got in through a hole in the chinking. Now they would have to go, and soon. Mice will drive you buggy by leaving crap on your well-polished counters. Running across your face in the middle of the night, they'll give you the fear of the rabid bat.

There were no mousetraps in the cabin, so I would have to build one of my own. All I needed was a lardpail, half full of water; an empty cream can stuccoed with butter and oatmeal, with a hole punched in top and bottom; a wire, and a small plank. These are all harmless ingredients when casually considered. But just add a touch of devious human ingenuity, and you have a water trap, a device that's been around ever since man first moved into permanent dwellings, and mice tried to move in with him.

The wire goes through the cream can, and across the rim of the pail. The plank, leaning against the rim, is the only access to the bait, smeared on the can. Now the trap is set. All that is needed to spring it is a little curiosity: something that both mice and men possess in abundance. A jumping mouse, a slippery footing, and the drowning pool waited below, merciless and serene. The barbarity of the device did not occur to me at the time. Scrubbing out the fouled cupboard, and throwing out a week's supply of food had soured any chance of reasonable debate between man and mouse. I could not see that I had created a paradigm of death, and not just the death of mice either. That recognition would come with disturbing clarity the next day.

I sat down at the table to record the day's events, the game observed, and the work accomplished, in my warden's diary, which was sent in to the Chief Warden every month, but I couldn't seem to concentrate on the work. The bucket in the corner glinted in the lamplight, reminding me of something, yet out of place—like a chamberpot in a church. Annoyed with myself, without knowing why, I opened a book of poetry, thinking to lose myself in literature. The book cracked open to page forty-three. I read, "and the mice are terrified/ We have set traps/ and must always remember/ to avoid them ourselves."

I thought of Bill Peyto then, imagining the malice that must have inspired him to take such chances with his body and soul, to set traps for other men. Yet, that was not what was troubling me. The bucket caught my eye again, and now I knew what it reminded me of. It was another kind of homemade trap I was thinking of, and the legend that lay behind its creator.

A few weeks before, clearing trail on the way to Yoho Lake, I had found a square hole chiselled four inches deep in the trunk of a mighty Douglas fir. The hole had been cut perhaps half a century ago and it was full of dead needles and moss. Curious, I had slipped my hand in, exploring, and something sharp dug into my finger and drew blood. It was a rusty spike, driven up into the hole at an angle from below. The point had been filed to a sharp splinter. It was an old marten-set I'd found that day, cut by a trapper at the turn of the century, before the park was established and trapping outlawed.

Gordon Rutherford had told me how the trap was baited with piece of tallow. Tallow wouldn't have much value to a marten, but it is an animal fiercely jealous of its territory, and nosy about any kind of intrusion. And so it would slip its sharp nose into the hole to sniff at the bait. The sharp spike would slip into its throat when it tried to back out, and its struggles would only impale it deeper on the spike until it had bled to death, left hanging on the tree that up until then had always offered a safe refuge. The trapper would pack the frozen body to his cabin, thaw it out and skin it. Later the pelt would decorate some wealthy lady's vanity. The carcass would be fed on by the ravens.

I turned the lamp out, opened the grate of the Quebec heater, and threw a log on the fire. The wind sighed in the stovepipe, and an owl hooted once over the roof. The flickering firelight threw my shadow in wavering outline on the log walls. I remembered the legend of the trapper that I had first heard about by a campfire on a windy night such as this.

It was up by Yoho Lake that he came upon the track of Mustahyah, the mighty bear. The tracks were ten inches long, and he knew from the scats of the grizzly that he was healthy and in prime condition. So he set his traps for the bear, but it was too smart to step on the pan. It seemed the bear could smell that iron no matter how carefully the jaws were hidden or how much the bait stank.

The trapper had fashioned a deadfall, triggered by a tripline, and armed with iron spikes. He baited the ground beneath the heavy logs with the ripe entrails of an elk. A few days later, he found the bear pinned under the heavy logs with a broken back. The bear was still alive. It gave him a terrible look that made him raise his rifle quickly and fire. The bear died without a sound, its eyes fixed on something behind the trapper, something he couldn't see when he turned to look.

A few days later, the trapper was working with his partner, cutting trees for a new line cabin. He was running out of the way of a falling spruce, when he tripped on a hidden root. The tree landed on his right leg, crushing the shin, and pinning him to the ground. His partner couldn't move the heavy tree, and in his haste to cut the trunk in half, he jammed the saw in the pinch of the trunk, and then broke the axe handle trying to free the saw. This was always wondered at afterwards, because this man was one of the best woodsmen in the country and had never been known to lose his head no matter what the emergency.

The trapper's face was white with shock. His partner covered him with blankets, left him a bottle of whiskey to kill the pain, and left on the run for Field, ten miles away, to get help. He planned on coming back that same night but a snowstorm and high winds caught the rescue party halfway up the trail and forced them to take shelter until dawn.

When they reached the place, everything was covered in a foot of fresh snow, and there was no sign of life by the downed tree. The injured man had vanished. Digging frantically in the snow, the rescuers found only the empty whiskey bottle, and one other thing, the trapper's right leg, amputated at the knee by his own skinning knife, and still pinned under the tree. But there was no sign of the man himself. All tracks had been obliterated under the falling snow. After searching for a few days they concluded that, delirious with pain, he must have crawled into the river and been swept away.

Full of remorse at the loss of his friend, the partner decided to give up trapping, and made one last snowshoe trip over the line, picking up traps as he went. The catch was poor. All he found were a couple of marten, and the usual assortment of squirrels and birds that wandered into his traps searching for food. In one trap was the foot of a rabbit which had gnawed itself free and crawled away to die in the bush. The sight nauseated him, but he picked up the trap and moved on.

When he came to the last trap, a wolf-set located near the tree line, he found something that turned his blood cold. A goat had run over the trap on its way to a mineral lick, and had been caught by one leg. This was unusual but understandable. The animal had been pretty well devoured by scavengers. What made his hair raise was the sight of the animal's hindquarters. A back leg was missing, neatly severed at the knee joint by a knife blade. There were fresh tracks in the snow nearby, mixed among those of the ravens and whiskeyjacks. One was a human footprint, the other the split hoofprint of a mountain goat.

The trapper abandoned his load of traps on the spot, and fled down the mountain to Field. He left that night on a train headed east and never returned.

But since that time, along about dusk, the odd traveller has caught sight of a human figure with long, white hair, moving along the ledges just above the timberline, but moving like no human could ever move along those thin angles, and recognized the Old Man of the Mountain, part man and part goat, with something that looked like a rusty knife held in his outstretched hand.

Or so the story goes.

Fact and imagination make fascinating partners and the legends they breed, though denounced as an unnatural child by both, still contain one or two features that testify to legitimate conception. The real trapper in that country was a man named Jack Otto, and it must have been he who drove the nail that pricked my consciousness sixty years later. In the winter he travelled these mountains on his snowshoes, sleeping at night in a pit dug four feet into the snow, with a fire at one end to keep him warm. Whether or not he'd ever been pinned under a fallen tree is not known. I do know that he didn't turn into a mountain goat. He and his brothers moved to Jasper, where they trapped, guided, and among other things, started the first Ford dealership there, and they built the first pool hall, which is still standing. Solid citizens.

Like all fables this one has a moral. The man who had lived on the suffering of wild animals had been trapped like an animal, and in his suffering had recognized a terrifying metamorphosis. The hunter becomes the hunted. Those who forget their kinship with the natural world and live only to exploit it will be reminded of their animal nature in frightening ways.

I remembered the story, but it didn't change my mind about getting rid of the mice. After all, a mouse may be a mammal but it isn't exactly a totemic figure like the bear. Besides, the cabin was not part of the natural order of things. It was man-made, and mice had no place in the layout. Still, the construction of the trap filled me with vague forebodings, a kind of unpleasant *déjà vu*. I mulled it over in bed, but made nothing more out of it before I fell asleep.

The next day brought harder riddles, grimmer portents.

I'd gone up to the Wapta Station to discuss some cabin repairs with Gord Rutherford. We were standing near the open door of the barn, talking in the bright sunshine that streamed in dusty rays through the conifers that lean over the corral. Bev, Gordon's wife, came hurrying out of her kitchen door a few hundred feet below us, and I wondered why anybody would want to run on such a hot day.

71

The air throbbed as a hummingbird darted between us, its brilliant wings shimmering in the sun. Gordon was forking hay to his horses and stopped for a minute, the handle balanced in his thick hands, to hear what she was shouting.

Her voice broke unnaturally loud in the clearing. " . . . a radio call for you. They say a man fell in the Kicking Horse! Down on the Big Hill!"

In the Kicking Horse. Might just as well say a flying saucer landed at Wapta Lodge, and the crew were in having a beer, for all the effect the statement had on the untroubled blue of the sky. Traffic whizzed by on the highway below the station. The white summits of the Lake O'Hara group shone on the green tongue of a moraine that swept down across the valley to lap at the shores of Wapta Lake, a touch of wind ruffling the green surface. Somewhere below the outlet of the lake, down below where it boils over the edge of the pass and beats itself into atoms in the dark canyons, a man was lost.

The day seemed far too bright to admit the darkness of death, and so we paused a split second, as if Gord's wife had said something amazingly bizarre. An afternoon wind gathered the green skirts of the evergreens in toward the corral, until they leaned over us like matrons who had overheard a four-letter word. Bev opened her mouth to tell us again, but by then we were already moving.

"Meet me at the truck," Gordon said. "I'll pick up a climbing rope in the house."

Midway down the Big Hill the river pours into a deep whirlpool, gathering its force for the final run down to the gravel flats two miles below. It pours in under a spray-flecked cliff, rushes down a rocky chute and hurtles deep into the bottom of the pool. It carries driftwood, heavy logs, fish, and the odd dead moose, and bats them playfully end-for-end on its spinning fulcrum. Anyone who fell into that pool would be battered to death in the chaotic swirl of rocks and debris. The icy temperature alone would kill a man in thirty minutes.

The water roars, murmurs, and chuckles to itself like a green living spirit under the mossy cliffs, and then flattens out in a final run through two six-foot-wide culverts that lead it under the highway and shoot it out into the canyon below.

It was into this pool that the victim, a middle-aged man, had fallen. A witness waved us to the view point above the pool, and indicated the exact spot. I tied a bowline around my waist and Gordon belayed me down the steep cliff to do a hasty search for the victim. For some reason, the man had tried to climb down a steep cliff, without a top rope and wearing smooth-soled street shoes. I moved down the thin holds, leaning out on the rope and straining to look under the overhanging cliff below me; but there was no sign of the victim. The roar of the water washed over my senses like a charm and I gazed, fascinated, into the violence of caged water. The green door of chaos whirled there, in a dizzy circle below my feet, while the brightly lit stream above disappeared under the shadow of the overhanging cliffs. Here was the vanishing point of half-sensed desire—Thanatos, the God of last wishes.

Then I saw a white scar on the dark rock where some loose stones had been pulled out of their bed, probably by the victim's hands. I was standing on the ledge where he had stood. Why had he come down to this dangerous place?

I will never know what it is that draws people to the very lip of a precipice, to gaze down under the spell of gravity. But I have caught them in the act of climbing over protective fences to get closer to the edge; I have seen them balancing on rotten logs to peer into a 1,500 foot drop. They stand or sit on the dry rock just at the lip of a waterfall, reaching out a tentative hand to feel the cold force of the water. A sudden wave will wet the rock beneath them; suddenly, they slip out into space and hurtle into the river below. Scarcely a summer goes by without a human fatality in the mountain parks, from this or similar causes.

The ledge that I stood on sloped down to the river, but it was wide enough to offer good footing. Then a slight disparity of the water, who knows from what cause, made the standing wave of the current break a few inches above its watermark on the cliff. The water flooded over the ledge, and turned it instantly into a greasy slide. My feet slid backwards, and the rope tightened on my waist. Then I knew that the ledge was the pan of a trap, but what motive lay behind its creation? I thought, then, that there is a power in the universe that plays with men, the way that men play with mice.

I left the place, hating the look of it. A shower of pebbles and dust pattered down from the top of the cliff. I heard Gordon shouting at someone to get back from the edge. The red flasher of the patrol truck was drawing tourists off the highway, the way a lure draws pike. I went up the cliff fast, the rope tight around my waist, as Gordon leaned into his shoulder belay, warping me up with his powerful back and arms.

73

I heard the radio crackle in the truck. Wardens Malcolm McNab and Bernard Engstrom were en route with grappling gear and a boat. The local Mountie, patrolling some distance away, would be there in a few minutes.

"I better stay here and control this crowd," Gordon said. "You check downstream."

Some local fishermen came up to offer help and I took them with me to act as lookouts by the culverts. A woman hurried out of her mobile home and waved me down and I stopped, hoping she had some news of the victim.

"Did you find the body?" she asked eagerly.

Her husband came up beside her. "I'll bet he looked pretty awful, huh?"

They were hoping to hear all the grisly details. Behind them was the victim's car with his children and wife sitting in the back seat, her face buried in her arms, mute with grief. The sight of the victim's family brought home the sense of helplessness I felt, knowing there was no hope her husband would be found alive, yet concealing this by an optimistic display of activity. In rescue work, we never pronounce anybody dead until the body is lying in the morgue.

The Mountie arrived with siren blaring, closely followed by McNab's half-ton. I left the two ghouls with their question unanswered and went to help unload the aluminum boat and dragging gear. Gordon and I stood by with heaving lines, as Malcolm and Bernie tied on their life vests. Bernie stepped into the bow, and Malcolm pushed the fourteen foot boat into the water. Some deadfall came hurtling through the white water, slammed into the culvert, and broke into two jagged pieces. Fearing that the boat would be pushed downstream and swept through the culverts like the deadfall, Gordon and I manned them with our lines, ready to catch the boat, but this precaution wasn't necessary.

There are some men who wear an aura of confidence about them that makes them the focal point of any rescue operation. Malcolm is that kind of man. The minute he appeared on the scene, the search shifted smoothly into gear, and my sense of helplessness was gone.

Malcolm McNab, grey-haired and rock hard from fifty-seven years of living with the sun and wind on his face, leaned into the oars, and the boat darted forward like a live thing. Malcolm was raised in the Lesser Slave Lake country with the sound of canoe water in his ears. Then he spent twenty-nine

74

years in the Arctic as a trapper, as a reindeer herder on the Arctic coast, and as a game warden. In all that time, water was the only highway he knew. In 1954, he transferred to Yoho Park, and had to learn how to drive a car for the first time in his life. So where other men would have hesitated at the sight of that whirlpool, Malcolm only glanced at it once, as he swung the boat into the current.

He inclined his weathered face slightly, watching the angle of the hull from under eyebrows black as a raven's wing, listening to the news of the water, the threats and triumphs of the river. In two short strokes of the oars the boat shot across the rapids, the bow angled upstream. He took it into the lee of the rock by the left bank, water and heat shimmering on the bright hull, and then nosed it around through the current into slack water at the outer edge of the whirlpool. There he held it steady with slight reverses of the oars, a graceful sleight of hand, while Bernie crouched in the bow with a grapnel.

Malcolm knew the ways of this kind of water, and he knew about bodies in whirlpools. He knew exactly where the body would be found, he had known it from the moment Gordon described the place on the radio. Since this man had been a non-swimmer, there was no chance of the victim being swept downstream unless, by some miracle, he'd managed to avoid the undertow of the pool. Malcolm told me later that in such cold water, a human body would sink immediately. It would take a couple of days for enough gas to build up in the body to float it up out of the depths, like a sullen fish.

The grapnel arched up, gleaming in the sunlight, and dropped into the centre of the pool. The line played out. Up on top the Mountie was busy trying to keep the traffic moving, so Gordon went up to control the bystanders who were pressing forward again toward the guard-rail, their cameras at the ready. There were not enough officers to control the endless stream of tourists. Gordon shouted for them to "get the heck away from there"—about the closest the big man ever comes to profanity, and a sure sign that his temperature was reaching a boil.

When the grapnel flashed out again, Malcolm moved the boat in a little closer. Their two figures were dwarfed by the high, polished walls of the canyon. All at once, the line went tight, snapping beads of water off the length of it leading in to the boat. Bernie leaned out over the bow, hauling the line in and said something to Malcolm, who let the boat swing into the current, taking it across with three strokes of the oars, deflecting and channelling its power with the glistening blades. Something floated heavily in the lee of the bow. Bernie kept it downstream, hidden from the tourists who watched from above.

The crowd was silent now, holding their cameras, but not taking any pictures. Some of them turned away, heading for their cars. They wanted out of there fast and, quite frankly, I wouldn't have minded getting lost myself when I saw the man's hair streaming in the current. But I was paid to stay.

"Give us a hand," Bernie called, and I scrambled down the bank and waded into the cold water up to my knees to shake hands with Death. I hesitated when his icy fingers brushed over mine.

"Just grab ahold, Marty," Gordon said behind me. "Let's skid him out of here before his wife sees him."

So we dragged him up the beach, Malcolm and Bernie carrying the boat beside us, to screen the body from the victim's family. The Mountie was keeping them back from us, getting them started for the hospital, toward the first acceptance of their loss.

We laid him down and Malcolm went to get a blanket, to hide the sight from the road. The saddest thing about the victim was his bright holiday clothes, dripping water on the dry white rocks. Those colours mocked the white skin, and the unbending formality of the arms. With a shock that made my eyes burn, I saw in the helpless attitude of the flesh, something of the child, and something of the boy, who had grown into this middle-aged body, that now had come to the sudden end of all dreaming. I saw how tenuously the line is drawn between human plans and callous destiny that metes out pleasure and pain in the same gesture.

The tasteful clothes, carefully co-ordinated now in their limpness, mocked the aspirations of the man who had worn them. The sight produced in me, a stranger, an overwhelming sense of loss, as if it was my own father lying there. More than that, it was as if, in that realization of kinship, it was myself grown to middle-age, lying there abandoned, the victim of a momentary impulse that now had ruined a family. It was my own death I saw lying there by the river, with the indifferent sun glaring in my open eyes.

There was no need to abuse the body with what would have been a travesty of artificial respiration. The local coroner came down the bank, bent over it, and released us with his legal pronouncement.

"Dead."

Malcolm covered the body with a blanket, and the hearse backed down the ditch to take it away. A man came down the bank from the watching crowd, holding a camera in one hand, and a light meter in the other. Moving with the assurance of one who is used to getting what he wants, he adjusted his camera as he came forward, not really noticing us standing a little way from the dead man.

The coroner moved between him and the body, and the man, startled, stopped short and looked at the coroner.

"What can I do for you, fellah?" the coroner demanded.

"I'd just like to get a picture," the man said matter-of-factly, and moved as if to go around him. The coroner stopped him with a hand on the shoulder.

"You with the police?" he asked, "Or the press?"

"No," the man replied, with a slight edge of irritation in his voice, "I just want a picture."

The coroner stepped into him then, pushing him slightly off balance, though he made it look unintentional. "You better get the hell out of here, fellah," he told him evenly, "or you'll get a helluva lot more than you bargained for."

His feelings plainly ruffled, the man huffed indignantly up to his late-model car and got in, slamming the door. He had a wife, and a load of kids in there and he wanted a picture of a dead man.

"Jesus," I marvelled, "where do they come from? Does somebody send away for them or what?"

But Bernie said, "There are lots more like that, so you better learn to love them, kid."

Then we loaded him in the hearse and they took him away. The cars drove out onto the busy highway with the sun streaming down on a scene that now bore no evidence of human tragedy, just a few men in green uniforms standing beside a river. "What do you suppose they're doing down there?" somebody might ask. And somebody else would say, "I dunno, probably just fishing."

A man had died.

The birds sang, people waved hello as they drove to their summer places, children, their faces bright flowers, waved at the wardens who waved back, "Hello, hello."

One candle snuffed out.

77

"You'll get used to it, Marty," Malcolm told me, "just like anything else."

Only you don't get used to it, not at all. You just get good at pretending you are. Having gained some new insights into the life of a park warden, I drove back to Takakkaw Falls thinking about blue skies and sudden death that happened as casually as the death of a fly swiped by a horse's tail. I sat in the moonlit softness of the cabin late that night, drinking whiskey from a glass to ward off the shadowy figures of the watching spruce outside.

After a while, when I lit the lantern, I saw the water trap and remembered how I had left it set that morning. There was a victim in the pail. A small figure slowly circled the metal canyon of the drowning pool. It was a deer mouse, still gamely swimming, his tail trailing behind for a rudder.

What kept it going? I wondered. Why didn't it give up and surrender to the inexorable pull of the water? There could be no chance of escape so it should have died as easily as the man in the river that morning. Nothing in its instincts would lead to the notion of mercy. It was beyond the mouse's comprehension, as well as its experience, to expect mercy from a predator. And yet, choosing to live to the last possible second, it swam on, in defiance of the giant shape that loomed over it. The deer mouse refused to acknowledge the rule of the trap.

I emptied the water carefully out of the pail, and scooped my small survivor out to dry in front of the stove, determined that something should be salvaged from the ruined day.

"No more traps in this house," I told it. "I've seen enough of traps today."

A scuffling movement caught my attention. Something was watching me from the dark corner. Slowly I reached out for the flashlight kept handy on the table. The beam revealed a beady-eyed mammal with a bushy tail, slinking along the wall with a spoon clenched in its teeth–a pack rat. The rat made a dash for the corner behind the stove, and I followed with the flashlight beam. There was the hole in the chinking I'd been looking for, made by the rat. He rushed for it, but it wasn't big enough for him to go through with the spoon which caught in the hole. He dropped it with a clatter, and was gone, running across the porch, heading for his nest under the tack shed. That's likely where I would find my watch, which had recently disappeared. Pack rats have a love for shiny objects. It would be buried in his nest under several hundred pounds of dried mushrooms that he'd been storing lately, for the coming fall.

The night grew darker as clouds scudded over the moon. Opening the cabin door, I felt the night cold settling in the valley, with more than a late August chill in its breath. The light showed a fine net of snow spinning in from the north. The snow would melt in the first light of the sun tomorrow, but my summer at Takakkaw Falls was coming to a close.

In the window was the reflection of a stranger, a healthier looking specimen than the boy who had stood there one day in May, with a bit more firmness around the shoulders, and in the line of the jaw. I raised my glass and drank a toast to youth and good fortune, to horses, waterfalls, Chief Wardens, and whatever or whoever it is that sends the moonlight streaming on river water. I fell asleep sitting by the fire in the open grate.

One day late in September, the horse truck came and took my two hay-burners back to the Ya-Ha-Tinda Ranch. They stood happily in front of the box, their manes flying in the wind, and never looked back. For winter was in the air and they knew their work was through. The larch trees were turning yellow in long necklaces of gold around the mountains. I boarded up the cabin, and headed east for Calgary.

In a few days I would be married to a lady who said she had waited long enough, that there were many fish in the sea and, for that matter, many seas she would like to fish. Maybe she'd be back, or perhaps she wouldn't. The relationship had been blossoming steadily for about five years, and neither one of us wanted it to end. So I went into hock, bought her a ring, and wrote an engagement song of enduring love. I yodelled it at her one night to the twang of my guitar, which had been loaned to me especially for that occasion by a sympathetic pawnbroker who was holding it as collateral on said ring.

She said, "Yes, I will."

One blustery fall day, the relationship was formalized to the satisfaction of all concerned. I never thought that the lady would marry a man whose first words to her had been, "What lovely teeth you have. Are they your own?" I had waited helplessly for the rebuke that would cut me to the bone, already preparing to ease out of my chair and slink off to throw myself under a bus. But she had smiled kindly at me and replied, "Yes, they are. My very own."

We went east for the winter, and it wasn't until the spring

that Myrna and I came back to the mountains. There were no openings in Yoho Park for a patrolman, so I applied for a position in Jasper National Park as a seasonal park warden, which was a grade or two above my previous job, meaning the pay was twice as much for doing one-quarter as much work and taking on one-third of the responsibility, at least most of the time.

So one May morning I sat in an office in Calgary across the table from three careful and dedicated men. Two of them asked irrelevant questions about the life cycle of the hoary wood bat. The other, veteran Chief Park Warden Mickey McGuire, said nothing, but listened carefully, while looking me over as if he would have loved to examine my teeth and hooves.

"Which theory do you think Parks Canada should be following?" one of the two asked me, "for the purpose of managing the environment? The evolutionary concept, with all its unpredictable connotations? Or a more dynamic approach, with active manipulation of the ecosystem?" And he settled back in his chair.

"That's a good question," I began, and tried to fend it off as best I could. It was a good question, because nobody in the entire parks service had the slightest idea how to answer it. McGuire gave me a grim smile. He had decided to rescue me.

"In other words," he began ironically, "in other words, if you looked out the window of the Athabasca Hotel and saw a fire coming for town at about thirty miles per hour down the side of Tekarra Mountain, would you go throw a bucket of water at it, or order another round?"

The other two interrogators stirred uncomfortably in their chairs.

"In other words," Mickey went on, "if you see a tourist feeding potato chips to a grizzly bear, which of the two would you boot in the behind? See what I mean? Is that what you were driving at, gentlemen?"

"Well, yes. In more simple terms, I suppose."

"Yes," said Mickey, nodding his grey-haired head, "I do like to keep things simple." Then he asked a few questions about my work in Yoho Park, while he leafed through my application form.

"I see that you're a married man now," he said. "You know, if I had my way, I'd have the wives in here with the men at these interviews. No sense hiring a man if his wife doesn't like the bush."

One of the bureaucrats cleared his throat with impatience. The Chief Warden had made a heretical statement, since under the new system of centralization, wardens and their wives were supposed to be moved out of the backcountry and into town. Their wives no longer had to have the slightest interest in the backcountry. But this Chief Warden fought the new system every step of the way and in his park there were still wardens living in the backcountry districts, which suited me fine.

"Does your wife ride?" he asked.

"Yes," I answered cautiously. After all, he never asked what.

"Can she shoot straight?"

"Like Annie Oakley."

"Split wood?"

"She's deadly with an axe," I answered.

"I don't see the point . . . " one of the others put in, but Mickey silenced him with a distasteful glance and turned back to me.

"Kid, it's always entertaining to be bullshitted by an expert. But, tell me the truth now. Is she a city girl? Would she like living in the bush?"

"She's right off the farm," I told him, stretching the truth by about six years. "She loves wood-stoves. She likes cold weather, prefers it to hot. She's one of those people who likes to get wet in the rain. She likes the wind on her face. Loves to hike, ski, ride, you name it. She's strong and she's tough." And this was all true.

Mickey eyed me with new respect and sat back in his chair, considering. Then he shot forward as if to catch me off guard.

"How tall is she?"

I wondered what this had to do with anything, but answered honestly. "Five foot ten."

McGuire was impressed. "Good," he grinned. "She'll be able to carry waterpails over the snow drifts without spilling them."

The interview was over and a few days later I got a letter telling me the job was mine. Somehow, though, I got the impression that my shrewd choice of a mate had at least as much to do with my success as my knowledge of ecology or my previous experience.

4

Something's Burning

"O western wind, when wilt thou blow,
That the small rain down can rain?
Christ, if my love were in my arms
And I in my bed again!"

anon.

We moved to Jasper Park where I was disappointed to learn I would have to spend part of the season working near the highway, with a chance of a move into the backcountry later in the summer.

And so I patrolled up and down the road, putting out illegal campfires, directing and correcting the tourists, chasing bears, collecting sheep crap for a scientific study, and arresting the odd drunk driver when the RCMP detachment was too far away to help.

The green uniform made me sweat. It was a dry, hot summer in the valley of the Athabasca, the summer of the fires.

Heat waves were dancing on the sandhills of Talbot Lake, seventeen miles north of Jasper on the Yellowhead Highway. The bighorn sheep, lying near their licks on Disaster Point, and resting in the afternoon heat, looked down on the highway and the wide stretch of the Athabasca where it winds beneath the big square of Roche Miette to the east, and the low, grassy hills of Moosehorn Valley to the west.

In a few more miles I saw sun glancing on the tiny silver box of Celestine Lake Tower, high above the valley. The tower man spotted my truck with his binoculars and greeted me on the VHF radio. The smell of woodsmoke in the air kept us all on edge. There were full Gieke bags of water and sharpened fire-fighting tools in the back of the pick-up, and I was expecting to use them that day. There had been several lightning strikes two days before which could have erupted into fires at any time.

The heat glared up off the pavement. It was hard on Myrna, who was five months pregnant, and we were planning to spend days off at a nearby lake, where we could swim, sip tall drinks, and relax.

Then, at 2:00 P.M., the radio crackled with a terse message from Jasper. Area Manager, Max Winkler, was calling all men under his command to report to Jasper immediately. Two fires had broken out almost simultaneously from lightning strikes, one on Whistler Mountain, near Jasper, and the other on Mount Quincy near the headwaters of the Athabasca River. The Whistler fire was steadily marching across the slopes and down the mountain, threatening the town of Jasper.

I swore out loud and picked up the microphone to acknowledge the call. Myrna would be packing the car right now for the trip we'd talked about that morning over breakfast. Now I would have to leave, not knowing for how long, without even saying goodbye. I called Jasper and asked them to telephone the news to her, then switched on my red dome light and punched the gas pedal to the floor, weaving in and out among the Winnebagos.

Twenty minutes later I arrived at Whistler Campground, the staging area for our fire-fighters. Jim Whyte, the fire boss, had to ensure camp was set up near the Quincy fire, while he planned and organized the fight. There were no senior men to spare, so when I appeared on the scene, Jim appointed me camp boss. Equipment for my thirty-three men lay in a chaotic pile, dumped by trucks from the park's central stores.

To get equipment and fire-fighters to Mount Quincy, Chief Warden Mickey McGuire asked for help from the Armed Forces base at Edmonton, Alberta. They dispatched a Chinook helicopter, which landed in due course at the staging area. The fire-fighters, an assortment of volunteers from Jasper, struggled in and began helping me load the equipment.

Our men, who were mostly young transients, were eager to work. It looked like some of them hadn't eaten in days, so I don't know whether it was the money or the prospect of free meals that attracted them most. I made a note for the fire boss to lay on the groceries without stint. This gang was going to be ruled by its stomach. I decided, as we filed aboard, that what we needed desperately was a good cook.

83

Jim Whyte was going in on the first flight with us to select a campsite from the air. The Armed Forces crew were nattily turned out in berets and spotless fatigues. My crew was casually clad in jeans and headbands, with shoulder-length hair and peace signs painted on their Hell's Angels-style jackets with the sleeves cut off. Some of them strove for a harlequin effect with multi-coloured patches stitched onto their jeans. Others sported faded trousers with the seat blown out. They wore a uniform of blue denim and were like an opposing army invading the green helicopter as they flashed a Churchillian V for victory at the grim-looking corporal in charge of the cargo. It was going to be a strange war.

A few of these men, as it turned out, were draft dodgers from the American Army. They were quiet and plainly apprehensive. Being in a military helicopter was not helping the paranoia of being on the run, even if it was a military that only had observer status in Vietnam.

It was late in the afternoon when the powerful engines started up and the twin rotor craft got under way. But something was wrong, we weren't taking off. Outside, I could see people running for cover. A packhorse, loose from its tether, crow-hopped around the infield. Our machine was rolling along on its two back wheels, the front ones pawing the air like a stallion penned in a corral. It was overloaded, but apparently not by very much. An order crackled over the intercom. One of the crewmen poised in the doorway, then leaped out. A hundred and eighty pounds lighter, the craft was immediately airborne, flying a few feet above the trees.

"That's pretty close," I told Jim nervously.

"Close enough for government work."

We left the highway below us in a few minutes, and turned to fly up the Athabasca, toward Mount Quincy. The plan was to land near the junction of the Chaba and Athabasca Rivers to set up camp. While we were doing that, Jim would fly up to estimate the potential spread of the Quincy fire, then return to Jasper to pick up the final load of men and equipment.

We could see smoke boiling up from a hanging valley on Mount Quincy as we flew on. The fire was holding its own, but it would lie down at night and be dormant until the sun and the winds began to work on it the next day. We were pushing our luck to set up camp at such a late hour, but if we could get on the fire early enough the next day we would have a chance to hit it hard while it was still weak.

84

We circled over the river, looking for a place to land. The pilot, being an army man, felt we should land a little closer to the "enemy," but not wanting to take a chance on the fire burning over us and converting me and my men into Rice Crispies, I asked him to put us down near the river junction.

There was a small peninsula jutting out into the river that looked like a good place to land. I assumed the pilot would set us down there, but should have watched to make sure that's what he did.

We landed. Jim stayed in his seat, talking to the pilot about the next day's requirements. I needed a co-leader from the volunteers to make sure the greenhorns kept clear of the helicopter blades when we got out. I appointed John Crawford, a professional wildlife photographer and former US marine, who had signed on as a fire-fighter for the duration.

We got out and started unloading the stuff. It wasn't until the helicopter took off that we realized we were not on the river bank at all, but on an island in the middle of the main channel.

In peace time, the military are scrupulous that landing pads must be absolutely flat, or so I was told afterwards. But I still wonder if the landing site had anything to do with the pilot's view that the long-hairs needed a bath, because there was no way of getting across the river without taking one. The island was about seventy-five yards long, and getting smaller by the moment due to the day's meltwater, still flowing in from the Columbia Icefields.

The crew waited for direction. I was their fearless leader, but I hesitated at the prospect of plunging into the rapids with a gas drum balanced on my head and a cry of "Follow me, lads" on my lips.

Crawford didn't hesitate, however, being the kind of man who likes to fill a vacuum with action. While we were stripping off our duds, thinking to keep them dry in case we didn't drown, the ex-marine leaped into the breach with a 100 pound tent on his head, for ballast.

John is a tall man but he didn't impress the Athabasca. It swallowed him right up to his chin, licking at his lips with the cold kiss of a melting glacier. He treadmilled on tiptoes against the current but it was sweeping him into a little right-hand turn that would leave him headed out into main stream.

With John in the thick of things, a few of us made a running leap at the far bank, which we missed by about forty feet. We flailed across somehow, found a pole for him to grab, and pulled him in.

With John safely landed, we waded back into the river and formed a human chain to relay the equipment across the channel.

The river had reached peak volume for the day. I could hear boulders rolling along the bottom and smaller stones clicking against them like billiard balls. The river was grinding its teeth. We were the meal.

Standing in the Athabasca River with the sun going down in flames over the rocky fangs of Dragon Peak was a staggering experience. It would have made a great photo for a beer ad, the kind that emphasizes cool refreshment. The glacial melt was around thirty-five brisk fahrenheit degrees. Just one shot of icy spray beading on our rugged profiles, as water lapped around our waists, would have the ad men doing handstands. But the camera would not have recorded the terrible fear we had that our cherished gonads might have permanently shrunk to the size of grape seeds.

A chunk of ice, fractured off a glacier upstream, floated gaily by, as we were swirled around in God's gigantic cocktail glass, the sight of it doubling our horripilation. We had to lean backwards to stay upright in that current, which broke over our backs at times, and washed down over our shoulders. Wet and slippery, the 100 pound barrels of gas tended to drag a man forward, especially if he was short, whereupon he would float away, buoyed on the barrel, and after a fierce flutter-kick and much nervous swearing, he would land in an eddy downstream, where Crawford waited, armed with the same pole that had fished him out.

Somebody said that he hadn't had this much fun since the time he caught his hand in the meat grinder.

I left John in charge and went to scout out a campsite near a drumlin lake spotted from the air during our flight in.

The site was perfect, with plenty of fresh water and firewood close by. There were also plenty of mosquitoes. A fish jumped out of the lake and caught one while I stood there. Good for you, I thought. Only four trillion to go. Slapping my neck and swinging my axe, I cut a portage path out of the deadfall that partially blocked the way to the island, and we ferried our tents up to the camp, where I showed the men how to set them up.

Slowly the camp took shape, as the crew of strangers got to

know each other, and began working together. A timekeeper had been sent out with us from town and he began initiating the men into the intricacies of getting paid by the government. All I needed was a camp cook.

The camp cook, or Bull Cook, is the key man in any bush camp, and depending upon how good his food is, he commands an inordinate amount of respect. The promise of good eating is one of the few pleasures in which men can indulge when isolated in a camp like ours. Meals are the high point in a day of simple, brute labour that runs from sunrise to sundown.

I looked around the camp and saw that one of the crew, a kid of about eighteen, had started a campfire. There's a latent Boy Scout lurking in every greenhorn. This one was boiling a couple of gallons of coffee in a steel firebucket, displaying initiative that could not go unrecognized. I rewarded him by appointing him camp cook.

"Oh no you don't," he said.

"Timekeeper," I said, "enter this man on cook's wages, starting right now."

Ernie, the reluctant cook, was a tall stringbean of a boy, who moved slowly to avoid wasting energy. He looked just about strong enough to stir a large pot of soup, but he had had experience, as we later found out, as a short order cook at a garbage food joint in town. He was a greaseball wizard, given the right ingredients: five gallons of hot grease, pre-cut, neutered, vitamin-injected capon, machine-xeroxed french fries, and Coca-Cola syrup. But he had never seen a surveyor's stove before.

It arrived at camp in a sack, looking like an oversized Meccano set with the crucial piece forever lost. It had to be bolted together and set on a bed of sand or rock. To the novice, it looks about as easy to assemble as an IBM computer. Ernie scratched his head when I showed him the stove.

"I'll never get the fat hot enough on that thing, man."

"Forget the fat, Ernie. We don't eat that greasy kid's stuff out here in God's country. We eat green vegetables and lots of protein. It's all laid on."

"But I always deep fried before, I never ... "

I quickly shushed Ernie and pulled him to one side for a pep talk.

"Look, Ernie, the Bull Cook gets paid full camp cook wages. That's $3.40 an hour, and bound to be lots of overtime. There's a cookbook in that mess kit somewhere. Read it when the crew's not looking. Bad for morale. And let's keep this deep-fry business to ourselves. Frankly Ernie, cooking with fat is simply 'not on,' as they say. What would Adele Davis think?"

"Who's Adele Davis?"

"Ernie, my wife believes that some day Adele Davis will be called upstairs as head Bull Cook on the right hand of Jesus. Nutrition Ernie. Noo-trishun is the word."

"Howdya spell it?"

"Don't spell it. Yell it! I want you to *become* the Bull Cook. Bull Cooks are mean. Anybody complains about the food, you let him have it. Beat on him with a soup ladle, throw a tantrum, thump your chest, and sulk for a day. Keep them nervous."

Ernie gave me a sick grin. I clapped him on the back and made a mental note to order him a hair net, for sanitation purposes.

I found Ernie a screwdriver and pliers to put together the stove, and gave him a diagram which had come in the sack, showing the stove in assembled form. He scratched his head, turned the drawing upside down, and went to work.

"What have I done?" I asked myself.

Down at the river, the helicopter was just coming in with the last load. The pilot had his landing lights on and the ship was a roaring shadow with red and green flashing eyes. Some of the boys used the arrival as an excuse to get out of the icy water, pretending that the pilot needed them to help direct his landing.

He was in command of a flying machine worth $1.5 million, with the lives of passengers and crew in his hands alone. It was getting darker by the moment and, as he came into the lee of Dragon Peak, the world dropped away below into a black pit. The luminous threads of two rivers joining were the only markers as he strained his eyes to find the landing pad. Something flashed in the last rays of the sun so he turned the ship gently to starboard against the cross-wind to have a look. The light was flashing on the white asses of six naked weirdos, hair streaming fantastically out like windsocks. They flashed him the V-sign. He frantically waved them off as he came in and they, thinking him very friendly, waved back. They were still waving when the prop wash from the twin rotors reached them and blew them over backwards into the river.

Jim got out last and looked blindly around, trying to orient himself. He did a fast double take at the sight of five naked men holding hands in the middle of the river. They were laughing through chattering teeth at six others apparently enjoying an evening's frolic a bit downstream. It must have seemed to Jim as if he had landed in a colony for frostbitten nudists.

Jim let out a roar of outrage and strode majestically into the water in full uniform, his stetson squarely admidships as his tie slowly dipped to half-mast in the rising tide.

"Uh, James, there's a helluva drop there," I warned him.

A wavelet washed through his mouth, cleansing it in mid-obscenity. I could see Jim was choked up about something as he grasped a tree root and hauled himself out on the bank, regarding me with a baleful glare. I had my pants off trying to get them dry, and was in the water, for about the tenth time, helping with the relay. We were all freezing.

"Where's your uniform, Marty?"

"Rig of the day is undress whites, Jim."

"Have you fruitcakes got the camp set up yet?"

"You might say it is set up. Shipshape and Bristol fashion it ain't!"

Jim walked up to inspect the camp.

It was now too late in the day to get the rest of our equipment and food in by helicopter, so Warden Gordon McLain was bringing it in by jeep up an overgrown trail that led from the Banff-Jasper Highway. He drove the mud-spattered, slightly dented jeep into camp later that night, bringing meat, vegetables, and a bottle of overproof rum. Most important, though, Gord brought us two experienced bush workers, kidnapped from the park maintenance staff. One of them was Bob Sculthorpe, who had been a logger since 1945 and a trapper since the age of ten. He was an invaluable man, as the next day's events would show.

Bob turned in early. Most of the others had also hit the sack, but Gord and Jim sat near the fire and planned the next morning's work. Too tired to participate, I went to my tent, scooped a hole in the hard earth for my hipbone, and burrowed into my sleeping bag.

A cool wind rustled the corners of the tent flap, swinging it open slightly to reveal the stars, so suddenly brilliant after the blind net of canvas overhead. Below us, the Athabasca whispered and whirled as it eddied slowly into the bank that held the camp. Across from my tent, the last man groaned under the aches and fears of the day, and wrapped the blankets more tightly around his neck. In a few painful hours, the young cook was going to find out all the horrors of cooking breakfast for more than thirty cold and irritable men. Fire still crackled in his new stove which was "burning in," like you would burn in a briar pipe to make it draw.

Except for our bizarre arrival, the camp could have been like many another pitched on this river shore; traders, survey-ors, and trail crews had all preceded us over the years. We had been baptized in the same cold green element as they. Ancient brules had forced them to ford that river many times on their journeys. The thread that bound us to the past was thin but strong, like the linen thread their old tents and our new ones were made of. The earth we slept on was our inex-orable connection.

The morning was clear and cold with light frost just begin-ning to glisten into water as we crawled out of our tents, only to scurry back immediately looking for warmer clothes.

As for Ernie, he was anything but cold. He had been up since 4:00 A.M. slaving over a hot stove, slinging hash.

There had been a trial and error period for a while there, as witnessed by several black-eyed fried eggs and a few cinders that had once been bacon. The new stove had a dent or two in it where Ernie had beat on it with a log to unleash his frustra-tions when it wouldn't draw. At least he'd had enough sense to start his fire in the firebox and not in the oven, which is the usual trick of novices.

Pots of hot food were stacked, steaming, on the coals while Ernie poured hot coffee into our tin cups with a tired but tri-umphant flourish. Lance, one of the thinnest fire-fighters, slyly lifted a pot lid, his greasy fingers sneaking in to nab a rasher of bacon. Ernie slammed the lid down with a backhanded blow of his egg turner. Lance yelped with pained surprise.

"Get your meat hooks outta that grub, and get in line," Ernie snarled. "And I trust you gentlemen have washed your hands," he admonished them. "Dirt is bad for the noo-trishun."

The men stared at each other. Mom was never like this. We had us a Bull Cook.

After breakfast, Jim divided the men into three crews, with Gordon, John Crawford, and myself as crew chiefs. Jim would be flying into Jasper to brief the Chief Warden on the opera-tion and supply of the Quincy fire, as soon as the helicopter had ferried us and our equipment up to the hanging valley that held the blaze. The Chinook soon appeared down the valley, and we were relieved when the pilot landed on a small peninsula that jutted into the river, instead of on the little island of the day before. We loaded our equipment and ourselves into the machine. Jim waved goodbye.

A mountain sun was coming up, red-eyed and mean, as we flailed our way up the Athabasca and circled upward toward Quincy. A black column of greasy smoke hung gloomily over the coming day. The helicopter rattled and shook in the crossdrafts, and our teeth chattered along in sympathetic harmony. I was convinced that will power alone was keeping us aloft, as the pilot squeezed his craft over the lip of Quincy Valley, fighting for a bit of graceful altitude over 6,000 feet.

The little valley before us had once been the bed of a tributary glacier leading to the ancient ice sheet that had carved the valley of the Athabasca thousands of years ago. The tributary ice had rived and scraped a box canyon in Mount Quincy some 4,000 feet below the summit of the peak. When the main ice backed away to the north, it had left a precipice between the canyon and the Athabasca Valley, a hanging valley with no access except by air or by a long traverse across the cliffs and meadows from the north on goat paths. Soaring portals of ice-polished limestone flanked our entrance from the east to an amphitheatre, three-quarters of a mile wide and a mile long. The west end terminated in a cliff presided over by the sphinx-like remnant of the glacier that had carved it out. A fall of shattered ice blocks testified that there was life in the white eminence yet.

The first thing we noticed was the water of Quincy Lake, winking up blue-eyed from the base of the fire. It was only a pond, really, covering a few acres, but that cool element was life and hope to us, compared to the inferno that had enveloped the forest above the lake. As we watched, trees sixty feet high blew into fiery mushrooms from root to crown. To the right of the fire was an old slide path, then a final cluster of trees growing on the edge of the precipice. We had to hold the fire at the slide path. If it reached those last trees, there would be a rain of fire that would set the entire Athabasca valley alight. It would make this fire look like a weenie roast in comparison.

Peering out through my narrow window, I watched and wondered. All I could see was fire punctuated with glimpses of glacier ice and rock. The sound of the blaze almost competed with the roar of our engines. We were interlopers there. The elements of wind and fire were loosed upon the slopes of Quincy. The great forests were purifying themselves, readying the earth for new growth in years to come. What appeared to be destruction was actually part of a monumental creation. It seemed that we would be annihilated if we tried to prevent it. In the scale of this battle, we would be like ants assailing a bonfire.

As we hovered, I could see that the slopes we had to work were inclined at forty-five degrees, with many steeper pitches. Up those fearsome angles we would have to crawl, carrying seventy-five pound hose bags, and we would have to run down them to free inevitable kinks in the wet lines of canvas hose.

While I mulled that over, our pilot circled near the valley entrance, trying to find a place to set us down close to the water. But there wasn't enough level ground; it was all trees and piled rock, alder brush, and deadfall. Up the valley we motored at tree-top level to the *cul-de-sac* at the foot of the glacier. There, the fire had come to the edge of the trees, where it had perished under the indifferent rule of the ice. Here was a brief clearing hemmed by rocks whose sharp spines reached up around us as we settled in; a most inhospitable reception.

Jim and I jumped out first to make sure the men kept below the deadly arc of the moving rotor. We hoisted our packs and took off, squeezing between rocks the size of outhouses or clambering over them when no other route offered itself.

Between the toes of various slides were little fens, a few square yards of mud and wet moss, where springs bubbled up to the surface. Soon these converged into a substantial creek. We followed it, wading back and forth at times to avoid pools of muskeg and pockets of fire that lay along the bank. The air was a smother of hot ash and smoke, filled with the dull roar and crash of fire coursing overhead.

In a stand of doomed spruce on the north bank, we came suddenly onto a trail. Hollows in the earth looked to be worn by the passage of human feet over countless years of travel in a place where men had seldom, if ever, walked. But these hollows, half drifted in with dead spruce needles, were eroded to twice the size of a human foot. This was the time-worn trail of grizzly bears. The secret of its existence had been passed on for decades from one generation of bears to another. Perhaps no human foot had ever followed that rough, uncompromising line through the dark forests. If I followed it long enough, I knew it would show me the route out of this box canyon in some great trans-mountain escape. The trail led down to the lake.

Above us, the fiery crown of Mount Quincy blazed on the cliffs, reflected below in the stilled water. Here we dropped our packs. The avalanche path was directly above us, guarded by an impenetrable tangle of dead trees that had been bulldozed to the bottom of the mountain by thousands of tons of sliding snow some winters before. We would have to force these rampikes with chainsaw and axes before we could reach the slidepath and clear a fire line.

The trail we had followed was burning up behind us. We had to build ourselves a landing site to guarantee an escape by air if things got too hot. There was always the lake, of course, which offered death by freezing as opposed to roasting. Gord and I broke out the pumps and organized some operators. Bob Sculthorpe started up his saw and began to fall trees from the jut of big rocks that formed the toe of the slide dipping into Quincy Lake. When limbed off, the trees would make a rough landing pad.

Falling trees with two dozen greenhorns milling around was a job for an old-time logger with plenty of experience. Men like that are getting hard to find, but I couldn't imagine doing the job without them.

Bob revved his saw and slashed a quick alley through the tangled debris on the avalanche slope. We sent most of the men up the mountain to the foot of the cliffs. From there they would cut and grub their way down to us, making a fire line, while the rest of the crew strung hose from below.

The men went up, weaving through the smoke. Each carried a shovel or Polaski, and every second man packed a heavy Gieke bag of water. This canvas bag has a length of rubber hose and a nozzle, activated by a sliding hand pump for shooting a needle of water into the burning duff. They had to stop at times and cut their feet free of the tenacious mat of shintangle that grew on the slide path.

It was slow work, and the fire was gaining ground, getting close to the edge of the open slope, which stood between it and the valley of the Athabasca that led ultimately to the town of Jasper.

Leaving Gord to supervise the pumps, John and I each

93

hoisted a bag of hose and took off up the mountain. We let the hose spill out behind us in 100 foot sections as we climbed up.

We went up and down the line, connecting hose. Finally it was ready, and I called Gord on the portable radio strapped to my waist. From the lake there came the sound that is music to a fire-fighter's ears, the infernal buzzing whine of a centrifugal pump, then the rising howl as the second and third units started up.

Some of the hose, however, had been moldering away in the park stores for too many years. When the water pressure expanded it, weak threads broke, turning it into 100 foot lengths of sprinkler. Cursing, I sent the men down to get some new lengths, while I slashed the brass fittings off the ruined stuff with my belt knife and tied the lengths into one double-boogered granny knot so it wouldn't return to haunt me again. While I was working, there was a faint cry of "rock" from above. I flattened behind a boulder as a big stone came crashing and bounding through the alder. I peered out from behind my salient and saw John's long form bounding, goat-like, up the mountain.

"Watch your footing, you crazy bastard!" I yelled, but he was out of earshot, and still going fast. Fuming away, I went up the slope following the hose line to check my crew.

A fire hose at the working end gives vent to fifty pounds per square inch of pressure so you want to have a good grip on it when that pressure reaches the nozzle. Up on Quincy, we could see the water crawling slowly up the flaccid line, which bulged upward like a boa constrictor swallowing a rabbit. I fought my way through the brush and stopped to glare down at Lance, who had draped his lean frame restfully among the rocks. He looked at me like I was the boss man on a chain gang and reluctantly got up with the nozzle dangling from one hand.

I smelled hair burning. Mine. Lance watched with interest for signs of pain. I followed his eyes and found the ember boring through my shirt sleeve. Screaming inwardly, I gave it a casual flick of the finger and flashed Lance a beatific smile.

"If you don't get a grip on that hose, fellah, you'll be wearing it around your neck."

"No sweat, man," he said. "Really. No-o-o problem."

"Far out, man."

Lance was from Haight Ashbury, with an innate distrust of all authority figures. I backed away out of range and watched, fascinated, as the water crawled up those coils, writhing with sensuous power and slowly flattening the brush with its weight. Lance posed with one hand in pocket, the other holding the nozzle as casually as he would a water pistol. At the first spray, the hose twisted from his fingers and zoomed into his chest, sending him sprawling into the deadfall. Then his partner, tending hose for him, went through a frantic waltz, leaping about to avoid the sinuous coils. I watched, grinning, as the nozzle whipped back and forth like a rattler, striking the air over their heads and choking them with cold water in the sauna heat of that fire a few hundred feet away. Finally, it caught under a dead limb. I showed the guys how to hold it with one arm over the nozzle as a guard, and the other hand gripped to aim it. Steam billowed out of the red coals as water sluiced deeply into the blistered earth.

In this kind of a fire much of the heat is generated from the ground. Cold air is drawn in by convection to fan the coals of burnt brush with fresh oxygen at the base of the trees. Spruce trees were like chimneys for this super-heated air that rushed in a bellow's draft through their tapering branches. They ignited as if soaked with gasoline. Thousands of glimmering red eyes were the blisters of burning pitch up and down their black trunks. When our water hit this nova, it turned into steam which burst over us and drove us back out of the trees into the open.

There was no protection from that heat. The sun's power was magnified and trapped in the amphitheatre, glaring up from the bleached rocks and pounding in a pressure wave on our heads. Our knees had long since turned rubbery, as we side-stepped that grade with water-filled Gieke bags, thankful for the coldness of the icy streams soaking through the canvas on our backs. The air we breathed was half smoke and one quarter fire. Drinking deeply from thin hoses, we washed the taste of ashes from our mouths and went on with our work.

Crawford drove himself like some kind of donkey engine at the forefront of his sector, leading by example with tools clutched in his big paws. Not content with merely supervising his men, the big American worked himself to the limit of endurance, as if anxious to find exaltation in extremity of pain. Those who tried to match his pace were soon lying on the rocks, gagging for breath. Then, they would pull themselves up and stagger after his form, vanishing in the smoke.

There was the odour of myth about John that created an unarticulated bond between him and the Americans in his crew. He seemed to embody the spirit of the vanished frontier, the old west of their boyhood dreams. They remembered that old faith, and followed John without question.

By noon, we seemed to be containing the fire to the west side of our guard. If we couldn't put it out, we were at least slowing the cycle of combustion by wetting and cooling the fuel. Up until noon, the wind had been gusting out of the north and east but, as the day grew hotter, the air currents showed a definite shift to the west. Soon, the few remaining ranks of spruce were burning on the edge of the slide. The fire surged forward. We were pushed back into the open, losing ground.

I left my crew and went up the slide with another man to check a spot fire that had apparently started from a small, burning stick. At first it seemed the stick had been blown out of the main fire by wind.

Then from below there came a shouted warning. We looked up in time to see a heavy deadfall plummeting off the cliffs in a wrapper of flame and flying rocks. A small stone caromed off my partner's hard hat, knocking it down over his ears. We hugged the rock, and watched the deadfall tumble through the thickets and smash apart in a rock pile. A dozen smokes instantly plumed up in its path.

Above us, smoke was building up fast on the cliff bands. The fire had been carried up there on rising currents of air, to broach the barrier of cliffs with airborne sparks. From time to time, old snags and flaming branches would topple over the cliffs, leap-frogging from ledge to ledge and spilling down on the slide below.

At the same time, smoke was rising up from the rocks on the east side of the slide where there was no visible vegetation. I rubbed my tired eyes at this spontaneous combustion. The very rocks seemed to be burning.

McLain picked his way through the rocks, to where I stood regarding the mountain, looking baffled. "There's squirrel nests down there, Marty. Dead spruce needles and leaves have drifted down between the rocks for years. Plenty of air and fuel down there. Looks like we got a weasel fire down below." He wagged his thumb toward the stand of spruce hanging over the Athabasca Valley. "That's where she'll surface, if we don't cut 'er off."

It was burning like a train of black powder spilled from a keg. Fire behind us, above us, and below. We were getting burned right off the compass.

I sent two men down to pack up a relay tank and a pump, while I pried boulders to make a level spot for the canvas tank. Once inflated with 200 gallons of water pumped from the lake, the canvas tank would act as a reservoir for our hose, strung yet further up the mountain. I threaded a siamese valve and ran a short hose and nozzle to work near the pump.

McLain slumped down on a boulder. Taking off his dirty white helmet, he wiped his eyes with the back of one filthy paw.

"It's a good thing we're hired on to be tough, Marty," he grinned, "'cause I'm sure as hell feeling weak."

I had to agree. Of course toughness, at least in males, is a much maligned state of being these days.

I swabbed my face with a bandanna and sank down beside McLain. "Gord, how far down do you think these boulders go before we hit the ground, if you'll pardon the expression?"

He peered around the slide, the ruins of a gigantic slab that had cracked loose from the summit many years before. The track of it was still visible as a narrowing fan of rocks pointing a quarter-mile-long arrow up at the whitened scar on the cliffs above us.

"What ground? It could be about twenty feet, thirty feet, in the hollows down to bedrock. Only thing we can do is pour it to 'er."

So we poked the hoses down between the rocks and poured it on. Steam came whistling back in defiant geysers when the ice-water hit the red-hot stones underneath. There were muffled booms as rocks cracked open under the shock. Often, when we had moved on to the next one, lifting sections of wet hose over the snarl of scree, smoke would come wafting up like a prayer flag from a pocket of coals burning under an umbrella of rock we couldn't see or reach.

A hoary marmot, about the size of a badger, perched on a chunk of limestone, gave us his long policeman's whistle, indignant at having his store of dried lupine wetted by our hoses. He scooped up the little row of plants into his cheeks with his front paws and scooted into his den—only to emerge again, slightly singed by the fire below. With heat downstairs and cold water above, the fat, yellow animal decided to break camp. The last we saw of him, he was headed due east with some dried flowers gripped in his teeth, for future reference. We gazed wistfully after him. He had more sense than we did.

Mount Quincy was one unpleasant surprise after another. A

sleight of wind had taken the fire to the cliffs and by late afternoon it had fanned to the east and was burning above a shoulder of timber; the last outpost of trees that grew to the 7,000 foot contour.

We pooled eight men from all the sectors and John led them up to build yet another fire break in an alpine meadow east of the trees. It was a gesture only, all that we could manage. We had strung hose as far as it would go until the strained pumps could no longer push it. The crew above had no water, except what they could pack from the end of the hose. They were hardly in position when the first fiery detritus began to slide down on top of them. The trees were soon taking fire in the crown beyond our reach.

The men were faltering. Fatigue was making them reckless. Becoming separated from their partners, they were no longer looking after each other and, punchdrunk, they were stumbling and falling head first after their axes. The aerial bombardment was checking us; a completely new tactic was needed.

As evening came on, the fire began to lie down. It wouldn't spread at all during the night. We cached our tools in the rocks and counted heads, then floundered downhill to the lake, there to soak blistered feet in the cold water, and wait for the helicopter. The sun had blinked shut for the day in a cleavage between Dragon Peak and Catacombs Mountain, that fearsome pair, when we landed by the river.

The night was cold, but one or two of us who couldn't stand our own smell ambled down to the river after supper to have a bath, or rather, to exchange silt, because the Athabasca was still flowing milky with ground rock flour washed out from the glaciers at its source. It would be well into September before the river level dropped and the water ran clear.

Anyway, I thought a coat of limestone talcum powder would sit better on me than the sackcloth and ashes I was wearing at the time. It takes a real loathing of dirt to force yourself into water that is struggling along barely above freezing point. The river behaved with its usual truculence, the current trying to push me into a hole and stifle me. It was "yelling water"—every time we splashed it on our skin, we yelled with the shock as it froze the fire out of our feet, leaving us in a state of agitated numbness.

I thought of Lord Southesk, the first mountain tourist and forerunner of today's ubiquitous hordes, who had come within twenty-four miles of this place in 1859. Southesk was suitably equipped to take care of his *toilette* with the delicacy of a man of means. Whatever the weather, he enjoyed a hot bath in a collapsible rubber bathtub in the steamy seclusion of his tent. There he snorted, soaked, and sported while his servants hewed firewood and hauled hot water to keep him comfortable. You might say that Canadians have been hewing wood and hauling water ever since, although today it's for multinational corporations not British potentates.

At least Southesk was a man who knew how to travel, I thought, as I burrowed my head in the silty Athabasca, and got sand in my ears and a crick in my neck.

That night some of the men straggled down to the little lake below the camp. Gord bulled in through the tent flap as we were sitting around the air-tight heater.

"Marty, you'd better check out those men of yours."

"What's up?"

"I think they got some of that weirdo weed out here. They're all sitting around in a little circle smoking and passing something around."

"Let's have a hit on this rum and talk it over."

"Well, they look pretty suspicious to me, Marty. Better show some leadership around here."

I cursed softly and left the tent. Why can't these people stick to rum like us mountainmen? Rum, man, rum's the stuff to drink when you're dead tired and your feet stink. Rum has an honourable tradition in these parts. Why, just over the mountain is the Athabasca Pass, where the Hudson Bay voyageurs used to make their long portage across the Great Divide, fortified by a dram of overproof against the chill of deep snow. Not far away is the Committee's Punch Bowl, a little lake right on the summit of the pass. There the men would drink a toast to the health of the King and the company, the Adventurers of England Trading into Hudson Bay, while their own health was ruined with pneumonia. There the Fur Trade Governor, Sir George Simpson, had committed the worst sacrilege of all time. He had smashed in a keg of rum with his hatchet to spite the men he thought were not moving fast enough, hampered as they were with seventy pound bales of beaver pelts and three feet of snow.

I bellowed, "Gord, it's black as the ace of spades out here. I don't see those jaspers around here at all."

Below me, in the darkness, came sounds of furtive scuffling.

A red spark flared out into the darkness and arched into the lake. Shadowy figures rustled into the greenery. A few minutes later, men casually emerged from the woods up by the cook tent. Obviously they had just been out for a midnight stroll, in ten different directions, and had returned coincidentally at the same time.

I went back to the tent.

"What were they doin' out there?"

"I dunno. Just havin' a smoke I guess."

"Yeah, but what were they smokin'?"

"Just smokin'."

"Well, that's okay, then. It would be a real shame to have to fly the Mounties out here. And then we'd lose our crew. They been workin' real good for us too."

"Gord, you're absolutely right. Now give us a hit on that bottle."

He passed it over. The rum burned like a slow fire all the way down, burning off the chill of the Athabasca River.

"Eeee hah! Now that's what I call coffee!"

Gord eyed me speculatively. "You know, Marty, I'm beginning to wonder about you . . . "

Down the valley a lonesome coyote called and listened for an answering voice in the stillness, but none came. I wondered about the crew. Perhaps they had a stash of exotic weeds somewhere around the camp. A serious business. One can't import such bizarre vegetables into the park without a permit signed by the Superintendent. It seemed irrelevant in these mountains to import dope where one snort of fresh air, laced with the sweet freedom of river smells and aromatic spruce, tends to hit the jaded blood of the city boy like a waterfall in the veins.

But different strokes for different folks. I prefer rum, refreshing, convenient, stimulating, and legal.

Gord shut off the lantern and we turned in for the night.

It was false light when Jim's yell of "Daylight in the swamp!" jarred the reluctant camp awake. Stepping out of the tent, I tripped over something that appeared to be a dead man, lying in a sleeping bag covered with a thin sheen of dew. Crawford disdained to share our contubernal bliss, describing the tent mildly as a "darn hothouse." So he used to roll out his bag on the ground, and conduct invisible conversations with us through our canvas walls at night. Starlight was John's favourite roof. He eased the zipper open on his bag, releasing a wisp of fetid steam, and stuck his head out to sniff the morning air like an old cougar hound reluctant to leave its kennel. A raven, perched on a branch over his head, squawked with umbrage to see its intended meal was still kicking.

"I'll let you know when I'm ripe enough to eat, you black sonofagun," John told it. The bird flapped off to look for a less lively breakfast.

Jim put in a radio call to Jasper, then came up to the cook tent to talk to us.

"I got some bad news and some good news. The bad news is that the Army helicopter has been called to fly elsewhere . . . "

The crew cheered and banged happily on their tin plates. "Hey, man, give us the good news," said Lance.

"Let's go fishing," someone laughed.

"The good news is that we got another machine. It'll be here in a few minutes, so eat up."

There was a collective groan of despair.

"Jeez, what a bummer."

Jim smiled.

McGuire, juggling his meagre resources to battle two major fires, had sent out telex feelers around the northwest, and finally scored in Alaska. The helicopter was a Bell 205, smaller than the Chinook, this one flown by a hard-eyed veteran of Vietnam. He had the face of a young man who had witnessed human barbarity at too close a range for too long, but he flew with an elegant precision that was beautiful to behold, a precision that earned him his nickname, the Iceman.

Up went the crew to Quincy, shuddering over the Athabasca, and now and then dropping in an air pocket down and down to the white-capped rapids that reached up like teeth and snapped on nothing as the chopper lifted again. White-faced, we held onto our breakfast with stolid determination.

Slowly we climbed into the morning, out of the shadow of the main valley, hidden from the sun, to go spanking along on the lip of a high plateau that stretches north and south below the summit of Quincy, before it joins the valley by way of a mile-long stretch of steeply sloping meadow. On our right side, alpine flowers winked up at us from a few hundred feet below while, to our left, the wall of the range dropped for 1,500 feet as if the plateau had been sliced by some celestial knife. Contemplating this two-faced landscape was a schizophrenic experience.

At the point where the plateau began to fall away there was

101

a little cirque containing a pothole lake of an acre or two. Fifty yards of meadow and a few larch trees stood between water and the edge of the precipice. This upper pond was some 1,000 feet higher than Quincy Lake. We looked it over, hoping it could be a source of water but the pond was sunk too deeply into the little cirque, and was at least a mile from the edge of the fire, too far away, or so I thought.

As we flew on to the south, a stream of white water glanced back at the rising sun. It was flowing from a waterfall far above us, which disappeared down the cliffs into the meadow below. The pilot took us in closer to examine the flow. From the base of the waterfall, it was a half mile to the fire guard. To use the water here would mean we'd have to tap it close to the cliffs before it faded into the meadow.

There was very little smoke coming up from the fire at this early hour and we had a bird's-eye view of the damage. Almost all the spruce on the north slopes had been wiped out. During the night, the bench fires had eaten steadily downhill. Beneath an envelope of cold night air, the fire slept fitfully, its ardour cooled by downslope breezes from the glacier. As soon as the sun hit these slopes, the convection of the sulking flames and radiation from the overheated earth would pierce the envelope of pressure. The result would be a bit like what would happen if a hydrogen balloon was punctured in the presence of a lighted match.

The Iceman left us on the hot shore line. The men picked up their tools and we started up the mountain.

Rising heat from the burnt earth was sucking the breath out of our lungs, the air was expanding around us. Little whirlwinds of dust went spinning joylessly, rousing malevolent red eyes in the blackened duff. In the upper burn, a score of hot spots glowed neon bright in the dark interstices of piled deadfall. The intense heat kept us back out of working range. Bathed in our own sweat for coolant, we tried to snuff the slag with dollops of gravel and dirt scratched from the meagre earth.

The sun was a fat, burning pig in the sky. We seemed to work in a flat smother of sound. Voices were blurred and scarcely audible. A deadening quiet, a surreal hiatus, held the mountainside. John suddenly straightened up and looked around wildly. "She's going to blow!" he shouted.

With his words, a whoosh of updraft came ploughing over the heather, rattling the tips of crossed widowmakers like knives clashing together. There was a shout of alarm from the men, as a burnt snag tilted slowly off base and came crashing and rolling toward us.

"Let's get the hell out of here!"

We scattered, leaping like deer over deadfalls to avoid the high roller. We yelled, grabbed, and shoved the men back to the fire line.

Black smoke spooled out of the sky's pierced vault. Soon the fire, with its enormous convection currents, was making its own weather. A steadily increasing wind blew at our backs, driving the fire uphill.

We needed water, a river of it.

Gord and I conferred on the radio and he decided to have our pilot water bomb the hot spots, by means of a monsoon bucket, a large nylon tank, which is suspended on a cable beneath the helicopter. In a while, we heard the machine approaching, and watched as it spiralled up from the Athabasca.

The Iceman hovered over the surface in his giant dragon fly, setting the bucket down, letting it fill. He lifted it off, 1,500 pounds of water, and circled up toward us, the tank swinging gently on the end of the cable. At this altitude he was flying close to the red line, meaning there was little power left over to correct pilot error. But the Iceman never erred.

Jim flew with him in the passenger seat, helping to aim the drop. The Bell hovered over a hot spot, heat waves shimmering on the green fuselage. The pilot hit his release button, and a wall of silver shot through the sun and hit the spot with a roar of steam and a crack of shattering rocks. The Bell tilted downhill and glided down to the lake, a miracle of modern technology.

The crew watched, delighted, as the Iceman cooled our fire until water ran in thin streams from the burn, carrying little boats of drowning flame.

It was a pleasant way to fight a fire, but unfortunately the idyll was interrupted when the Bell developed a fire of its own. It was hovering over the lake when the cockpit suddenly filled with smoke. The pilot groped around in the murk, trying to find out what was burning. He raised the ship and hit his release button but nothing happened, the monsoon bucket stayed full. He knew then that the hydraulic compressor under Jim's seat was overheated and burning. Jim discovered the fire at about the same time, through a sudden pain in the ass. The two men were sitting in a flying time bomb of Turbofuel.

They could not land on the copter pad with the bucket, there wasn't enough room. The pilot would first have to quick-release his bucket, which would tear apart the electrical and hydraulic lines.

The Iceman had about two minutes to do something. He considered the chances for a few seconds, then swung the Bell a hundred and eighty degrees, and dove it over the cliff, down to the river.

For Jim Whyte, it was an especially frightening two minutes, strapped to his fiery connection, and unaware of what was going on. The pilot didn't have time to do any explaining. But once down on the flats, where there was plenty of room to land, a few shots from the fire extinguisher killed the blaze.

That was the end of the monsoon bombing. It had been enough to help hold the fire in for another day, but wisps of smoke from the thousand little pockets in the duff reminded me the job was far from over.

I had an idea, and the more I thought about it, the more I became convinced it would work. It involved setting up a gravity cone at the base of the waterfall we'd seen that morning, and running the water collected by the canvas funnel, down the hose line to the fire.

I told Jim and Gord about the plan that night over a cup of hot grog. That rum was powerful stuff, and to this day I blame it for the resulting fiasco, it and my youthful enthusiasm. Newton's apple danced before my smoke-reddened eyes, as I waxed on about the beauty of using the simple law of gravity to put out this fire once and for all.

"Just give me the men and the hose, Jim," I said expansively, "and then stand out of my way."

"Sure, kid," said Jim. "Anything you say."

The next morning, while most of the crew continued the attack with hand tools, led by Crawford and McLain, I took six men and started stringing two thousand feet of hose from the waterfall downhill to the edge of the burn. "What a perfect place for a gravity cone," I thought to myself, as I pried stones out of the way at the base of the wet rock, and tied the big cone in place in the rush of icy water. My only concern was that the tremendous pressure generated by the drop in altitude between waterfall and fire might blow my hose apart.

Everything was ready. Water surged down the hose line, and in a few minutes there were shouts of triumph on the radio as water reached the end of the hose. My chest puffed out with righteous pride, as I hiked down the line to the fire.

The wind was picking up. It was blowing in our favour, driving the fire back on itself. But soon it was blowing cold enough and strong enough that we had to put our jackets on. Then I noticed the hose. It had gone flaccid! Where was my water?

Glancing up the cliff, I saw the stream disappearing in a plume of spray. It was evaporating right before my eyes in the dry wind. It was then I remembered the story about a railroader on the CPR, who had climbed up to the foot of Mount Stephen to fill his tea kettle. As he held up the kettle, the water evaporated just out of his reach, tantalizing and frustrating him. I wished I had remembered the story earlier.

There were no more happy shouts from the small figures slumped dejectedly across the steep green meadow. The water was gone. I had taken too much for granted.

Back at camp, Jim and Gord carefully said nothing. After supper, we were laying around the tent scratching ourselves, bored stiff, and desperate for a good time.

Jim cleared his throat at length. "Well, how'd you and the gravity cone make out?" he asked.

I went outside and got some logs for the fire so they could laugh and get it over with. From the tent came the sound of hoots and muffled giggles.

"Coupla school girls," I muttered angrily, and took the wood back in.

Jim winked at Gord. "Now that you've got all that hose laid, what are you fixin' to do with it?"

"Can't let it drop, eh?"

"Not 2,000 feet of hose," Jim answered mildly.

I sighed in exasperation. "Well, I was thinking of trying to run hose from the upper lake. But I don't know if it would work." Then, in total defeat, I asked, "What do you guys think?"

Jim cleared a space in the dirt with the edge of his boot. He picked up a stick and scratched a circle with the point. "There's your water," he said, and scratching a much bigger circle, "there's your fire. Now, how were you planning to connect the two?"

"Well, I thought I could pump up to the stream bed and from there it would mainly be downhill to the burn."

"Anything in your way?"

I thought for a minute. "Yeah. About a 200 foot vertical rise spread over 400 feet. Then it's gradually uphill to the stream bed."

Jim nodded his head patiently. "So what do you need?"

"I need two pumps and a relay tank. One I would place at the lake here and the other pump and tank would work from the top of the hill above the lake. If that doesn't work, I'll move to the stream bed," and here I looked up, a thought occurring to me, "where you told me to set up that relay tank today. Why didn't you tell me that the gravity cone wouldn't work?"

Jim took a swig of coffee. "You never asked."

So that's what we did the next day. Bob Sculthorpe kept an eye on both pumps and their operators. We strung another 2,600 feet of hose to connect at the stream bed, making more than a mile overall. It took a while to get it all together. We had to ease the pumps into synchronization. The upper station tended to suck the relay tank dry faster than the head could build up from the lake up a steep slope. Frustrated, I galloped down the hose line to confer with Bob. The problem was one of an untrained hose operator doing his best against 400 feet of back pressure. The pressure was pushing against the vanes of the centrifugal pump and heating it up like a car trying to climb a hill without snow tires. We were going through a 100 foot section of lined hose every fifteen minutes.

The only thing that was holding the fire was the wind. But should it suddenly shift, we would find ourselves back at square one. Meanwhile, the stream on the cliffs was producing nothing for us but a colourful rainbow against the weeping rock. To hell with Newton.

Bob took over the pump at the lake. The first thing he did was to drain the water through the siamese valve and get rid of the back pressure. Then he started the pump and gradually opened the siamese.

"Let's try it without that second pump running for a while," he said.

Water crept slowly up the hill and went out of sight over the crest.

That was our watershed, our great divide. I wasn't thinking of the siphon when I heard the pump start to race, and I doubted that Bob had ever heard of Newton. But I'm sure he had had occasion, at one time or another in his variegated career, to dip a surreptitious hose in the odd gas tank, with the other end draining into a gallon can. Maybe it was the smell of gas that gave him the idea.

"What the hell's wrong with that pump, Bob?" I asked him,

expecting bad news. He indicated the hose through which water still pulsed as he throttled down to run just above idle. The radio came alive. I could hear the guys whooping it up on the other end.

"We've got water here now. Keep it coming!"

We had created a siphon a mile long! Though our little lake was 200 feet lower than the meadow, it was still several hundred feet higher than the top of the fire. Half a mile of gravity was pulling water through that mile of hose. I looked at Bob's weatherbeaten mug and, slapping him on the back, pounded a grin on his face. When it comes to fire-fighting, a college education will never hold a candle to forty years of horse sense.

That's how we put out the Quincy fire, with a lot of help from the wind and the force of gravity. When it was all over, and the crew were washing ten days' dirt off their skin, a dark cumulus cloud rolled up to camp and ripped itself open on the fang of Dragon Peak. It rained so hard on us and on the blackened timber, that you could hear the dust hiss on the scorched earth. All we could do was stand there and curse, tears of rain streaking our grimy faces, until the water drove and flayed us before it into the shelter of the leaky tents.

The next day we flew out to Jasper and said our goodbyes. Most of us would never see each other again. It seemed a shame, somehow.

5

The Squaw Hitch

"Memory rides a quiet horse
With a gentle hand at the rein ..."

Ray Bagley
Those Other Days

While I was battling fires, Myrna had been fighting a different kind of war, slugging it out with a couple of hundred mice and one black bear, while she baked in a tin trailer located in a mosquito-infested swamp near the east gate of Jasper Park. The place was known as the Pocahontas Warden Station, named after an extinct mining town which had been named after Longfellow's Indian princess. The romance of the name was lost on Myrna as she watched the deer mice crawling across the screen doors late at night, hunting the giant luna moths that fluttered around the outside light.

Every night, after the mice and the moths were dormant in the cool air, the resident black bear would come through on his way back to the swamps of the Athabasca River. Grunting with satisfaction, he would stop to scratch his behind on a corner of the front steps, making the trailer rock violently as if it had been transformed into a boat caught in a rough sea. This irritated Myrna who found herself slightly seasick as she reeled towards the door. She would grope for the porch light, turn it on and, with a yell, bounce a stick of firewood off the old boar who took this as his signal to amble back through the willows to the river where fat pike, held by the spell of the full moon, loitered close to the bank.

When I opened the trailer door, I found her sleeping sound-

108

ly, although it was the middle of the afternoon. There is something ponderously tender about a pregnant woman, especially in the drowsy heat of mid-summer. She didn't stir when I called her name and the depth of her sleep was evidenced by something I saw on the floor by our bed near the back door, something that made me stop and heed the scolding of a squirrel in the spruce trees outside. It was the muddy footprint of a bear, pressed in sharp outline on the waxed linoleum, that sent me hurrying outside just in time to see a black shadow drift into the woods at the clearing's edge.

On the back steps there were more tracks, and I pictured him standing up on his hind legs pushing the door open with his weight. I imagined him taking that one step into the room, leaning over my sleeping wife, to sniff at her with his enquiring nose. I wondered how long he had paused there, what sparks of comprehension had drifted through his brain before he turned again to wander out into the meadow. He had meant no harm, though had there been any food lying out in the place, he would certainly have bypassed the sleeper and ransacked the kitchen.

I sat for a while and watched her sleeping, trying to decide which of the two would have been more frightened—Myrna, if she had suddenly awakened and seen that furry, man-like figure standing up to try the fridge door with its yellow claws, or the bear. It was not an amusing thought at the time. I was already worried about her because our move into the Tonquin Valley, postponed until the fires were out, had now been approved by the Chief Warden. We were to pack into the Tonquin the next day, and the dangers of taking a pregnant woman into the isolated valley on horseback preyed on my imagination.

Soon she woke up, and after welcoming embraces I broke the news about the transfer.

"Great!" she cried. "When do we leave this dump?"

I hesitated and she guessed the reason. "You're worried about taking me along, aren't you?" she asked disappointedly. "And after all the times we've talked about it . . . "

To change the subject, I pointed out the track of the bear, "That one is getting far too friendly. It should be live-trapped and moved further into the bush."

Her eyes widened at the sight of the tracks, as she realized how bold the bear had become.

Sensing a weak spot, I pressed further, "There's grizzlies up in the Tonquin as well as blacks." But I should have known better than to mention that bogeyman to her. She was a warden's wife, after all, and knew a few things about the grizzly.

"You know damn well there's grizzlies all through this park," she scoffed, and added lightly, "I saw one down by the river the other day. I forgot to mention it."

"What the hell were you doing down there?"

"Picking berries."

I was alarmed but knew that remonstrations would be useless. "Look, you keep your ass out of that berry patch when the bears are around. They take a dim view of competition when those raspberries get ripe. And don't tell me you're picking berries," I added lamely. "It's against the law in the park."

She looked at me boldly. "I was across the line, on provincial land."

My wife is a terrible liar when it comes to raspberries.

"All right," she said, her voice now crisp and level, her eyes flashing, "but as far as the Tonquin goes, if you think you're going to go up there without me, you can think again."

That ended the argument.

I gave it up. "Who said anything about going without you?"

"Why you . . . ." The clouds exploded in the downpour that had been threatening the valley all afternoon, and the rain whanged on the tin roof and drowned out her reply. A leak began in a rusty section over the kitchen with a steady plop onto the floor.

"We do have running water up in the Tonquin," I told her, as we watched the dripping water. "There's a creek that runs right by the front door."

"Close enough," she laughed. "Let's get out of here."

The leak increased to a small waterfall, and it looked like the mice were going to need life preservers. We got up and started packing. In an hour, we had the truck loaded and, without a backward look, headed for Hinton to buy a month's supply of food.

On our way, we speculated what life would be like in the Tonquin. Jasper was one of the few parks that still encouraged wives to live with their husbands in the backcountry. In electing to live in the backcountry, Myrna was entering the spirit of an old Warden Service tradition that was only a memory in the parks like Banff, where the wardens had been moved into town for the sake of efficiency.

110

The old-time wardens of the mountain parks were a breed apart. Civilization had driven them into the sanctity of the mountains as it had done some years earlier the buffalo, the grizzly bear, the wapiti, and the wolf, and the mountains were the last stronghold of men like Bill Peyto, who once shot a grizzly through the eye with a single bullet from a .22 calibre rifle, men like Frank Wells and Frank Bryant, who had curled up in the snow like wolves all night for the chance to catch poachers and then chased them for twenty miles on snowshoes, finally running them down. They were jealously possessive of their lonely districts and, if they saw more than one person during the course of a winter's travels, they'd complain about "too many goddamn people spoilin' the peace and quiet."

Of necessity the women who married these men were as strong-willed and self-reliant as their husbands. In addition to keeping house in the bush, such women were expected to lend a hand on the trail with packing the horses or fixing phone line. In later years, as the number of people travelling in the backcountry gradually increased, the warden's wife acted on his behalf when he was absent, by selling fishing licences, giving information, registering climbers, and manning telephone and radio links to town in cases of emergency. She received official recognition from the parks branch, and no pay. In effect, the government gained two employees for the price of one. A married warden could travel more freely and efficiently in the bush with his wife "minding the store" in a headquarter's cabin. Obviously, such a woman required considerable patience, and most important when dealing with the public, a sense of humour.

We stopped to say goodbye to one of our neighbours at Pocahontas, an old-time mountain woman who took the life of a warden's wife in her stride. Mona Matheson is known to some of the natives around Jasper as "one of the greatest gals who ever laced on boots." She lives in a cabin near the Yellowhead Highway in a clearing of pine and aspen forest with a commanding outlook toward the mountains she has known for most of her life. Though they have dominated her existence for over fifty years, they have never dominated her spirit. Having outlived her husband, Charlie, she stays on in their cabin alone.

Mona met us at the door and invited us in for tea. It would be the last chance we would have to talk with her for several

111

months. She's a slender, grey-haired woman of medium height with a pert, pugnacious nose, and she moves with an ease and lightness that is at odds with her age.

Mona poured cupfuls of tea, the drink that serves as a conversational lubricant in the mountains.

Myrna was full of excitement about our move to the Tonquin Valley, and Mona told her not to listen to my objections because she herself had raised a child in the Warden Service. That had been in the days before helicopters, when the hospital was many days away, and a mother had to be both nurse and doctor to her children in cases of emergency.

I mentioned Charlie and at once her expression changed, her eyes looking inward on a private pain—but only briefly.

"Charlie." She said the name softly, with a depth of feeling that made clear how great the loss was. She had been prepared for his death, though, because she had nursed him through several years of illness.

They had met at Medicine Lake in Jasper Park, where Mona and her sister, Agnes, worked as cooks in a trail-ride camp for Fred Brewster, a Jasper outfitter. The wardens used to drop in for coffee on their patrols to Maligne Lake or the Rocky River. There was a stack of well-worn magazines in the tent for the dudes to read and the men would leaf through these at times, waiting for the coffee to boil, pretending they were reading. Mona noticed that Charlie was the only warden who held his magazine right side up. It seems the others were just using it as a lecher's screen while they ogled the young cooks.

"We didn't like the way they looked at us," she said, and we laughed with her.

Mona soon decided that Charlie would make a good partner, although Charlie, sixteen years her senior, seemed set in his bachelor ways and would be a difficult man to convert. But Mona was determined. She once helped him jingle his ponies at 4:00 in the morning when they pulled out on him at Jacques Lake. She walked and ran nine miles in thin running shoes to help round them up, chasing after the faint tinkle of the lead mare's bell in the timber. Her feet had been slightly frostbitten in the process but Charlie, though sympathetic, was not entirely convinced about matrimony.

While he was making up his mind, Mona and her sister talked Fred Brewster into hiring them as horse guides. They had picked up skills of that trade by watching the cowboys working around camp and practising what they learned on their days off. After a brief confrontation with the Chief Warden and the Park Superintendent, who were alarmed at the idea of women doing what had always been a man's job, Mona and Agnes got their licences and became the first female guides in Jasper Park.

"I wonder why more women didn't apply for those jobs," said Myrna.

Mona thought for a minute. "I don't really know. Maybe they were afraid to try. Nowadays it's different so I'm told."

"In some ways," said Myrna, with a smile, "but in lots of ways it's still the same."

"Well, you see, I've never been afraid of anything. I don't know why, but it's true. Guiding turned out to be a lot of trouble and hard work. But for me, it was worth it. Just to know I could do the job."

The sisters were just supposed to guide dudes on backcountry horse trips and Brewster was to provide them with men to do the packing and horse wrangling. For some reason, these men never showed up. Mona never said why, but knowing a bit about cowboys, I wonder whether there wasn't a bit of male conspiracy there, to test the sisters by seeing if they could do all the work involved, not just the horseback riding. It was a man-size task since each had to do the packing and wrangling as well as guiding for two outfits, totalling thirty-five head of horses. They were up each day before 4:00 A.M. to catch, feed, saddle, and doctor their animals. They had to pack all the food and equipment for the dudes as well, which included everything from thundermugs to outboard engines. They saw each other occasionally in camp that summer, the rest of the time they worked separately, guiding or packing.

Mona, a former cook, slaved away the long hours in her exalted position as head guide, while the new camp cook sat on a log and watched with interest. Holding a heavy pack box in her arms, the diminutive guide had to stand on a stump to reach the back of a tall horse. She was able to lift everything but the outboard engines needed for fishing at Maligne Lake. The motors weighed 200 pounds but Mona's cook, a big strapping man, used to lift them up onto the horse for her with ease.

"Teamwork," said Myrna, giving me a significant glance.

"That's right," said Mona. "As long as he could lift them, I could get them tied on, and as long as it was tied on good, the horse would carry it."

I glanced at Mona in covert admiration. The key to the horse business has always been the skill of the handler, not his or her strength. Still, as a large mesomorph, who once had my hands full just dealing with two horses, I was feeling slightly overwhelmed as Mona modestly described how she packed from ten to fifteen head at a time.

Charlie too had been impressed, so they were finally married.

Mona's skill with the diamond hitch came in handy on many occasions, but none so dramatically as during the dry, hot summer of 1935. That year she and Charlie were stationed at Maligne Lake, thirty-two miles southeast of Jasper townsite.

"We had gone up to the narrows of the lake with our boat one Sunday. About noon, here comes Harry Phillips from the camp at the north end, with two kickers [outboard motors] on his boat, going like blazes. He told us a fire had broken out on the Horseshoe Bend."

Horseshoe Bend is on the Maligne River, between Maligne Lake and the Athabasca River, a good fifteen miles from the narrows, ten by boat and five by horse. They went down the lake as fast as they could. Charlie took some tools and two horses and galloped off down the trail. In an hour he was scouting the fire's perimeter and he saw that he couldn't contain it without help. He had his forestry field-set with him, so he climbed a tree to the phone wire, hooked in his set, and rang up Jasper.

The Administration Building was in an uproar. Sixteen fires had broken out in the park that day and all available men were already committed. The Chief Warden told him to hang on, that he would send him a crew the next day. Charlie fought the fire all day, and late in the afternoon, worn out, he rang up Mona and asked her to bring him his outfit with tents, teepee, blankets, and enough food to last twenty men for three days. Alone, with the fire building up around him, Charlie was lucky to be married to a horsewoman like Mona who could look after this chore without him riding back to help her.

The horses were pastured in the Opal Hills, a high meadowland above Maligne Lake, in the shadow of the 9,000 foot Leah Peak. Mona moved as fast as she could, but it was 7:00 P.M. before they were in the corral and she could start saddling up. It took a while to gather up all the equipment and it was hard work packing the heavy teepee cloth, the bulky crew tents, the boxes of canned goods, wool blankets, and fire-fighting tools.

The job had to be done carefully. It's dangerous to have a load slip on the trail, especially in the dark. Mona worked on into the night by lantern light, finally topping off the packs with some empty twenty-five pound lard pails, which would be cooking pots for the big crew.

Late that night she took the string out of the yard, heading down the Maligne River, which led her like a starry carpet through the darkness. She gave the mare its head and kept hers down out of the way of the low branches that swept over the trail. Just before dawn they rode out into a little meadow and, suddenly, there was a rush of heat rising from the ground. A lake of fire stretched out before her, no flames, just the embers scattered like fallen stars along the earth. There was a clink of metal and a shadow drifted across the red coals, little arrows of flame fanned in its wake.

"Looks like hell, don't it?" cracked Charlie, adding, "Thanks, Mona."

They started setting up camp at dawn. The crew came in by boat from the head of Medicine Lake early that morning and Charlie shook his head when he saw them. They were boys, the oldest being about seventeen. Charlie asked Mona if she would stay and cook, since the administration wasn't supplying a camp cook. Mona took on the job.

"Now we had no cook tent," she told us, "and we had no stove either. For a table, we used a pack mantle spread out on the ground. I cooked everything in those twenty-five pound lard pails hung over an open fire. What a job! There were three shifts of fire-fighters to be fed three times a day and only one cook. That fire burned a whole month. It went right over the top of a mountain and down into some blind hole."

As she talked, I pictured the camp, the dirty, exhausted boys lying on the ground, the blackened pots smoking over the fire, and the bulldog flies and mosquitoes clumped in the air, living clouds of torture. I pictured Mona rolling out of her blanket in the teepee before dawn to start the breakfast fire and working late into the evening, the smoke of thirty days' work stinging in her eyes.

"What did they pay you for that, Mona?" I asked.

"Pay!" she exclaimed. "Ha! That's quite a joke. Oh, the fire-fighters got paid, of course. Charlie got his regular wages, I think $130 a month. No overtime either. They hadn't invented that yet. He had to stay on that fire twenty-four hours a day, until it was dead out."

"Yes, but what about you?" Myrna asked. "Didn't you get paid at all?"

"Well, they didn't quite know what to do with me. I was the warden's wife, you see. I guess they figured it wouldn't look good, putting me on payroll. People would talk. In the end, they decided I should get something, so they gave me a cheque —for five dollars."

"That's terrible," Myrna said, stunned. I sat back in my chair, shaking my head.

"It was about what I'd expected, and anyway, I was doing it for Charlie, not the service. Charlie and I, we shared everything, including the hardships. It was no picnic for him either, at times, but it brought us closer together. I have no regrets, though it was kind of hell at times."

There had been no trace of bitterness in Mona's voice as she told the story, only a kind of ironic amusement at the memory.

"I remember I bought a dress with the five dollars. I called it my fire dress. It was a lovely shade of blue . . . ."

On a table near the window there was a picture of Mona as a young woman of twenty-seven. She wears bush clothes and a peaked woollen hat of the kind popular in the thirties, a wool shirt, Ironman pants, and a long hunting knife on one hip. There are leather moccasins on her feet and she stands with her snowshoes held up beside her, a pair of long Cree shoes used in deep-snow country. She has shaken the snow off them at the end of a trip, and having finished this gesture, looks steadily into the camera, completely at home in the scene, a part of it, like a tree or a wolf. No. A cat, I decide—a cougar. There's the same kind of watchful alertness, the same feline grace.

Late afternoon sun streamed through the window, playing in a mellow glow over the varnished logs of the cabin. It moved gently over Mona's face, diffusing the lines of age, and I could see again the face of that young woman in the picture, her confident, steady look, a match for that of my young wife who sat across from her, marvelling at the cost of one blue dress.

Seeing our interest in the photograph, Mona began to reminisce about the winter it was taken, the first winter of her marriage. It had started out unhappily, with Mona ill in town with the flu and Charlie miles away on a solitary patrol of the Brazeau country, some 400 square miles of high mountain terrain that lies seventy snowshoe miles southeast of Jasper. Though

116

Mona was a beginner on snowshoes, she had planned to learn the craft by travelling with her husband. Now she faced the prospect of living without him until spring break-up. It was a rude end to the honeymoon for a young wife, when she realized that Charlie had a mistress she had to compete with, and that mistress was the wilderness of Jasper Park.

Mona got mad. She got mad at the hired girl Charlie had left to look after her and she got mad because Charlie wasn't there to help nurse her through her illness. Then she got mad at her body for letting her down and ordered it to get well, at once. As soon as she felt strong enough, she sent the girl packing and called Charlie on the forestry telephone to tell him to clean up his cabin and get ready for her arrival. Astounded at the idea of his wife snowshoeing seventy miles by herself to join him, Charlie made her promise to wait for him at the Upper Sunwapta Cabin, which sits near the foot of the dangerous Poboktan Pass, a place where the high winds and the avalanche mete out life or death with equal indifference to winter travellers.

Mona packed her rucksack and prepared to leave. At the time, she didn't even own a pair of snowshoes, but she knew that the Superintendent's wife had a pair hanging over her fireplace to decorate the wall. Neither woman realized at the time that those pretty snowshoes with their gay red tassels were strictly built as ornaments. Only after many stops and many repairs with haywire and leather thongs would Mona learn the truth about them, yet she was to travel all the way from Jasper to the Brazeau on shoes that were more ethereal than real.

The first part of her trip went well. The cabins along the way were stocked with food and blankets, and the only event that cast a shadow on her trip was a storm that piled snow up to the eaves of one of the cabins and forced her to hole up for three days. Despite the delay, the two arrived at their rendezvous within ten minutes of each other. She informed him that she didn't think the life of a warden in winter was so bad, and then Charlie gave her the bad news.

He had been travelling with a big dog named Smoky. Smoky, who was part wolf, earned his keep by carrying extra food and a double sleeping bag in a canvas pack. During the storm the two of them had become separated and now the dog was missing, along with his precious cargo. There were no blankets in the primitive shelter where they slept that night, and without the extra food, their rations would soon run low.

To keep warm, one would wrap up in a square of canvas, while the other stoked wood into the air-tight heater, a small barrel-like stove that was supposed to heat their shelter.

The temperature was forty below zero. The log walls, which looked like something thrown up by a desperate man in a hurry, were covered with two inches of hoar frost, and the cracks were plugged with the last warden's discarded underwear and socks. For a bed, they had a pile of spruce boughs in one corner and the repose on it they described as "burn and turn," the side nearest to the stove getting scorched, while the side next to the wall got frozen.

If the sleeping arrangements were rough, the eating arrangements bordered between laughable and intolerable.

At home, Mona kept a well-stocked pantry and an array of pots, dishes, and cutlery. Charlie, who was used to travelling alone all winter, did without niceties, to keep his pack light. He lived out of a frying pan with a blackened billy tin for making his tea, and one mangled fork.

They sat in the windowless shack at night, cooking over the glowing top of an old tin heater, with the door open to the storm to give them enough light to see, and with the howl of timber wolves for dining music. Blowing snow eddied in with a bracingly cold draft which had the advantage of clearing out some of the smoke billowed from the rusty stove-pipe, and Mona drily asked Charlie whether he preferred death by suffocation or death by freezing. A little sheepishly, Charlie coughed and conceded it might be wise to pack in a new stove-pipe and a lantern or two, next trip.

They ate supper, taking turns using the one fork, until it fell out of a numbed hand and disappeared in a crack in the log floor. They looked at each other and laughed. Mona drew a line down the middle of the frying pan with a stick, and they dug in with their fingers.

"How do you like a warden's life now, dear?" asked Charlie, and when she looked up to answer, he tried to sneak his fingers across the dividing line.

A sense of humour was probably the greatest commodity for anyone in such bad times, but sometimes these situations are only funny in retrospect.

They ate their worst meal one afternoon below the summit of Poboktan Pass in a blizzard. Mona's wool clothing had gotten wet, then frozen in the cold wind so that she could hardly move, and her feet had lost all feeling in the icy moccasins.

118

They stopped as soon as they got back down to tree line, and Charlie quickly built a fire while Mona stripped down to her bare skin and changed into dry clothing from her pack.

She rested, sitting on her pack and inching her toes forward to reach the fire, which was slowly melting its way down into the ten-foot deep snow that was packed into the neck of Poboktan Pass. Soon she had slid part way in after it, fighting the smoke for the sake of a little heat.

"Are you hungry, dear?" asked Charlie tenderly.

"Starved," was the plaintive reply.

"I'll fix a nice lunch then," said Charlie, worried about the health of his young wife, and trying to do his best for her, according to his lights. He hung the billy tin over the flames to melt snow for tea water, then he got out their sandwiches. These were frozen stiff, of course, which he was used to. Mona watched with alarm as he stabbed his belt knife through them and held them down to the fire until they were thawed enough to chew. As she bit into the cold, soggy bread, Mona allowed herself a moment of doubt about the wisdom of leaving a warm house in town to be a backcountry wife.

There could be no turning back, however, and after a night spent untangling the phone line by moonlight, where a moose had torn it down with its antlers and wrapped it around a half-dozen trees—a not uncommon occurrence, as she soon found out—they arrived at the comfort of the Brazeau Station, a real log house with windows, cook stove, pots, forks, and plenty of blankets and food.

Their relief was spoiled, however, when they discovered that a pound of butter had fallen out of the pack at their last stop, seven miles back up the trail, butter they needed to spread on their hotcakes and on the fresh bread that Mona had promised to bake.

They cooked themselves a big meal and ate. Then Charlie tied on his snowshoes again and walked seven miles back down the trail to get that pound of butter before the birds ate it. The mountains of Jasper in winter were no place for the weak. All mistakes, however slight, had to be paid for in extra sweat.

Now as we sat in Mona's kitchen, the teapot was empty, and the story was told.

Outside the window we saw a squirrel and chicadee quarrelling over a chunk of suet that lay on a feeder outside the kitchen window.

119

Mona told us that a few months before Charlie died, there had been an unwelcome visitor at the feeder. She was sitting at the table one day, enjoying the afternoon sun, when a shadow fell across the room. She looked up, half expecting to see a cloud drifted across the sun, but was startled to find instead a grizzly bear standing up to sniff the suet, his broad head seeming to fill the window frame. Mona has seen plenty of grizzlies in her time, but seldom at such close quarters.

"It gave me a nasty surprise, and when I opened the window to tell him to scat, do you know that old beggar just stood there and squinted at me? He sure took his sweet time leaving."

Myrna and I exchanged glances. I was picturing Mona shaking her small fist under Mustahyah's nose and ordering the mountain king to "scat."

"The next night," Mona went on, "I was sitting there writing a letter—I had just put down about the bear being there the night before and I hoped he wouldn't come back, when I looked up. And there he was again, big as life and twice as ugly! Well, I let out a shriek that time. Poor Charlie. He was going to bed and he must have jumped six inches off the floor. But at least I scared the bear away."

We got up to leave and Mona walked us to the door, wishing us luck in the Tonquin Valley. We thanked her for the tea and the stories and, after promising her we'd drop in again when we returned that way, we got in the truck and drove down the road.

As a warden's wife, Mona's life had not been easy. Myrna reminded me of something Mona said when I had asked her why she hadn't chosen to stay in town like some of the other wives, rather than live in the backcountry.

She'd answered, "I'd rather face the elements any day than face loneliness."

Now she was facing just that and doing it remarkably well.

We arrived that night at the Cavell Warden Station which sits on the west bank of the Athabasca at the foot of Mount Edith Cavell, six miles' south of Jasper. That was the kicking-off point for our trip into the Tonquin the next day and the headquarters of my new boss, Tony Klettl.

We moved our stuff into the bachelor quarters in the back of Tony's garage, cooked a quick supper, and before going to bed we loaded our packboxes for our trip into the Tonquin Valley.

120

The morning was clear and cold as we drove up the road to the trail head the next day at the 5,500 foot level of Mount Edith Cavell, where our horses were waiting. There was a glistening sheen of light frost, hanging in a silken web on every leaf and branch. The willow bush had the limpid in-between shine that it gets a week or so before the first yellow of approaching autumn tints its leaves, and the air held a keenness that makes your nostrils prickle; a keenness that will hold the scent of an animal in the air for a few minutes after it passes by, like a calling card.

Long ranks of evergreens marched down the flanks of the mountain to the Astoria River, brawling its way down to the wide Athabasca far below. We rounded the last switchback and suddenly confronted the diamond crown of Mount Edith Cavell. Angel Glacier, washed blood-red on its pillory of solid rock, seemed to hover over us, as if set free from its union to the cirque that holds it prisoner, below the summit of Cavell. We looked below us and saw the same image again, mirrored in the still water of Cavell Lake. I turned the truck to drive down to the outlet and over a small wooden bridge, wrapped in wisps of morning vapours, rising from the green trout-stream below.

We got out of the truck at the corral. The horses pricked up their ears and moved slowly up from the water trough to get their oats.

"That sway-backed sorrel is yours," I told Myrna.

"He's beautiful!"

I looked at him again, but he still looked ugly as sin to me, though in a durable and endearing way. "His official name is Rusty, but mostly he goes by the handle of Seldom Swift. Due to his speed."

"Look how fuzzy he is!" She stroked his whiskery old chin. Truly, one would suspect it to be December and not August, if they went by the length of pelt on that gelding. He was prime.

I showed her how to slip the leather halter on and she led him over to the saddle. "I think he's trying to tell us something," I told her, for the air at that altitude held the breath of the north wind.

I strapped on my spurs and caught the other two horses, Toby and China, both geldings. Toby was a white horse, which is handy in the mountains, when they're hobbled and kicked out to graze. A white horse shows up better in the forest or against the backdrop of green meadows. China was a wall-eyed pinto.

Now I found myself in the role of riding instructor, despite my conviction that there should be a law against husbands trying to teach their wives anything. "Fold the cinch over the saddle, like this, before you try to throw it on, Myrna."

"OOF!"

"What's wrong?"

"It's my belly. It gets in the way."

"Let me do it for you, then."

"No, thanks," she pushed me gently away, "I want to do it myself."

I could hear struggling and puffing noises while I saddled the other two.

"Hey," she called. I looked up. "How'm I doing?"

"The rigging's caught under it."

"What's rigging?"

"The back cinch. Also, the blanket's too far back. Best rip it off and start again."

"Hell."

I got her a stump to stand on and pointed out how the blanket sits forward on a horse's withers. I started packing the pinto, while she hoisted the saddle back on and fiddled with the cinch. The sun came up, the light frost melted to a dew, dripping off the roof of the pack shed; I wanted to get under way.

"Huh," she grunted, "I can't bend very well it seems."

"Well, let me help you."

"No! I want to do it myself."

"What the hell are you so stubborn for?" I flared at her. "Now what's the matter?"

She stomped off. There was the hint of sudden tears in her eyes. I dropped the pack mantle and hurried after her.

"What's wrong?"

"Don't talk to me like that," she said, her voice sounding scratchy. "I'm not one of your pack animals." There was a fierceness in her eyes that obviated the tears. I had touched her pride with my impatience, and I felt like a fool for spoiling such a day.

"I'm sorry. It's just that I'm used to doing this a certain way. Look, we'll work it out. It's a beautiful day, let's start all over again, okay?"

Embraces, endearments. I discovered that having my wife along was much better than travelling with another man who, if you gave him a bear hug out of sheer enthusiasm, would probably respond with a sudden punch in the eye. I helped

122

her adjust the cinch and the stirrups and finished packing the pinto with a promise that I would teach her the diamond up in the Tonquin, when we had more time. Then we set off, I leading the way, China following, and behind him my partner, wearing her sheep-skin coat. Every time I turned around to check the packs, she responded with smiles and assurances, instead of insults about the quality of my packing, which would have been the case with a warden. Nothing was lost on her quick eye; no spray of fireweed, no arrangement of rocks and moss or movement of game and birds beside the trail escaped her attention. Rusty took to her immediately and she spoiled him, I'm afraid, refusing to toe him in the ribs or make him lift his head up and step out. She wouldn't brook any complaints about that either, so she lagged along behind, completely happy.

We rode down the long traverse that leads to the Astoria, with the warm updraft lifting the horses' manes. At the footbridge, I met Tom Vinson, a barrel-chested outfitter in a badly bruised stetson, coming out with his pack string from his fishing camp at Amethyst Lake. Tom ran a critical eye over my outfit as we splashed across the ford, and offered his hand as I reined in beside him.

"There's an owly old grizzly sow up above there," he said by way of a hello, "and she put some pilgrim up a tree. She ain't as bad as he makes her out though, should you run into him up at the lake."

He caught sight of Myrna, who was crossing the river behind me, and his sunburnt face cracked into a smile.

"I see you brought your better half along."

I introduced them.

"Ma'am. Pleased to meetcha. It's about time you dragged this desperado up here.

"Anyway," Tom continued, "this dude was following her around with his camera, snapping away like a goddamn mousetrap—pardon my French, Myrna. He was just too close."

"Yiii! They don't like that clickety-click sound at close range," I said.

"No, they sure as hell don't. She's got three cubs and between them and the people that's crowding in up there, she's about run ragged. She was backed down into Chrome Lake, figurin' to stay clear of the campers, I guess, when this dude showed up. She finally turned and put the run on him. Lucky for him he found a good solid tree."

"Was he hurt?" Myrna asked.

"Nope. He's minus the heel off one boot, though."

"That's pretty close," I said.

"Just close enough to smarten him up a tad, and still leave him with a story to tell."

"If she has a taste for boot leather," I told him, "it could get a bit ugly around here."

"Yep. And there's enough people up above to keep her in leather. They're camped all over the place—everywhere except where they're supposed to be—buildin' fires way up in the timber, cuttin' trees, buildin' lean-to's, scatterin' garbage. There's enough abandoned sheets of plastic from their lean-to's to roof a greenhouse in hell. It's blowin' all over the meadows. They come down to my camp to try and bum a meal and bitch about my horses damagin' the ecosystem. Me and these horses been gettin' along with the ecosystem long before most people around here were old enough to wipe their own behinds." Tom thrust out his jaw as if daring me to challenge his statements.

There was a broken log handrail on the footbridge above the ford. Tom pointed it out to me, in case I'd missed it. I hadn't.

"Some hiker must have bucked his pack off," he said drily. "I see you got a saddle axe there."

"Yeah. I've got some six-inch spikes too."

"You'll do," Tom grunted approvingly and, with a promise to Myrna that he'd drop by the cabin for coffee, he spurred his horse into the river and disappeared into the far trees, the packhorses following.

Myrna watched our horses while I stepped off, axe in hand, to find a spruce pole for the handrail. As I worked, I mulled over what Tom had said. The plight of the grizzly sow was a familiar pattern to me by now: too many people, and not enough room for a bear to make an honest living. The situation would have to be watched carefully, for the sake of both the grizzly bear and the people.

I finished spiking down the new handrail, and we took the horses up the Astoria River, checking the forestry line as we went, riding into the shadow of Throne Mountain to the south, which dominates the valley, gradually working our way up the slopes of Oldhorn Mountain on our right, over rockslides and up sets of steep switchbacks. I got off to lead the horses on the steep ascent and, as I walked, I threw deadfall and rocks off the tread, stopping here and there to block some man-made

124

shortcuts with barriers of dead branches, to prevent erosion of the trail. Breathing hard, I led the gelding over the shoulder of Oldhorn Peak, and through a big rockslide that leads into a meadow. There it was.

I turned and watched Myrna's face as she rode over the hump, to suddenly confront one of the most beautiful arrays of mountains to be seen anywhere on earth. She stopped, astounded, her mouth dropping open.

"Good God!"

Indeed he is. Old Kosmos outdid himself when he took his chisel of prehistoric ice and carved the Tonquin Valley. It's said that the Indians regarded this range as the lodges of strange creatures and evil spirits. The first white men had been awestruck too at the sight of those castellated cliffs that rise sheer above the blue waters of the two Amethyst Lakes to form a wall over 3,000 feet high and three miles long. To white men, the dark, crenellated towers, studded with short rivers of ice hanging on their cloud-embattled walls, were like the fortress of some medieval warlord. So the range was named the Ramparts, and the peaks that form it were given names like Barbican, Drawbridge, Parapet, and Redoubt.

Long, rolling uplands stretched away on either side of where we sat above the valley, green hills swept with acres of alpine flowers that rippled now bright, now dark, in the patches of light that played between high, white clouds. They flowed in a sea of colour up to the grey barriers of rock and glacier that ringed the valley on three sides. A few miles to the west, the open end falls away down Tonquin Creek and Meadow Creek, to the Frazer River and British Columbia on one side and to the Miette River in Alberta on the other. We were looking at the jagged backbone of the Great Divide. Ripples of wind blew in arcs a quarter of a mile wide across the surface of the water below. The two lakes are joined by a narrow channel and near this narrows was the red roof of Tom Vinson's lodge, shining in the sun. Dotted here and there along the meadows were the tiny red and yellow squares of backpackers' tents and below us, near the outlet of the lake at Surprise Point, was the log warden cabin, dominated by the walls of the Ramparts that seemed to rise right out of the log corral behind it.

"There's our home until the snow flies, Myrna."

"I don't believe it," she said, drinking in the scene, "I didn't know there were places like this left in the world. And to think they pay you for being here!"

125

"Yeah, the poor fools, but they get their money's worth, don't worry. And the banker doesn't exactly rush out to welcome me when I go to cash my pay cheque, either."

"I know. But still, we're lucky to be here."

I laughed. "We're both hooked now, Myrna. Once you get a taste of living this way, you'll never be satisfied with the modern world again." But I only said it with half a smile, because there is pain, as well as joy, in that addiction to living in the past.

The horses stepped down through the fields of yellow paintbrush and blue forget-me-nots to the cabin. Seeing the glow of health in Myrna's face and the delight she took in every aspect of the cabin was a pleasure that made up for the drudgery and grimness that had been our lot in the first part of that summer. We sat up late on the porch drinking hot rum, listening to the murmur of the creek in the front yard, and watching the first play of aurora dancing over the ghostly heads of the Ramparts.

"I could stay here forever," she said.

Those days had wings. The trails were suffering badly from heavy use and the phone line was cut in several places by washouts and deadfall below the cabin on the old Astoria River trail. In a few days, Myrna learned how to rope a deadfall and skid it off the trail with her saddle horse when I'd swamped the limbs off. She worked with me on the phone too, tying on to the wire with her rope and stretching it with a dally around the saddlehorn so I could splice the broken ends together. Seldom Swift was unflappable and worth his weight in oats, "foolproof," as they say in horse parlance. He seemed to sense Myrna's delicate condition and allowed her liberties that he would never permit me. He'd let her stand on the saddle with the reins looped over the horn while she nailed up an insulator. But when I tried it, he stepped out from under me, leaving me hanging from the wire, springing up and down like a yo-yo. We got the phone going in time to call a helicopter to evacuate a middle-aged man who'd had a stroke while fishing in the lake, dramatic proof of how important communication can be in such a remote area.

When we were home, Myrna kept the tea kettle boiling and any traveller who came by the cabin was suitably tanked up on the staple mountain drink before he left for the final mile hike to the campground. A cup of hot tea on a rainy day is the cheapest way I know of doing public relations work for the park. The presence of a warden's wife removes the mask of anonymity that hides the civil servant from the public and puts a human, therefore understandable, slant on the park regulations. A warden's presence in the area demonstrates that the department cares about the park and the people in it and intends to look after the environment. It makes people think twice before they start destroying things.

A month sped by. One day I got a call from Tony who said he had a load of winter supplies for me to pack in from the trail head. He also had a message from the doctor that Myrna was due for a check-up, so the next day we saddled up and dead-headed down to Cavell Lake where Tony had left a truck for our sixteen mile drive to town. It was a strange sensation getting into a truck again and, unnerved by the sudden rush of cars that whizzed by like a horde of angry wasps, we crept down the first miles of road.

After a month in the bush the town of Jasper in the tourist season, even in the tail end of it, gave us an overdose of future shock, with its car horns, line ups and rubbernecking crowds. Myrna went to see her doctor, and then we went to the grocery store where we ran into Julie Winkler and her husband, Max, the Area Manager of the townsite. We got to talking about the joys of backcountry living and Julie invited us over for lunch.

The talk centred on the days when they had lived in the Brazeau district, former stomping grounds of the Mathesons. Julie, a talented wood carver, has the introspective temperament of an artist. With short, dark hair and aquiline features, she has the intensity and self-assurance of a woman who knows herself well.

For Julie, living in the backcountry was a turning point in her life. Max was away most of the time, and Terry was just a baby, so she couldn't travel far from the cabin in winter. The wilderness makes psychological demands that equal the physical challenges for people living in isolated cabins and Julie was forced to fall back on her own resources of spirit.

Like most modern women, Julie was untrained for life in the wilderness, in an environment that had disappeared years earlier from most of North America. She found herself using the tools of housekeeping and survival that had been forgotten everywhere else since grandmother's day. She had to learn to live with wood for heat, candles and coal oil lamps for light, and horses for transportation. It was an alien world and at first she didn't know whether she could cope with it, but old times are only a few decades away, after all.

Julie found herself attempting things that she thought she couldn't do, found herself doing them anyway, out of necessity, and marvelling at the pleasure this gave her. Discovering that she could cope with the bush gave her a new freedom and self-confidence. Suddenly, life seemed full of possibilities that had been overlooked. Brimming with these new ideas about herself, Julie longed for the women friends she had left behind, wanting to tell them about her changed life. In the evenings, she wrote long letters to them, letters that couldn't be mailed anywhere. Her imaginary conversations in these letters served as a journal and as a way of staying in touch with people she loved and longed to see.

"You tend to exist very much in your own mind out there," she told us. "The letters were an attempt to break through the shell of isolation. You can lose your voice if you don't use it."

Max brought out their photograph album to show us some of the things they had recorded over the years.

"This is Terry, age three," said Julie.

"Riding a horse at that age!" Myrna said with surprise.

"The country was far too rough for him to walk through," Julie explained, "and he was getting too heavy for me to carry all day so he had to learn to ride early."

"You must have worried about him when he was little, so far from town."

"I did. Because once the snow flies, you're completely cut off. We did have the phone line—when it was working. But you couldn't rely on helicopters coming in there or anything. If you had a serious accident and you were alone, you were as good as dead."

Her face darkened. "I made a mistake once," she said. "I left some pills out on the table, and the baby got them. It was just at the time when he was learning to stand and the first time he stood by himself, he got the pills. I came back in from the spring, and there he was smiling and gurgling at me, with the empty bottle in his hand—I was absolutely terrified."

But Julie couldn't afford the luxury of hysteria. She made a salt-water solution and forced it down the baby's throat until he had thrown up most of the poison, crying with shock at such rough treatment. Then, slowly, the cries quietened, the small head lolled and the baby lapsed into unconsciousness.

128

Julie rang up Jasper, shouting over the static on the line for the dispatcher to get a doctor on the phone.

Seventy miles away in distance and in time, the doctor's voice was hardly discernible. The telephone line, buffeted by the wind that blew tree limbs against it, was the single strand that joined Julie to the twentieth century, to the world of doctors and hospitals that began at Jasper, Alberta. The vagaries of wind and snow, the crackle of static electricity, toyed with the doctor's voice.

"Give ... emetic. Bring ... Jasper ... must ... hospi ...," as if he could hope to reach back that far into time and space, into the lost fragment of the world that was the Brazeau Station; as if he could order the past to be reasonable.

Julie struggled to catch his words. It was not so much the advice she needed, as contact with another human being because she had already done everything she could for the child. The voice she heard, the weak but at least human voice, strained thin as the silver wire that carried it over the mountains, kept her from falling into uncontrollable panic. As she listened, her eyes lingered over every slight rise in the baby's chest, each shallow breath. It seemed to her then that her mind was stretched as thin as that wire and that it would snap if she put down the receiver. How, after all, could a human voice expect to enter this solitude, a voice other than that of her husband, who was still a day away from the phone line as he patrolled the farther reaches of his district? How could a voice travel through seventy miles of spruce and pine, dipped from tree to tree on a swaying wire no thicker than a clothesline? Yet the voice lived in the wire, the wire faithfully tended by Max with muscles and schemes, with cuts and bruises, and most of all, with anxiety.

Julie listened to the doctor's voice. He wanted her to bring the baby out, she realized; he had no idea of the impossibility of that demand. To carry the baby thirty five miles on snowshoes to where she would meet the nearest warden patrol was impossible. The trip would kill them both, or an avalanche or frostbite would. Travelling with a sick baby was something to be tried only under the best of conditions and with the help of two strong men towing the toboggan, equipped with ropes and shovels to get through the steep cornices that hung over the lip of the pass.

She shouted back at the doctor to tell him it couldn't be done, but his voice faded altogether, like a lamp going out. On

129

the receiver there was only the static of the winter night, star talk crackling across the mountains, the pulse of aurora borealis. A cosmogony that allowed no place for human beings leaned along the cord of the telephone line, and it bound her heart only to universal night. So it was as if the voice had been an illusion after all. The reality was her child, drifting away from her into a terrible darkness, and only she could call back his spirit. She was alone.

But Julie was a fighter and she had been alone before. She was a tough-minded blend of common sense and almost mystical faith in the power of the human spirit. So she stoked the stove, massaged the child to keep his blood moving and bathed him in her love. The hours passed but she would not give in, until, as if aroused by the sheer force of her will, the baby stirred at last, unsettling the weight of poison in his veins. He trembled, whimpered, and began to breathe more steadily.

The wind stirred in the trees outside, spruce logs cracked in the stove. The wind would be blowing mares' tails of snow from the plumed peaks that no man would see that night. In the dark valley, one light shone back at the stars, defiantly. It threw a square of tender light, weakly but steadily, onto the indifferent snow.

"I guess that was the longest night of my life," Julie said, bringing us back to the present. We had been sitting entranced, captured by the strain of her ordeal.

Max reminded me we were due back at work. Our horses were waiting at Cavell for the trip back into the Tonquin Valley. Before we left, Julie showed me a poem she had written in the Brazeau Cabin, a remarkable statement about what that life had meant to her, though perhaps too passionately tender to reproduce here. I remember the last lines, which convey what a home can mean to a man and a woman, even in the most isolated wilderness:

> ... here is all warmth
> All friendliness, and food and fire
> Bounded our world in joy, our element
> All known, all new, and sweet as warmth is sweet
> Our world is all encompassed in our arms.

As we headed the horses down toward the Astoria River later that day, I thought about the poem again. What I admired about women like Mona, Julie, and my own wife, was their toughness, determination, and self-reliance, which I realized were the things I admired most in wardens. What I had nearly overlooked was their tenderness, their generosity, and their ability to give of themselves. I thought again of Mona saying, "I'd rather face the elements any day, than face loneliness." It was the kind of statement that puts physical hardship into perspective, for surely loneliness is the greatest hardship any human being faces, regardless of where he lives.

So the story of these women turns out to be a love story. For me, it was a fascinating discovery to learn that the common ingredient that made them able to transcend the limitations on their freedom by society and on their bodies by nature, was not the tough blend of will power and stamina that I had expected, but a more fragile and infinitely more profound resource—love.

We spurred the horses over the ford and started up the long hill. It was well after dark when the stars came out and lit our way down to the cabin at Amethyst Lake.

6

Mustahyah

"I had some Indian packers working for me when I
guided around Grande Cache, and they used to call
the grizzly 'Mustahyah,' which meant 'the mighty
bear.' In their stories, the bear was also referred to as
'our brother across the river.' You know, when a grizzly
is skinned out, it does look a bit like a naked man."

Mac Elder

In the Tonquin Valley, the warm days of Indian summer were
coming to an end, and we savoured each one with special relish, knowing that in a few weeks the seasonal job would be
over for the year. Our future was undecided. I had applied for
a full-time park warden job, and though I was reasonably sure
of getting one, there were no openings in the mountain parks
and, as a new man, I would be subject to transfer anywhere in
the western region, which included the prairie and northern
parks.

One Monday evening toward the end of September Tony
Klettl rang us up with the news that I would be laid off, effective Wednesday. The next day would be our last in the Tonquin, and I would make one final patrol before we locked up
the cabin and packed up for the trip out.

The next morning we woke up to find that the brilliant red
and yellow hues of autumn had been transformed to a dazzling and elegant white. The sun poured into the cabin through
a veil of thin icicles that hung from the eaves above the windows, and the light rippled and wavered between streams of
meltwater that ran from the snow on the roof. Two inches of
light powder, the first of the coming season, lay on the ground
and on the boughs of the spruce trees. Outside, a raven,
perched on top of a gaunt, dead tree, greeted me with the mu-

sical throb of song those buzzards are capable of in their happier moments. No doubt it found the prospect of winter cheering; winter is good to the ravens, there is always meat somewhere on the season's white plate.

Down below the cabin, the lake water was tinted black in contrast to the white clarity of its banks, and a belt of cloud girdled the Ramparts, ermine against their royal purple. It was a great day for climbers wanting to plan new routes. The light snow had etched out every rough line in the towering walls that had appeared smooth yesterday. Now, every ledge and bulge that would hold snow or a climber's foot was sketched out in bold relief. I took the water pails down where the creek smoked in the chill air and stopped in mid-stride at the sight of a message printed for me in the snow.

There were tracks all around the cabin and tracks around the tree that held our meat cache, a wooden, screened box lashed high off the ground. The tracks looked as if a big man and three kids had walked barefoot around the cabin while we slept. There was a wide sole mark, and five toe indentations in each print, just like a human foot. But at the tip of each toe was a round hole poked through the snow and into the soft earth beneath it, made by the four-inch-long claws of a grizzly sow. The tracks of three cubs followed hers around the cabin.

"Prrrr-ock," went the raven from its perch and was answered by its cohort in a stand of trees to the north that separated the cabin from another wide meadow. I looked to where the bird pointed like an animated weather-cock, and saw between the trees four black shapes already a mile away, the big sow moving steadily toward the forest edge, the three cubs rambling after.

The snow had made her restless. She had stayed down near the head of the Astoria for as long as the range would permit, feeding on the carcass of a moose she'd killed. The ravens led me to the carcass, half-buried under dead limbs and moss the sow had raked over it; the bone marrow, an unhealthy grey, showed it to be an old or a sick animal. Easy prey. Now she would change her range for a while, maybe head down Meadow Creek to get below the snow belt, and feed on what was left of the berry crop at that lower altitude. She needed plenty of high calorie food, because from now on the need to lay on fat would dominate her existence until the real winter set in, driving her and the cubs into their winter den. Her ap-

133

petite was stimulated by the five-month-long famine that would soon be upon her, and nothing would distract her from trying to satisfy her belly, not even the demands of motherhood.

Few animals are as well adapted as the grizzly bear for survival in an inhospitable environment that is only free from snow for three or four months of the year. The grizzly is a prodigious and eclectic eater of almost anything, equipped with the killing tools of a predator, the opportunistic instincts of a scavenger, and the omniverous tastes and digestive tract which allows it to exist on a largely vegetarian diet. It will graze on grass high on an avalanche slope, acting more like an old cow moose than a fierce predator, licking up any insects it encounters along the way, and digging up plants with its powerful claws to eat the succulent roots. It loves carrion most of all, relying on the wind to bring news of food to its highly developed nose, since, with its dim eyesight, it may not see the message of the wheeling ravens. Grizzlies don't often kill big game animals because, unlike wolves, they lack the instinct to hunt together and drive the quarry into a pocket where it can be cut down. But when conditions are right, if the game is in some natural corner, or is weak or sick, the bear has the speed to run it down, and will kill it with crushing bites of its powerful jaws. A grizzly has the speed to outrun a horse for a short distance and the stamina to run straight up an avalanche slope for a thousand feet without stopping. But it is a careful opportunist; it won't expend energy on the chase unless its instincts tell it the chase will be rewarded.

Both the grizzly and the black bear have a built-in respect for man. Only one thing draws bears to man and that is the smell of human food, including garbage, which to the bear is a delicacy.

Fortunately, there were no campers left in the Tonquin Valley. The rain that had preceded the snow had sent them packing down to the highway. But there was always the chance that more people would be hiking in via Portal Creek and Maccarib Pass, coming in to the Tonquin where Maccarib Creek flows in at the north end of the lake. The bear was headed that way so I decided to follow her and learn what I could about her routes and her temperament. If I met any hikers on the way, there'd be good opportunity to prevent run-ins with the bears by making sure they kept a clean camp, with their grub tied up in a tree.

The horses were out of sight. "Ho, boys!" I called and heard the "pong" of Toby's old brass bell float to me across the meadows, but the sound echoed from the mountains on both sides of the valley, and you could never fix his direction from the first note. "Oats, Toby!" I yelled, like every morning, and heard the bell go "pong, pong," as he lifted his head and nodded a yes to his belly at the prospect of grain. The horses had drifted up the lake shore toward Tom's camp. I thought tonight I'd feed them in the corral, in case they tried to pull out on me, and head down Meadow Creek for Dominion Prairie. That was down on the Yellowhead Highway, safe from early snow. Even with hobbles, they'd pull out if they sensed a blizzard coming, jumping like kangaroos with the front feet moving together, a trick any mountain horse knows well.

I went out with a halter to where they had turned to watch for me, the snow still clinging in patches on their rumps, steam rising from their wet backs. I slipped the hobbles and haltered my saddle horse and the others followed, walking stiffly at first, taking small, shuffling steps as if the hobbles were still on their front feet. We went up to the cabin.

Myrna had seen the tracks. "I'm going to follow her for a while," I told her. "I want to see where she goes, figure out her range a bit better."

"I guess you'll have to bushwhack," she said.

"Probably. I doubt she'll stay on the trails. I may have to lead the horse and climb if she goes up high."

"It's all right. I wouldn't mind taking it easy today. Really," she added, seeing my contentious look.

I'd been expecting more of an argument; she fooled me, as usual.

After breakfast, I buckled on my leather chaps, then went out and tightened Toby's cinch. Myrna brought our coffee out on the porch and we drank it in the sunlight, savouring the flavour of the brew and the smell of spruce and wet meadow grass. I watched the horse pawing impatiently at the snow, anxious to be moving in the chill air. I finished my coffee and set my cup down.

"Hold the fort, sugar," I told her and went over to the horse and untied his lines, "it may be dark before I get back."

"Write if you find work," she said, watching me swing on. "Shouldn't you take the rifle?"

"Naw. The trouble with that rifle is that once you have it, you have a tendency to think you're safe. Bears don't like the

135

smell of gun grease. Best not to get close enough for them to smell it in the first place."

"Good advice," she said. "Just see that you follow it."

I grinned and rode out on the track of the bears. The snow made it easy work, but it would be melted by mid-afternoon, so I took a short-cut across the meadow at the trot, aiming to pick up her sign on the far side again. Just before the tracks led into the woods, Toby shied at a dark object half hidden in the willow shrubs. It was a dark green pile of bear crap, splashed with the brilliant red of soapberry. I got off to have a look at it because a bear's droppings will often give insights into a bear's state of health that would be dangerous to try to obtain by means of a more intimate inspection of the animal. The crap on hand was still conveniently firmed up by the night's cold, despite the enematic effect of the soapberries on the bear's digestive tract. What they see in those acridly bitter lumps of poison is beyond me, but they will spend days gorging themselves at berry time, using their claws as rakes to gather in the berries, or simply eat them branches and all. The size of the scats identified them as the sow's and not the cubs', and the green colour meant she'd been feeding almost completely on vegetable matter, not flesh, which gives a characteristically dark blackish colour to the stool. With a stick I broke it up, looking for bone fragments and animal hair and checking for parasites, but found nothing but vegetable fibre. The sow was healthy, which was good, since it made her less likely to try and steal human food out of desperation.

A big rock fell and clattered down the wall of Paragon Peak on the far side of the lake. It rolled down the talus slope and into the lake with a splash. The sun was fully up, and the good tracking would not last long. Tom Vinson's chainsaw rattled a half mile to the left, as he cut deadfall on the wood permit I'd issued to him. He would buck it into eight-foot logs to be skidded to his camp when the snow was deep enough for them to slide easily.

The bear tracks led into the dark woods, and I reined in for a moment to let my eyes adjust to the dim light, after the dazzle of snow in the bright meadow. The tracks meandered indecisively on the trail of a marten, backing up in disgust from the marten's pissing post where the pungent weasel scent had assaulted the sow's nose. We came out into a narrow meadow at the foot of an avalanche slope. Here the trail, which had been steadily gaining altitude, as if to bypass the campground, detoured abruptly down a creek to the first tent site, where much scuffling and arguing had gone on over some fish guts that somebody had heaved into the creek, and where one cub had been roundly cuffed out of the way and sent rolling down the slope like a ball to learn some manners. There were a few bright scales clinging to the rocks; other than that, the camp's water supply, fouled by man, had been purified again by the bears, our resident sanitary inspectors.

The sow knew all about campgrounds. She had taken the cubs on a tour all around the tent sites, and their tracks were in the snow on top of the camp tables. I had cleaned up that campground just a few days ago, burning the paper and bagging cans and bottles to be packed out on the horses. The place was spotless, free of human pollution, or at least that's how it appeared to me. The critical nose of the bear mocked my efforts. All through the campground there were little pockets of snow and earth dug up and in each one was a garbage souvenir that campers had buried under a pile of leaves, covered with a rock or stuffed down a ground-squirrel burrow. The sow had scented each one out and dug it up for me; an orange peel, a chocolate bar wrapper, chewed into a wad and spat out again, tin cans, plastic bags, beer bottle caps, and Kleenex—soggy, pink, and ubiquitous—all scattered obscenely on the immaculate white of the snow. I slumped in the saddle and sighed when I came to the old garbage pit that one erstwhile group had dug with their trusty war surplus trenching tools. They had filled the pit in behind them with a couple of feet of dirt, probably figuring that the garbage had been neatly disposed of for all time. Two feet of loose dirt is not even a fair test to a bear's nose. Contemptuously she had raked it all out, spreading broken glass, tinfoil and plastic bags from hell to breakfast for me to clean up.

I tied the horse up and worked for an hour gathering up the smaller bits and pieces that would fit in Toby's saddlebags. The rest I stuffed into a burlap sack carried for that purpose, which I cached in the fork of a tree to be packed out later. Patches of grass were showing through the snow by the time the job was done, and the tracks were erased from the meadow beyond the camp. Back in the saddle, I circled the camp until we cut her sign, picking it up on a higher contour where the snow was shadowed from the melting warmth of the sun under a canopy of spruce. She'd gone up the mountain in a straight line, headed for timberline and the higher meadows that lay beyond. The trail was an overgrown tunnel through the forest, the moss deeply indented by the feet of her ancestors, made impassable to us by the overhanging limbs and deadfall. A big spruce at the entrance was blazed and gouged by the claws of bears that had come this way over the years. A tuft of black hair was stuck to the trunk, glued in a stream of pitch that had flowed out of the wounded tree; memento of some old humpback that had paused to rub its back against the rough bark, relieving a colossal itch.

Toby stopped, his nostrils twitching, smelling bear. "Gitup," I told him, and we went switchbacking up the mountainside, working our way through the trees as we climbed back and forth across her trail, snapping off dead limbs and being generally about as quiet as a bull moose in rut as the horse lunged through the shintangle. The end of a snag slipped under the stirrup leather and Toby stopped, breathing hard. I got off and pulled it out, then began climbing up on foot, leading him. The sweat was running down my face by the time we made it out to timberline, walking through a stand of larch trees, their black branches wrapped with the spun gold of their changed needles. We contoured across to the north until I picked up her trail coming out of the timber near the edge of an old rockslide. She was hunting ground-squirrels and the hunting had been good. We came to a fresh dig where she had shifted a boulder weighing a quarter of a ton to get at the burrows beneath it. There were blood stains and a wisp of gold fur on the dirty snow, all that was left of the ground-squirrel colony.

The horse snorted and backed up nervously. Even I could smell the musky taint of grizzly bear in the ravished earth. An afternoon sun was warming the slopes, and the wind had changed in favour of the sow; blowing up my neck and carrying our scent towards her. A pika, a diminutive relative of the rabbit, squeaked and chittered with alarm from its vantage point halfway up a rockslide. Sensing the bear was near, I quickly got back on the horse and spurred him forward below the slide to where I could see a good line of escape leading down toward the valley of Maccarib Creek. Toby was skittish, worried now that he could no longer get wind of the bear, and not knowing in what direction to look.

She was watching us, but from where? I was sure that she wasn't below us in the timber; she would feel safer if she kept above us. There was nothing in sight on the steepening arc of the horizon; the green line of the meadow was marked only by scattered patches of dwarf spruce and the sharp ridges of Mount Clitheroe rising beyond it. I reined the horse in and waited; no sense moving until we figured out where she was. A flight of pink snow birds spiralled up from the forest below and flitted in a rose-coloured cloud across the patchy snow to land, noisily quarrelling on a clump of dwarf spruce two hundred feet above us. The sow stood up then with a roar and the small birds scattered and tumbled like pink fluff from her shoulders with high pitched, frightened cries.

Toby's ears went up like rockets and he took one step back and froze with his front legs braced. My feet tightened involuntarily in the stirrups, as I began to ease his head to the left again, wanting him pointed the right way, in case he ran into the timber, bucking. Standing seven feet high with her yellowed claws held out in front of her, the sow dominated the horizon, her black form etched against the snow and the blue of the sky, her silver-tipped ruff fanned out in the light. She weaved her head gently back and forth and sniffed sharply, reading our scent, and the sound shivered the air like a bone whistle or the note the wind will make on the lip of a chimney. I shook the reins lightly and Toby took a step sideways, wanting to keep his head toward her, watching. The cubs walked out of the bush then and stood up beside her. One of them dropped to all fours and walked a little ways down the hill towards us, curious to find out what we were.

Her hair was up. "Easy Toby," I said and kicked him around, urging him forward. She noticed the cub, dropped to all fours and came down the hill without warning, letting out a bellow when she ran over the cub in her haste, continuing on in a line that would take her to the right of us. The speed of her charge precluded any motion from us until she had already pulled up and turned to go back to the squalling cub. She cuffed him once, driving him uphill, and he shut up fast, scurrying after his siblings. Then they were gone over the crest and I knew the charge had been a bluff, made out of fear for the cub.

There had been no time to feel fear but now that she was gone I saw my hands trembling on the reins and felt the slightly nauseated churning in the gut that follows a surge of adrenalin and an accelerated heartbeat. "Close enough, Toby," I told the horse and he stepped quickly down the slope following the tree line by way of an answer, snorting and shaking his head as if to say, "I told you so." In a few minutes we reached the mouth of a steep-walled ravine. Looking up, I saw the bears a quarter of a mile above us, moving quickly across the top of the meadow at the base of the cliffs. But she would have to go lower for a while to feed before taking them up to dig a winter den high on an avalanche slope. How long she stayed out after that would depend on her fat and the weather.

We rode down through the meadows, wary and alert, feeling the tension in the air that the presence of a grizzly creates, a tension that hones the senses to a sharp edge, so that they quicken to the slightest movement, the faintest noise or scent.

"Know how to tell a grizzly bear from a black bear?" an old timer asked me, many years ago. "Just climb a tree. Black bear will climb up after you. Old silvertip, he can't climb; so he'll just shake you out of the tree like a plum, if he don't tear it out by the roots."

In his hyperbole there is a serious message. Allowing the bears to roam at will admits a risk to existence that is at odds with the carefully controlled environments of men outside bear country. Here, the bears make the rules, and though the black bear is usually timid, and a tree is usually a safe refuge from the grizzly, you can't ever count on being completely free from danger.

Wilderness provides us with insights into our own animate nature, that we can experience nowhere else. Without the grizzly bear, the last great predator of lower North America, there is no wilderness, only tame, empty playgrounds that mock the pretensions of the adventurers who wander through them. While the bears survive, those of us who love wildness still have a refuge to retreat to from the sea of madness that surrounds it and cuts its corrosive channels more deeply, year by year.

The grizzly bear sow and her cubs were part of a race that once roamed North America from Mexico to the Arctic Ocean. In western Canada, its range extended as far east as the Red River in Manitoba, where it ruled on the plains as it did in the mountains, without fear of natural enemies. The spears and bows of the Indians were seldom effective against the mighty bear, a totemic animal that they both feared as an enemy and worshipped as a god. With the coming of the white man and his fire arms, the plains grizzly went the way of the buffalo and what remained of a vast population was driven into the mountains, its last stronghold. If not for the national parks of Canada and the US, it seems likely that the grizzly would have been extinct long ago in lower North America. It is still hunted when it ventures out onto provincial lands, shot or trapped when it prowls into the grazing leases of the provincial forestry reserves in Alberta. Even in the parks, the bear's future is tenuous at best as more and more people flock to the mountains and compete with the grizzly for elbow room. The high valleys that man finds most beautiful are in short supply and this is the very country the grizzly needs, each bear requiring a twenty-five-square-mile chunk of land to roam at will in order to survive and reproduce.

Now you cannot admit millions of tourists into the domain of one of the most ferocious predators in North America—only the polar bear is more fearsome—without having accidents and, from the play that the slightest incident gets in the newspapers, the park visitor might easily expect that he is taking his life in his hands the moment he ventures into the mountains. The first question that most people ask when they arrive in a park is "Where are the washrooms?," and the next one is "Are there any bears around here?" The truth is that one's chances of ever seeing a grizzly bear on a trip in a national park are minimal, though you can guarantee being visited by a black bear in the main campgrounds, if you leave enough garbage lying around your campsite. The injury rate for run-ins with grizzlies for the eleven national parks in North America that have grizzly populations, was one injury per two million visits for the period 1872 to 1969, according to biologist Stephen Herrero of the University of Calgary. In that period of ninety-seven years, seventy-seven people were injured, and five killed. Not bad odds. So why all the hysteria about bears? Well, an animal that can disembowel an elk with one swipe of its paw, or crush a man's bones with one bite, makes good copy. Stories about the savagery of nature, rare as they are, allow us to forget the savagery of a civilized world that once murdered six million people and, up until a few years ago, was busy dropping jellied gasoline on straw huts where babies lay sleeping; such stories also allow us to forget that our chances are about one in a hundred of even getting to the mountains safely in our automobiles.

Nevertheless, the grizzly is an animal that demands respect, notwithstanding the statistics. The only way to keep the accident rate low is to have district wardens in the field, identifying individual bears in their districts and monitoring the

141

movements of both campers and bears, to prevent the two from getting on a collision course wherever possible. We could never guarantee there wouldn't be accidents which, if not fatal to the person, are usually fatal to the bear, for it was departmental policy to destroy bears that have grown aggressive or have injured humans, because the mandate of the outfit is to protect the visitor from the environment as well as to protect the environment from the visitor. The warden can't do that job while sitting on his ass in town. That's why it was worth taking the risk of meeting the sow up close, getting to know her moods, trying to predict as closely as possible what this unpredictable beast might do in an encounter with the most unpredictable of all beasts, *homo sapiens*. As a warden I couldn't afford to underestimate the savagery of the bear, for the Tonquin Valley is where one of those five people had been killed.

I took my binoculars out of the saddlebags and glassed up towards Maccarib Pass. There were the four tiny figures, moving across the meadows in a long arc that would take them around to the north and lead them eventually out above Meadow Creek.

After an hour's ride, we came on a game trail and followed it down to Maccarib Creek. I urged the horse across the ford and up to a little point of land above it with a commanding view of Amethyst Lake on one side and Maccarib Pass on the other. This had been the site of the old warden cabin when the pass was the main route of entry into the valley. Now there is nothing but a few scattered logs and some trees blazed by travellers many years ago. Behind the cabin site is one other memento, a tombstone set in a little chained-off enclosure whose epitaph reads:

PERCY HAMILTON GOODAIR
1877-1929
"We cherish his memory in our hearts."

The grave was overgrown with orange paintbrush flowers and wilted alpine buttercups—all that was left of the season's blooms. Most of the year, Goodair has the place pretty well to himself except for the odd warden stopping by to pay his respects to a guardian of the mountains who died with his boots on and was buried in a place that he loved. The wind blows over his grave and the water purls over an old beaver dam in the creek below; there are voices on the air, stories on the wind.

142

On September 12, 1929, Warden Goodair stepped out of his cabin and headed up the creek in the face of a blizzard to look for his horses. When he didn't show up in Jasper a few days later to pick up supplies, as scheduled, a party of three wardens was dispatched from town to look for him. They found him near his cabin, buried under two feet of fresh snow, his side ripped open by a grizzly. He had made a vain effort to plug the wound with a bright coloured sash that he habitually wore, voyageur style around his waist, but the claws had gouged too deeply, the damage was too great. Alone in the snow, knowing that help would never reach him in time, Goodair had composed himself to die. When they found him, his hands were folded over his chest and his legs were lying out straight in front of him. He had tried to make the spectacle of his death as easy on his friends as he could, imposing on his last remains the stamp of the courageous soul that passed out of them.

There had been a sow with two cubs in the valley around that time, and she habitually passed by the cabin, travelling between feeding grounds. The searchers concluded that Goodair, his vision and hearing obscured in the storm, had walked between the sow and her cubs and that she had come at him before he had time to even suspect her presence. Typically, the sow had not fed on her human victim but, once satisfied he posed no threat to the cubs, she had left him alone. Goodair might have survived the attack, as other victims have, if he'd seen her coming and dropped to the ground to roll himself into a ball, but the storm and fate had conspired against him. The sow was never seen in that valley again.

Goodair had the unlikely distinction of being the only warden killed by a grizzly bear in the history of the service. There have been plenty of near misses and close calls over the years, though; everyone who has travelled extensively in the mountains has a story to tell about old Mustahyah, the king of the hills.

The stories have all the elements of myth because nowhere is the confrontation between man and nature so sharply focused as it is in the meeting between man, the tamer of the wilds, and the grizzly bear, the savage, rebellious spirit of the wilds made manifest.

I shook the reins and headed Toby down toward Amethyst Lake, checking him with the bit as he tried to turn south for home. We would check the second campground on the way home, to see how the firewood was holding up. The snow was nearly gone and there was still a week of good camping left, when the wisest hikers travel to avoid the flies and the tourists which go into hibernation after the first frost of the year. I stopped the horse from time to time, once to glass a small herd of caribou trotting across the mouth of a high basin on Mount Clitheroe to the east, other times to note materials and man hours needed to repair wet sections of the trail.

It was near dusk when we made the campground. I checked it over, then lit my pipe and gave the horse his head, thinking over the day's events. The horse had been good with the bear, had been alert but steady, seeming to sense that the rush would only be a bluff. With the benefit of hindsight, I could see that there had been something nervously oblique about the way the sow had charged us, that the mighty bear was afraid of us, despite its advantage. If the horse could talk, it could have told me much about the grizzly and how to read its moods. It must have encountered bears often, grazing at night in the meadows, for bears, like elk and moose, will graze right alongside horses in the mountain night like so much cattle when the grass is good, in mutual tolerance. On a dark night, it's best to rely on your nose when you walk out to check your horses, not just your eyes. A grizzly on all fours may look like a horse when there are only the stars for lamps.

An old-time Jasper warden, Ed McDonald, took the situation to its logical, if frightening, conclusion, in a high, lonesome valley one night. He went out in the dark to get his horses in for an early start the next day and walked toward what he thought was a horse cropping grass a few yards away. "Ho, pony," Ed said softly, so as not to spook the horse by surprising it, "easy now, big fellah." He stepped up to its shoulder, and reached out with the halter but froze when he felt long, shaggy fur instead of horsehide. The bear snarled once and, chopping its jaws together with a sound like a steel box closing in an empty room, it moved quickly away to find a less crowded place to feed, leaving Ed shivering with the halter still held in his outstretched hand. If Ed laughed over that one, he must have waited until he got down to the old log shack in Jasper, where, in those days, the wardens used to rendezvous to drink whiskey and swap stories. The shack is gone now but the stories live on.

For most of Ed's career, he had the Rocky River district which stretched from the Athabasca River, up the Rocky, and along the east park boundary to the limits of the Brazeau district at Southesk Pass. The area was, and still is, some of the last unruined wilderness to be found south of the Northwest Territories. It's a land of narrow valleys, bisected by swift-flowing streams like the Rocky, Restless, and Medicine Tent Rivers. But it isn't the fast water and big lonely mountains staring down that make it wild, it's the track of the grizzly to be found in the high passes and in the tributary valleys of the Rocky River. There were many bears in the district back then, and Ed came and went among them without giving it much thought.

Having once tried to halter old humpback, and having lived to tell the tale, Ed lost his fear of the bear. Once, Ed's doughtiness, and a couple of machinegun bullets he'd been carrying in his leg since the First World War, combined in an accident that nearly cost him his life.

One day in June of 1937, Ed was returning to his line cabin on the Medicine Tent River after a day spent siwashing up to the head of a nearby creek. It was part of the warden's job then to explore and map every brook in his district so as to monitor its potential for fire protection and to discover what big game animals ranged its upper slopes and at what time of year. Ed couldn't stand not knowing about every creek, valley, and meadow in his district. An unknown place pricked at his peace of mind like a sliver under a fingernail; he couldn't sit still until he had probed it out completely.

It had been a long day. Ed's fifty-seven winters combined with the warm sun of late afternoon weighed heavily on his eyelids, so he drowsed in the saddle, riding with a slack rein. Sometimes he loosed his right leg from the stirrup and let it trail free, because the chunks of steel-jacketed lead the Army doctors had overlooked pinched the nerves at times, making it painful to bend his knee. Now and again the horse, sensing that its rider was dozing off, would stoop to steal a mouthful of grass along the way but mostly it stepped along quick enough, headed for the cabin and a bait of oats.

Ed's dog Willie, a six-month-old collie pup, ran along under the stirrup. Ed trusted the horse. It was a seasoned animal that knew the country well and knew the dangers too. They had seen a silvertip earlier that day, feeding on the broad leaves of cow parsnip at the edge of a small meadow near the trail, but Ed had passed it off as just another grizzly. The horse had never run from a bear before. This time, though, it must have come on to the bear sign too fast, or perhaps the wind changed suddenly and the horse got too much bear stink all at once, because it suddenly shied violently, and Ed, not having a good seat, with one leg out of the stirrup, found himself flying off before he could gather rein. He lighted on his back right on a dead tree that lay beside the trail. Something gave with a snap that made him yell with agony and, winded, he lay still, wondering what had hit him. Before he could move, the horse came by him, bucking, and kicked him hard on the hip bone. Still unaware of how badly he was hurt, in the numbness that sometimes follows a serious injury, Ed tried to get up but found he could not stand. His pelvis was broken.

Old Ed had hit the jackpot and he knew it. He eased himself over on his stomach and felt his mind clouding with a pain that smoked along his hips and burned along the fuse of every nerve. He was in need of a doctor and a hospital but the nearest medical help was forty-two miles away. Considering the shape he was in, it may as well have been on the moon and he knew that a week might easily go by before anyone came looking for him. It had been a warm spring and the rivers were beginning to flood with runoff. In Jasper, they might figure a section of phone line had been washed out and they would allow him enough time to fix it, maybe five days, before they got worried and sent somebody looking for him. That's what had happened to Goodair. Ed's eyes focused on the wire that waved slightly in the breeze, twenty feet above him. He wished he had had his field-set with him but it was back in the cabin, only half a mile away. Surely he could make it half a mile, such a short distance. He tried to get up again but it was as if, in order to stand, he had to slide his groin along the sharp edge of a knife. He fell back, moaning with shock.

The horse had settled down and was feeding on the trail behind him. It would have to pass close to him to get up to the cabin where the pack ponies were picketed in the meadow. He saw the shape of an eleven-inch-long grizzly track, pressed into the wet earth between his hands, the track twice as big as his own palm prints, and he then knew what had frightened his horse. A twig snapped behind him and he felt the warm breath of an animal on the back of his neck. He yelled with fear and rolled over to meet it, reaching for his belt knife. There was the dog, backing away from him, terrified.

Calling the dog to him, he lay still, fighting the pain, until the horse drew near and the reins flicked over his arm. While the horse stood patiently, Ed hauled himself up on the stirrup leathers until he was nearly standing. Though he tried repeatedly, he could not get into the saddle. At length, he pulled out the cinch knot, dropped the saddle and blanket to the ground, pulled off the bridle, and with one hand on a nearby spruce lowered himself to the ground where he lay, soaking wet with sweat from the pain of the wasted effort. He wrapped himself in the saddle blankets, and covered himself with his slicker, not having the strength to crawl around gathering wood for a fire. The dog lay down with him, offering its loyalty and the meagre warmth of its body. The dog growled steadily at something in the woods by the trail that Ed didn't want to see or think about, though he knew it was the bear.

Two days passed while Ed lay under a spruce tree, hoping that he would improve enough to be able to move, or that help would come from Jasper. On the evening of the second day, the weather changed, and a light rain fell on the two miserable figures lying under a spruce tree. With the cold of evening, the rain turned to snow. During the night the bear came closer but the dog never left Ed's side to provoke the grizzly into attacking. In the morning the whiskey-jacks looked down on a circle of bear tracks printed in the snow around the two huddled figures blanketed in white. From time to time, the dog lifted its head from Ed's shoulder and growled at the form that moved slowly through the thickets nearby, feeding on willow shoots and the green grass that poked through the spring snow.

Later in the day, the sun stirred Ed awake and it came to him that he would die where he lay, if he didn't try to move. He began to move with the slow reluctance of a creature wrested from hibernation. He blinked at the snow, forgetting where he was, then felt pain stirring in his body and he remembered the accident. Heat and cold played with his nerves; his tongue was swollen with thirst, lying in his mouth like a dead mouse, and the sound of his voice made the dog cringe.

The stiffness in his hips was the first paralyzing rigour of death and his abdomen was abnormally swollen and discoloured with infection from the damaged tissues inside. Fever made him sweat and shiver by turns. How would he find the strength to move? Then he heard the sound of the creek, its murmur amplified by the delirium of his thirst. He scooped some fast-melting snow into his mouth and the slight taste of water goaded him to try. He looped the blankets over his back, knowing that he would die of exposure without them, and began to crawl. He crawled, propped on his elbows, with the dog running up to lick his face now and then, trying to join in the game.

His mind could no longer deal with the distance there was to the cabin, so, like a crafty strategist, he promised himself he would only go as far as the creek. The dog ran to the creek occasionally through the day for a drink, returning with its fur wet from wading in the sweet water.

In the late afternoon, a roaring began in his ears. He stopped, but the roaring went on, so he kept going; but the roaring grew louder. He held his hands to his ears and yelled to drown it out. When he looked down, there was the creek a few feet away. He slid into it belly first, breathing in the water, letting it wash over his burning head, then he forced himself to wait, to drink the ice cold element in slowly, filling his inflamed stomach a little at a time. Then he crawled across the shallow ford, hauling himself up on tree roots, and laid his burning head on the cool, damp earth. He slept.

It was near dawn when Ed woke to the low, steady growl of the dog which strained against him, frightened. He looked around and saw two shapes standing in the morning mist of the creek a few yards away. He opened his mouth to speak and, hearing a low, moaning cry, he was unsure whether it was his own voice or a stranger's. Then, the two figures dropped to all fours with a splash and he heard them coming up the bank through the alder bush on either side of him and he heard the rattle of their long claws on the stones. He felt the thin earth trembling under his back as they passed him and went up the trail. The bear had brought a friend.

All that day the bears walked beside him in the thickets on either side of the trail, while the dog circled him, bristling and growling as he crawled. Their interest kept him going, for he knew they wouldn't bother him until he gave up completely. Then they would drag his corpse off the trail by the scruff of the neck, cache him under a pile of debris, until he got ripe enough to stink, before they fed on him. At dark, he heard the horse whinnying at the cabin and knew he was close. Sometime after that the bears left him and the only sound was his own harsh breath and his body dragging along the ground. By dawn, he reached the clearing and the cabin. The horses winded him first. Snorting and whinnying with hunger, they watched him crawl into the yard and they pawed at the earth with impatience, having eaten the grass down to the roots for twenty-yard circles around their picket pins.

148

Ed ignored them, concentrating on the few yards of ground he had yet to win. The thought that the telephone might not be working had been in the back of Ed's head for four days. He had kept the idea at bay, but now it suddenly pushed against his will with a clarity that made him stop and cry out. He shook his head as if to clear the notion away by a physical effort, and kept going. All night, he had been thinking about the cabin, the food and the dry blankets, and about the telephone on the wall, high on the wall. He inched his way to the cabin door where he stopped and picked up a stick, using it to open the latch above him. The door creaked open; light poured in through the opening, glinting on the shiny metal of the telephone.

The set was on the end wall, five feet off the floor, looming overhead with the metal crank on the side that he must reach somehow to call for help. Praying that someone might already be talking on the party line, he used a broom to knock the receiver off the hook. It dangled on its long cord just over his head and, miraculously, there was Charlie Matheson's voice.

Unable to speak at first, Ed gathered his strength to shout, "Charlie. It's Ed McDonald. I'm hurt. I'm hurt real bad."

A pause, then, "Ed! I hear you, Ed. Hang on! I'll get help to you right away!"

Ed watched the black receiver swinging over his head from its cord; he could hear the voices talking faintly above him. They had heard him, they were coming to help.

He got a can of fruit and a bottle of overproof rum from the cupboard under the phone, hacked open the can with his belt knife and drank the sugary syrup, washing it down with a jolt of rum. Then he opened a can of meat for his half-starved dog.

What Ed did next may leave the reader incredulous, but the facts are a matter of record, and they show the true mettle of Ed McDonald. He knew that his horses were starving, so he dragged himself out to the darkening meadow, slashed their picket ropes and crawled back to the cabin where he wrapped himself in the blankets and lay there nursing the bottle of pain killer.

In Jasper, a rescue party was organized. Charlie Matheson was ordered to form a party with two local men, Joe Weiss and Roy Knutson. Frank Wells was dispatched from Jasper with Dan Blacklock and Bruce Otto, two mountain men noted for their strength and stamina, and Dr. Donovan Ross. They had a thirty-mile ride to make at night, so they pressed on through the blackness. Frank said Ed McDonald was more dead than alive when they got there, sometime after midnight; the outside of his stomach was black, green, and yellow, and his urine was nearly straight blood. The doctor fixed him up as best he could, before tending to his own injuries–saddle sores.

They laid over a day, building up Ed's strength for the journey while the men built a travois to sling between two horses in Indian file. Ed started to feel better, raising hell with the boys for putting his pots in the wrong cupboard and not washing his cups thoroughly. At 8:00 the next morning they wrapped him in blankets and canvas and loaded him in the travois. They said Old Ed knew where he was the whole trip, although his face was covered by the canvas to keep out the rain. He could tell where they were by the sound of the horses' feet and kept himself occupied telling the men to watch for a fork in the trail they were coming to or giving them hell for trying to sneak by his drift fences without putting the bars up.

The travois was too long to go around some of the corners. They would have to stop, untie the poles from the rear horse, and carry the travois on one man's shoulders, a feat that only strong men and expert horsemen could accomplish because, with a broken pelvis the slightest motion can cause the victim excruciating pain. After what Ed had suffered, it was miraculous that he survived the thirty miles in the travois. At Medicine Lake, they transferred him to a boat which took him to the end of the lake where an ambulance waited to drive him to the hospital.

Old Ed recovered and he wardened many years after the accident. The story got into the press about Ed sleeping with the grizzly bears and he got letters from all over North America, full of the wildest speculation about the savagery of the bear. I think, in the end, the letters wound up making Ed a little owly on the subject because, afterwards, whenever anybody talked about how vicious the bear could be, he would say, "Hell, don't tell me they'll slap you down and eat you up. They could have had me and my dog for supper four nights running and they passed us up."

This casual dismissal of bad luck by a man who had nearly died because of one mistake on his part, was typical of the old-time wardens. Ed McDonald died at ninety-three in an old folks' home, although by all rights he should have died the night he tried to halter the grizzly bear or the day he fell asleep on his horse.

My thoughts were interrupted when Toby shied violently to one side of the trail. I looked around apprehensively, half expecting to see a bear rise out of the shadowy thicket, but all that was there was a grouse, clucking at us from the branches of a spruce.

I urged Toby forward, wondering what it is in the nature of horses that they will stand their ground before a grizzly bear, and practically faint at the sight of a fool hen. We rode on, the lengthening shadows of coming night warning me to be more cautious and pay attention to the trail. My thoughts returned to the old timers, some of whom were notably uncautious, like old George Busby, a warden who had seen the beginnings of Jasper National Park. According to Frank Wells, Busby was a man who didn't like cabins very much. He wasn't one to lock his door to anyone or anything. As a matter of fact, he never bothered to shut his door at all most of the year, content to let the four winds blow through his beard at their leisure. This open-door policy can cause certain problems in the bush, where the creatures tend to move in to any space, man-made or not, they find open to them, expropriating it for their own purposes. Thus, Busby shared his bed with many a nocturnal traveller and was as likely to wake up in the morning with mice nesting in his straw mattress as he was to wake in the middle of the night to find the luminous yellow eyes of an owl watching him from the rafters.

Busby was stationed at Miette, on the west side of the Athabasca, about thirty miles downstream from the town of Jasper. It's a beautiful, moody place of big, open meadows and thinly timbered hills full of elk and mountain sheep. It is also a haunted place, for just a few miles upstream, on a day in 1830, the last of the Snake Indians were massacred by their rivals, the Assiniboines, who had tricked them into coming to their camp to sit around the council fires and make a lasting truce.

Many a fur brigade had passed that way in the old days and, though it was wild country, it had the feel of a land where men had been, although few traces of them could be found except for a few cut logs mouldering in a ruin, a brass cartridge case, or a half-buried arrowhead. So to these presences, Busby left open his door, letting it wave in the wind, his ironic salute.

One night as he was sleeping with an ear cocked to the breeze like a true old scout, a rustling noise in the cabin startled him awake. He opened one eye and looked around but saw nothing. The only sound was a log crackling in the heater

151

and the sigh of the wind in the meadow grass outside. He was drifting off to sleep when the noise came again, this time closer and louder. Busby whipped off his blankets, jumped out of his bed to investigate and one foot landed squarely on a porcupine, which had been lying under his bunk, gnawing on his boots to get at the salt in them. Busby let out a roar and grabbed his axe, hopping after the quill pig as it rustled out the door, but giving up the thirst for revenge quick-like when he banged his foot with the embedded quills against the door-jamb.

Busby lit a candle, swearing with pain. His foot looked like a pedicurist's nightmare; there were thirty quills buried in there. Busby had to cut the top off each one to release the pressure that kept the barb extended in his flesh, and then he had to pull each one out. Gangrene developed in his foot, and it took a long time to heal. He was a stubborn old scout, though, and when he got back to Miette, he continued to leave the door open as he damn well pleased to let the air in or the devil himself enter. And the devil, wearing a long fur coat, did just that. Here's the way Frank told it.

"He woke up at 3:00 in the morning one time, and he had company. There was a great big old grizzly come through the door and was helping himself to the jam and whatnot in the cupboard. Old George smelled him good, and he lay in his bunk afraid to move a whisker. After a while, though, he reaches up easy for his rifle, which was always kept hanging just above his head. But the old grizzly heard it slidin' on the peg, and turned quick to get out. Well, it was a small shack and a big bear; when he swapped ends he hit the door with his behind, which slammed it shut. Now he couldn't figure how to get out, and neither could George, at least not in one piece.

"So old George and the grizzly was roommates, and every time George would go to reach for that rifle, the bear would be makin' a circuit of the cabin, dancin' around in there on two legs with his head near up to the roof, and cuttin' a swath with his paws as wide as a scythe. And this goes on, if you'd heard old George tell it, for about two hours, and the more he told it, the longer it goes. But finally, George manages to get that rifle down, and it was a helluva rifle too. One of those old war surplus jobs that'll kill at both ends. Well, the bear backed up into a corner, snarlin', and its head was outlined against the starlight in the window; he was too big to go through it. George said his prayers, and let 'er rip. Shot that bear through the head, dead as a hammer. George takes his blankets outside and crawls under a spruce. Figures it'll be a lot safer there, in case the bear has relatives to come lookin' for it. 'I never did like these goddamn cabins,' he says to himself.

"Well, the story doesn't end quite there. He had to get that bear out of the cabin, and he couldn't do it by himself 'cause it weighed well over 700 pounds. So in the morning, he went and gets his favourite old packhorse, Ned. He hung the skid-harness on him, and had to blindfold him too, because every time Ned got near the cabin, he gets a snort of grizzly, and would bolt. But he finally got him backed around and got him connected to the grizzly. Then he started him up, but just then the blindfold must have slipped off, and Ned turned his head to see what he was skiddin'. Well, lo and behold! When the grizzly slid out of the door, old Ned went over the top of George, right over the hitching rail, and went galloping across the meadow, towin' the bear and the hitching post behind him. He must have figured the devil had him by the tail. George never found that horse for three days and when he found him all he had left on him was the collar."

Frank didn't know whether Busby left his cabin door open after that or not, or whether he gave up on cabins altogether and just slept out under the stars from then on.

The sound of water pails jingling together brought me back to my own present tense. I found I'd been travelling like Ed McDonald, letting the horse and the voices in my head take me where they wanted. It was dark, and a square of light shone down through the spruce trees from the cabin, where Myrna was making a late supper. The smell of woodsmoke and fresh-baked bread drifted on the wind, as Toby pulled up at the hitching post, and I slid off.

"Hello dis place," I shouted.

"Hello yourself. Supper's on." She came to the doorway and talked to me as I unsaddled Toby.

I buckled his bell on and gave him a can of oats. The other two would stay in the corral for the night, since the weather was uncertain and the smell of snow rode on the wind. Inside, the cabin was warm with the heat of a wood-stove. I backed up to it gratefully, feeling the warmth soaking through to my chilled bones while I regaled Myrna with an account of the day's events, carefully understating how close the brush had been with the sow. The truth would have earned me nothing but a cold shoulder and a hot tongue-lashing.

After supper I wrote a report for Tony on the encounter, giving the bear a strong reference as a good mother and an honest animal that still had a healthy fear of man, when left unprovoked. She would be safe now from human interference until it was time to take her cubs into the winter den though, like all grizzly bears, she lived tenuously year by year, her future dependent on good luck, as well as good wardening.

I finished the writing, then helped Myrna pack our boxes for the trip out in the morning. We were subdued that night, saddened at the prospect of leaving. We had had hopes of spending the winter there, but it was not to be.

With the boxes packed, we stood outside for a while watching the northern lights play in wild silence over the Ramparts for the last time, before rolling under the wool blankets to keep each other warm, and listen to the mountain night breathing against our log walls.

7

Kiss Your Ass Goodbye

"To qualify for mountain rescue work, you have to
pass our test. The doctor holds a flashlight to your ear.
If he can see light coming out the other one, you qualify."

Willi Pfisterer

Myrna and I left the Tonquin for Calgary with no plans and
only a little money. I got a job teaching English composition at
the Institute of Technology for a while, hammering grammar
into heads that were blissfully ignorant concerning the union
of subject and predicate.

In March, our son Paul Kelsey was born, legs slightly bowed
from riding the range the summer before. I sat, male and re-
dundant, holding Myrna's hand in the delivery room, watching the sutures of my son's skull expand as his head emerged
into the light. It was the profoundest moment of my life. After
that happens, there's no turning back.

When summer came, the Warden Service called me back to
Jasper where we were stationed in a log house on the Snake
Indian River. Having a baby complicated our life in the backcountry, so I patrolled alone for twenty-four days at a time between the Miette Cabin and Moosehorn Valley, living mostly
in the tiny Moosehorn Cabin. My two horses and one 600
pound grizzly bear roamed nearby and kept me company.
During the day, I followed the sheep hunters to make sure
they did their hunting outside the park boundary on provincial land.

When summer ended, I was promoted at long last to full-
time warden, and transferred by the department to Prince Al-

155

bert National Park in Saskatchewan. There we lived at the Boundary Station in an old house above a beaver pond, surrounded by deep snow, lakes, birch trees, and timber wolves, seventeen miles by four wheel drive from the nearest town, and thirty-five miles, as the crow flies, from park headquarters.

Game and fish were plentiful in the national park and in the provincial land around its borders. Hunting pressure by treaty Indians, who could hunt all winter regardless of official hunting seasons, was heavy along the park boundary. Any moose, elk or deer that crossed the line was fair game.

Several white trappers had lines that ran right up to the boundary. To make sure nobody succumbed to the temptation of slipping into the park to take game, I was out most days patrolling by truck, Ski-doo or cross-country skis.

To us, the deep, silent woods were a winter paradise, but the Park Superintendent proved to be the serpent in our frozen Eden. He had been infected by the centralization virus, which was sweeping through the national parks like an epidemic, and now he wanted his wardens to bite into the same poisoned fruit.

One day he called us all into the headquarters at Waskesui and told us, "Men, the days of the district system are over. I'm not going to leave you stagnating by Walden Pond, contemplating your navels." The park would be managed much more efficiently, he told us, if the wardens and their equipment were all centralized into Waskesui, so we could all work together on resource management studies and problem-solving sessions. He filled a couple of blackboards with complex looking graphs and charts that he must have picked up at some management course in Ottawa. The stuff was more arcane than a wizard's cabbala and, in my opinion, just about as useful. Then he ordered us to start packing.

Soon we were all living in apartment buildings and duplexes in Waskesui, a dreary, dead town in winter, contemplating our TV's by the frozen shores of Waskesui Lake.

There were no resource studies or problem-solving sessions. Instead, I wound up driving thirty-five to eighty miles each day just to get back to my former district to start patrolling. Then I would roar out into the bush on a Ski-doo for twenty or thirty miles to make up for lost time, unable to see anything through the driving snow, hear anything over the roar of the engine or smell anything but the stink of gasoline.

156

Around spring breakup, I was offered and accepted a transfer back to the mountains. When the ducks and geese were starting to migrate back to the northern lakes, my family and I migrated west to the mountains of Banff National Park and drove into the yard of the Bankhead warden residence on the east slope of Cascade Mountain, which towers over the town of Banff.

High above the small clearing that holds the house, spring avalanches roared out a mountain welcome from the wide cirque of the east face that arcs over the skyline.

The Bankhead house was too modern to be lovable but there was a garden behind it. Lashed with a few yards of manure, it would soon produce the green things that Myrna loves to grow and which, as we soon found out, the deer and black bears love to eat. Indeed, they managed to eat much more of it than we did, no fence being quite high enough for the former to jump over, or for the latter to rip their way through, accompanied by growls and munching noises in the dead of night.

We soon moved in our battered furniture. Myrna tied a harness and a rope on the baby, drove a peg into the ground for an anchor and gave him a hundred feet of slack to go exploring. Within half an hour, he had passed inspection by a resident mule deer, a Clark's nutcracker and a magpie, and was being fought over for right of possession by two squirrels as he threaded his way in and out of their territorial imperatives. We were home again in the mountains.

Next morning I put on my green uniform and drove down the hill to Banff to report as a full-time warden in Canada's oldest, most celebrated, and most maligned national park.

It was an inauspicious beginning. The Banff warden headquarters is probably one of the ugliest buildings in the entire national parks system. Its square, flat-roofed, yellow brick exterior is exceeded in dreariness only by the dirty façade of the park garage which rises, or rather squats, just behind it.

At the east end of the building is a long frost fence which separates the visitors' parking lot from a store's yard full of condemned, rusty equipment. The warden office is the kind of bleak, featureless building you'd expect to find in an industrial park. The whole look of the place suggested a smug utility imposing its inscrutable will on a once beautiful natural setting. I wondered how Parks Canada could hope to impress on private developers that the appearance of a building shouldn't intrude on the natural scene and still justify their own architectural Edsels.

It was as if the creator of this brick lemon had arrived blinkered and deaf to the sights and sounds of high mountains and green forest, as if his inspiration had driven him to build a Woolco store in the mountains. If that was his intention, he had failed. Woolco stores are more attractive. In their native ambience of asphalt and smog, they blend in beautifully, their wide windows allowing the shopper to keep an eye out for hub-cap thieves in the parking lot, as he browses through the latest plastic gimcracks on the groaning shelves of excess. But this brick box, with four small windows in a wall fifty metres long, not only denies the existence of the scenery, but prevents the viewing of it from within most parts of the building. I stared at it, non-plussed. This was where the wardens, those rugged outdoorsmen, were supposed to report for work every day at 8:00 A.M., before working on their shift near the highway and the busy town of Banff.

Overwhelmed in the face of such banality, I opened the front door and walked into the air-conditioned reception area with its sealed windows and its commanding view of the gas pumps and garage where many park visitors get their first, and often their only, impression of the Banff Park Warden Service. The dispatcher pointed me to the warden's common room.

Despite the appearances, this was still Banff, the place where Canada's national parks began, back in 1885, the second national park to be formed anywhere after Yellowstone in the USA. Knowing this, and knowing something of the strains of running a park as subject to heavy visitor use and political interference as Banff is, I expected to find an élite Warden Service, and Banff to be a model of a well-run park. Typically, Banff had been the first park to abolish the old district system, wherein each warden had lived in and looked after a 200-square-mile-piece of the park. I thought that perhaps the bugs might have been worked out of the new centralized system by now, though my recent experience in Prince Albert Park inclined me to doubt it.

I looked around. Several wardens were busy at desks, writing reports, while others laboured over light tables, with maps and drafting materials spread out beside them. There was a blackboard on the wall that showed the location where various culvert traps were set to apprehend wayward bears. On the walls were numerous maps, studded with pins that repre-

158

sented game movements or indicated where trails or facilities required repair. I was suspicious of all these impressive looking plans because, as most of the wardens appeared to be in the office, I wondered who was out doing all the work.

"Well, cheesus," said a familiar voice, with a slight Austrian accent, "the more they come, the vorse they get."

I looked up, relieved, and met John Wackerle's friendly grin. He was a twelve-year veteran of the service whom I had met during one of his visits to Jasper Park.

John welcomed me to the outfit, and showed me where my locker was. I then learned that I was due for an intermediate level course in mountain rescue that was scheduled to start at 10:00 that morning. We went to the park stores where I picked up climbing boots, knickers, climbing harness, and an orange uniform anorak. By the time I changed, the class was gathering in front of the rescue room to help load the portable winches, steel cables, and climbing hardware into the trucks.

All wardens in the Canadian mountain national parks are trained to proficiency in mountain rescue techniques by two Alpine Specialists, both professional mountain guides. These two Alpine Specialists maintain the high standard of competency in rescue work that were first set for the service by the late Walter Perren, a Swiss guide.

When Walter joined the service in 1955, wardens were generally hired on the basis of horsemanship rather than mountaineering abilities, since horses were relied on for transportation in the backcountry. As a result of this, many of the wardens were former cowboys from the flat ranchlands of Alberta and Saskatchewan, and they had little use for the world of the mountaineer, the world above timberline where no grass grew.

But mountain climbing accidents were increasing at an alarming rate in the national parks, in proportion to the rising popularity of the sport, and the responsibility of rescuing the injured lay with the Warden Service.

It is the greatest tribute to Walter Perren that in a few short years he was able to transform a bunch of cowboys into the first professional mountain rescue group in Canada. One of the techniques Walter had introduced was the cable rescue method, and we were going to practise it that day on Tunnel Mountain.

It was a grey, overcast day, good weather for climbing accidents, as Alpine Specialist Peter Fuhrmann pointed out.

At Tunnel, we parked the trucks and started backpacking the heavy spools of cable and hardware to the edge of the mountain, whose steep east face rises straight up from the banks of the Bow River.

After a brief refresher course in knot tying, to ensure everybody was using Association of Canadian Mountain Guides knots, and not something they used for calf roping, Peter and two veteran wardens showed us how the winch should be anchored. There were several large spruce trees available, and the winch was tied off on two of these with double climbing ropes, ready to lower.

Warden Monte Rose had walked down to the foot of the mountain on a hiking trail, to act as the "dummy." Now all that was needed was a dummy to go down on the cable and rescue him. In a real situation, of course, the victim would be a stranded or seriously injured climber or hiker.

"Volunteers?" Peter asked.

The winch site was a hive of activity; suddenly everyone was very busy, including me.

Peter grinned. "We'll send the new boy down," he said, and motioned me forward.

Peter told us that being a good climber is not enough to make a good rescue man, it just makes a good place to start from. On a rescue team, there is no room for prima donnas. Mutual trust, knowing that the other guy is guarding your ass, is the only thing that makes a rescue team work.

He showed me how to put on the Gramminger rescue harness and clipped me into the cable. I soon found out what he meant by teamwork when I reached the edge of the mountain and leaned out over the 300 foot drop. Far below was the river and beyond that the green fairways of the Banff Springs golf course. Monte Rose was down there somewhere, under the overhanging roof of the Gonda Traverse, a well-known rock climb on the east face, but I couldn't see or hear him. I hesitated, not sure of how to move on the cable. In a rappel situation I'd always regulated my own descent by braking on the climbing rope. Here, I had no control. I looked at the winch party, working under Peter's careful eye. One man would control my descent by allowing the cable to run on friction around the wooden lowering block. Another held an emergency stop device in his hand. I'd never seen the two guys before that day. Suddenly I was anxious to get to know them.

"What are you waiting for?" said Peter. "Lean back against the cable and step off."

"Step off?"

"Right. Give him a little slack, Bill."

The slack forced me to move backwards to keep the cable taut. I took a step and found myself over the edge.

"Lean back some more," yelled Peter.

Then the winch team was out of sight over the rim and I was alone on the wall, walking backwards down the cliff on the end of my tether.

The cable played out fairly fast and I had to keep moving. Once I made the mistake of stopping on a ledge to rest and found, to my horror, that four feet of slack had accumulated in a loop beside me. The ledge was too tiny to stay on for long, anyway. I closed my eyes and jumped off, coming up with a bang hard on the harness.

Then I discovered the necessity of staying directly in the fall line, like a plumb bob, avoiding the temptation of going down at a slight angle, seduced into that by the prospect of easier footing, like ledges and bulges of rock.

My boots hit the rock and I went swaying across the face, doing a slow half turn, smacking my helmet into the limestone. I shook my head like a prize fighter and kept moving; there was no other choice. In two more steps, I came to the overhang, stepped down this natural eave, and found myself hanging in space. There was the "victim," Monte Rose, sitting on a ledge below, smoking his pipe. I could see a rusty piton on the traverse under the overhang, and the black streaks of rubber left by climbers' boots. I was hanging like a spider on a thread, slowly descending while Monte watched.

"My hero!" said Monte with a fake female trill, as I touched onto the ledge, and felt my tiptoes, ball of the foot, and finally the heel set down firmly on the earth. I introduced myself.

"I'm Rose," said Monte. "Welcome to Banff National Park. It's always nice to have new blood."

I sat down on the ledge so Monte could get into the canvas rescue diaper and called on the radio strapped to my waist to prepare for hauling up. Monte strapped himself in and I rolled to one side, eased a knee under my gut, and struggled upright, piggy-backing him. With the radio strapped to my waist, I called for tension on the cable and soon felt it tighten on the carabiner hooked into my rescue harness. We lifted off the ground, Monte's weight taken off my back, and transferred by his hook-up onto the cable.

One can't just be hauled up without effort, however, because it would mean getting all the hide scrubbed off your body by the rough rocks. With my waist bent at a right angle and feet spread wide apart, I began to walk up the vertical wall, toward the overhang.

I discovered two things immediately: I learned how hard it is to stay exactly in the fall line, while balancing two bodies against the force that tends to pendulum you across the face, and I also found out about Monte's sense of humour. Monte is a veteran of many dangerous rescue operations, and some equally dangerous recoveries of the mortal remains of people who had fallen a long distance and landed very hard. As a result of his grisly experiences, Rose tends to be somewhat cynical about mountaineering in general and rescue work in particular. He has the blackest sense of humour I have ever encountered, and I was alarmed to get an earful of it, on this our first and most unlikely meeting.

"Well here we are, completely helpless. Couple of babies dangling on an umbilical cord. 'Specially me. I can't do a thing to help you, you know, if anything goes wrong."

"Yuh," I grunted, well aware of the fact, as I moved my left foot four inches up the rock. My knees were already shaking from the strain of keeping balance for two. I told myself "don't look down." The sight of the rocks far below us was paralyzing.

Soon the angle of the cable leading from the overhang swung us out into space. With no solid ground to balance against, we began to spin with increasing velocity as we were hauled up. My head was swimming. Monte cheerfully called out the number of turns, reminding me that we had to spin ourselves in the opposite direction as soon as we stopped, to unkink the cable.

"Each turn means one kink," said Monte. "One kink in a cable is dangerous. We got twenty of 'em."

Dizzy from twirling and untwirling, we were drawn slowly up. Monte sucked on his battered pipe and, resting a bony elbow comfortably on my shoulder, he mused happily on our situation.

"Look at how thin that cable is, Marty. No thicker than a lead pencil." He let me think it over for a few seconds, then, "Can you imagine what we'd look like if that thing broke?"

"Jee-sus!" I imagined it all too well and reminded myself that the cable had a breaking strength of 4,000 pounds and our combined load was probably only about 350. "Four thousand pounds," I said under my breath, like a litany, "4,000 pounds."

"They say it has a breaking strength of 4,000 pounds," said Monte, who was relentlessly psychic. "I think that's just to make us feel good, don't you?"

I decided to try and ignore him.

"Besides, they only measure that on a straight pull in a lab. What do you suppose would happen when it's bent over a sharp edge, like that overhang above us, and a great big boulder comes hurtling down from somebody's clumsy foot up there, and goes CHUNG! right on that cable?"

"Good God!"

"Oh, we'd see Him all right. Or more likely the other fellah, the one with the horns and the pitch fork." He paused, considering, and blew a cloud of pipe smoke which billowed around my face. "I can see it all. First we'd give a yell. Then there'd be a split second where we'd sort of be clutching each other, looking down. Our lives would flash before our eyes, like in the movies. Especially the naughty parts . . . "

"A i e e !"

'They say it's not the fall that kills you, it's the sudden stop at the bottom," he chuckled.

I had broken out into a cold sweat. I glanced down between my legs at the jagged rocks far below, and felt my hands tighten convulsively on the slippery, thin strands of the cable. The rocks gaped up, God's teeth. I shuddered. There was no way out, no solution but to keep on moving.

Then the cable stopped and we swayed helplessly out under the roof of the overhang, over which the cable led and disappeared, as if connected to nothing.

The harness straps were biting into my thighs, cutting off my circulation and my legs were tingling, going to sleep. There was a ledge on the wall in front of us, my boots touched tantalizingly near the edge of it, but I could get no closer. The crew, out of sight above us, were changing the winch angle to get a more direct line on us and all we could do was to hang in space until they were ready to haul us up. I ran my hands over the harness straps wondering how strong the stitching and the rivets were.

"See those golfers down there, Marty? Lookit 'em. Beating that poor little ball to death with their big clubs. Just flailing away."

The description appealed to me in spite of my fear and I craned my neck, peering out from under my red climbing helmet, like a turtle, to see where Monte pointed with his pipe stem. Sweat ran into my eyes. Pebbles of rock, knocked off the cliff by the cable's slight motion high above us, whistled past like rifle bullets as we swayed awkwardly back and forth, the cool wind from the Bow River far below blowing up our backs.

The golfers were beetling up and down the fairways in their electric wheelchairs, looking no bigger than bugs from where we were. They were down there in their Jantzen polo shirts and Spalding golf shoes, sipping Chivas Regal out of silver flasks, sucking on Montecristo cigars, and grumbling about the latest stock market quotations. I hated them with a fierce, unreasonable hatred. I would have given anything to trade places with one of them at that moment.

"See 'em?" Monte asked.

"Yeah, yeah. I see 'em."

We were moving again. I turned back to the rock and felt my skin creep when I caught sight of the cable smoking where it had worn a groove in the soft limestone rock of Tunnel Mountain.

Monte had noticed it too. "Don't worry about that. It happens all the time. As long as it don't get too hot and start to glow red. If that happens, you can kiss your ass goodbye.

"Like I was saying, they'd hear us yell. And when they looked up, kinda irritated, you know, like they get when their stroke is spoiled, they'd look up, and there we'd be. Two tiny figures, falling. First our little hands would be making hand over hand motions on the cable. Then our little feet would be making climbing motions in mid-air. Then they'd see our little arms, flapping like mad, trying to fly. Can you imagine?"

"Oh boy!"

Monte cackled. "Yep. Just two blobs of jam. That's all that would be left of us."

Obviously the cable didn't break or melt, although I have learned by experience that given the right sequence of mistakes conjoined with the wrong arrangement of your lucky stars, it is possible for even that carefully constructed lifeline to part, with most embarrassing results for whoever is dangling from it at the time.

After a week of clambering up and down mountains, of being lowered into crevasses and sliding across canyons on a pully suspended from the wire, and after one hair-raising flight, dangling from a climbing rope underneath a helicopter, I graduated, having gained some frightening new insights into mountain rescue work.

Experience with a genuine rescue operation would not be long in coming. In the meantime, I settled into the routine of summer patrols in the front country, or the urbanized part of Banff Park—the townsite, highways, and campgrounds, where most of the park visitors spend their time and where, as a result, a Banff warden spends much of his.

I soon began to think of Banff in the summer rush as a kind of outdoor theatre of the absurd, with a cast of thousands, marvelled at by an audience of resident deer, coyotes, black bears, and mountain sheep. Man acts out his little part in this amphitheatre of high mountains under the eyes of the forest, that watch curiously from the green mountainsides. It is mainly melodrama, lots of comedy, with the odd tragedy thrown in.

Every kind of human character can be seen walking down wide Banff Avenue, an absurd promenade, with its bowling alleys, souvenir shops, beer parlours, and, incredibly, a wax museum where you can admire dummies while listening to muzak. This town, which is supposed to serve as a convenience centre to help the tourists to enjoy the natural attractions of lakes, rivers, and high mountains, has itself become the number one attraction to a very large number of park visitors.

A large part of the park budget is spent on servicing the town. For many, the high peaks of Cascade and Rundle, which tower over the roofs of Banff, form only a colourful and vaguely comprehended backdrop against the urban attractions of the town. Only a few of those visitors, in the end, can imagine wilderness beyond the last street light and fewer still venture into it, for which I give thanks.

Banff is many things to many people. To some, it's drinking beer and trying to get lucky in the Cascade Hotel pub. To others, it's a place to score a bag of grass, eyes wary for the resident narc, a young RCMP officer who carries a snub-nosed .38 under his faded denim jacket. To others still, the curio shops and cabarets contain the only impressions they will carry home with them at the end of their vacation. For them, the town may be summed up in a souvenir statue of a red-coated Mountie with "Made in Japan" stamped on the bottom. To the increasing numbers of Japanese tourists that come to this town, the significance of buying such a monument to the age of tourism is perhaps a poetic irony they might not appreciate.

165

Among the crowds that elbow along the sidewalks, or crawl through the weekend traffic in their vans and mobile homes, there are family groups, campers, hikers, vacationing firemen, travelling minstrels, Hare Krishna dancers, hustlers, golfers, pushers, good people and bad people, young and old. Two million visitors pass through this gypsy town each year. It is, as much as anything, the thousandfold expectations of this transient population, this demand that the town and the park should be all things to all people, that accounts for the air of unreality that Banff takes on in the summer. How can all these factions possibly be satisfied?

One kind of visitor who often gets in trouble is the Intrepid Mountaineer. He can be seen any day of the summer, usually a young man dressed in new boots and knickers. He can be found standing on some street corner, a bright new Kelty pack on his back, loaded with gear. Like most of his generation, he's an equipment freak, counting on the latest technology to help him conquer the wilderness. Inside the pack is everything needed to survive the elements; five pound dacron sleeping bag, good for sixty below, primus stove, first aid kit, Buck knife, hatchet, arctic-proof down jacket, waterproof match container, Silva compass, ten pounds of granola, and a copy of *Walden*. A selection of the latest hardware, all of steel alloy, dangles from a nylon sling with a rock hammer. This array of gear would turn a veteran rock climber, usually poor as a beggar and dirty as a skunk from the material demands of his chosen vice, green with envy.

Over his shoulder he carries a new perlon rope, blue as the summer sky above Mount Rundle.

He walks down the street, ignoring the curious looks, bound for the heights. Though he hasn't been in town long, already he has adopted the attitude of contempt that some of the transient workers in Banff hold for the tourists to whom they owe their daily bread and butter. It's expressed on a T-shirt decal that has appeared on the streets lately, reading "Please don't talk to me, or ask me any questions. I'm not a tourist, I live here."

If you overhear the young climber talking to a friend, you'll hear him refer to the passersby as "gorbies." A gorbie, as defined by Banff native, Jon Whyte, " . . . is a word used by someone who's been living here for a month to describe someone who's only been here for a week."

Somewhere along the line the kid will no doubt get his

lumps. If he would confine himself to admiring the limestone facings on the Cascade Hotel, trying the edge of them with his new waffle stompers he would be just one of many ridiculous but harmless exhibitionists on Banff Avenue this summer.

The other day I saw him clanking around the golf course, in danger of being brained by a stray golf ball, and gazing resolutely up at the peak of Rundle as he fingered his pitons and eyed the famous knife ridge of rock that carves the clouds into long streamers adorning its majestic profile.

Mount Rundle draws the young men with their bright ropes and brighter hopes. The ones that go to it with no experience and no climbing partner, with nothing but shiny new equipment, are the ones it sometimes keeps, the ones it chews up and spits out.

One day, two hikers on the trail above the Banff Springs Golf Course, climbing the mountain on its gentler west side, looked up a watercourse and were startled to see something looking back. It was the skull of a young man who had been the subject of a full-scale search back in 1965 and whose body had not been found until then.

Now another would-be climber of Mount Rundle surveys the summit. I wished him better luck. In him I saw myself at seventeen, walking around theatrically with the same new rope slung over my shoulder, ignoring the advice of the local people to find an experienced partner or go to a rock climbing school to learn the basic skills of the mountaineer. A boy feels the animal energy rippling in his muscles and he thinks he is going to live forever. On a solo climb of Cascade Mountain in the summer of 1965, I fell thirty feet and very nearly broke my leg. Taking five hours to creep down a descent route that would take an uninjured man one hour, was all I needed to make me aware of my own mortality. Maybe the kid would be lucky too. But it seemed quite possible, given his attitude and his experience, that he would have to learn the hard way and maybe wind up represented as a coloured pin on our map of the year's accidents; yellow for stranded, green for injured, or red for dead. Already there are three red pins stuck in the map.

As the summer went on, I learned that life on the "high-visitor-use" shift in Banff Park was a bizarre mixture of ennui and grim terror, depending on the weather, and the number of mountain climbers that were registered out for climbs on any given day.

167

After a few glimpses of what can happen to the human body after it plummets and bounces for a few thousand feet down a mountain, the rescue man tends to have plenty of sleepless nights, when he lies awake in a cold sweat, thinking, in lurid detail, of all the possible things that can go wrong with the equipment he uses, or pondering the inevitable human error that could cost him his life.

Of course, rescues are only one aspect of the job, although there might be some sixty missions in Banff Park during the summer.

I dreaded the rescues, but even worse was the regimen of routine patrols by truck along the highways of the park, fighting crime, looking for illegal campfires and litterbugs. We were like firemen in a way, half in love with the idea of a fire. Slow days, when the bears were holding some ursine convention far from the campgrounds, and the tourists were behaving like disciples of Aldo Leopold instead of the descendants of General Custer we knew them to be, were a kind of purgatory of the psyche. We were trained and ready for action, all dressed up with no place to go.

The place I most wanted to go was out in the backcountry, but my shift out there was not scheduled for weeks yet. In the meantime, I was struck in "high visitor use," as the urbanized part of the park was called. We had another name for it: "high visitor abuse," which was a hell of a lot closer to the truth. Problems occurred where there were the most people, which is why centralization had come about, to keep the men close at hand to deal with emergencies, especially mountain rescues.

"The squeaking wheel gets the grease," said my partner, John Wackerle.

"Maybe so, but I wish I was out in the bush," I complained. "I didn't hire on this outfit to be a half-ton jockey. I wish ... "

"Why wish your life away?" But when he thought I wasn't looking, he snuck a little spoonful of Maalox, the panacea of frustrated, twentieth-century man, chalk to smother the smouldering fire in the guts. John was a fine warden, but a poor liar.

Sometimes a bizarre event would take place that signalled the end of a boring stretch of time, like the day the black bear bit our Superintendent. He had been sunbathing, half asleep on his lawn, when the little runt ambled out of the woods and nipped him on the forearm, to try and find out, I suppose, whether he was alive or dead, since, if dead, he might qualify as grub. On the other hand, maybe the bear just wanted to play with him, since he hadn't broken the skin.

The Soup jumped up, and the bear ran off, but the Area Manager came in to the office and said somebody would have to tranquillize the runt, and relocate him out into the bush.

"Why don't we tranquillize the Soup and relocate him?" came the query from one corner of the room.

"Yeah. Preferably to Baffin Island."

The Superintendent, at that time, was an *éminence grise* who was not that popular with the Warden Service because he seemed to support the expansion plans of a local ski resort, an expansion which many of us viewed as a prostitution of the environment by commercial interests. This lack of popularity was probably unfair because it was obvious that the Soup was carrying out orders from high up the ladder that the expansion should go ahead, despite the howls of outrage made by conservation groups.

"It just goes to show that black bears have no taste," sniffed one old timer.

Monte and I went out to clean the trap with a steam hose to get rid of the smell of the last inmate, a large grizzly bear. When we finished setting the trap, we stopped back at the office for coffee break.

As I followed Monte in the door, a young man came striding out, a blue climbing rope over one shoulder and a loop of pitons dangling from his waist, though the ground was safely flat and free of precipices for half a mile in any direction. I recognized the Intrepid Mountaineer, whose presence here meant bad news. He had come to register for a mountain climb.

"What the hell was that?" Jim Deegan greeted me from behind his dispatch desk. "I saw it, but I don't quite believe it."

"That was stupidi dangerosi, Banff variety. The reason why we have to hang around on these horrible cliffs."

"Don't knock it," said Rick Kunelius, who was younger than I and still loved adventure. "It's a living."

I smiled at this enthusiasm. "Dying is a living? Maybe for an undertaker."

Jim showed me the registration book. The boy was headed for a solo climb on Rundle Ridge the next day. I found myself wondering which pitch he would fall off. Maybe tomorrow we'd be climbing Rundle Ridge with the portable winch strapped on our backs. Jim had tried to talk the boy into trying something a little less dangerous and his advice was based on many years of living in the mountains. But Jim was a senior citizen standing in a room that looked more like a bank than a place genuine mountaineers would frequent. The boy only came there because registration was required by law. He didn't want any advice, nor did Jim have the power to deny him the freedom of the hills. The kid had to work out his own fate.

We went in to the coffee room, where Jim Davies, the local helicopter pilot, was talking with some of the wardens about a rescue they had done the night before on the cliffs near the Cascade waterfall. This is a much admired and photographed landmark several miles east of Banff near the Trans-Canada Highway. Quite a few people are drawn to the falls, and some of them scramble up the cliffs. It's always easier to climb up a cliff then it is to climb down because of the inherent difficulty of moving backwards against the pull of gravity when you can't see your holds. Two young men had become stranded on the cliffs that night about 1,000 feet off the ground. They called for help and a tourist down below heard them and came into the office.

Lance Cooper and Tim Auger took the call and started climbing up to reach the higher of the two stranded men, who was in the most dangerous position. More wardens were needed to reach the second man before he panicked and fell from the ledge where he stood clinging to the mountain.

It was a Saturday night and many of us were out on the town for the evening. Jay Morton was home throwing a little party for two, which was well advanced by the time the dispatcher called him up.

"Are you sober enough to do a rescue, Jay?" came the question.

There was a silence for a moment on the other end as Jay considered. "Hell, I'd rather do them drunk any day," he said.

Promising his lady friend that he would return immediately after saving a life or two, Jay wobbled over to the office where he chugalugged two cups of coffee and pulled on his climbing pants. There he was met by Keith Everts and Jim Davies, who would land the two wardens as close as possible to the second victim.

Davies landed Keith and Jay on a wide bench part way up the mountain. Above them was their quarry, clinging to his ledge. Keith belayed Jay as he started to climb up to the frightened pilgrim. Davies took off again, headed for Banff, to await further developments.

"Last I saw of Morton," Jim told me, "he was standing on a knife ridge at the foot of the cliff with nothing on either side of him but altitude, wobbling back and forth like Humpty-Dumpty."

Jay came into the room at the tail-end of the story. "I'll bet that straightened you out in a hurry, Morton," said Jim.

"You got that right."

After the rescue, Morton went directly back to his party and celebrated the miracle of his survival well into the early hours.

It had indeed been a miracle. While Jay Morton and Keith Everts were helping the lower victim, Tim Auger was still climbing to the second, belayed by Lance Cooper, and wondering how the stranded greenhorn had ever managed such difficult holds without experience. The rock was rotten and suddenly a big slab, an unavoidable feature of the route, peeled off at the touch of Tim's boot. Unable to prevent the rock fall, Tim held onto his hand-holds and let the slab push his legs out and fall clear.

Lance saw it coming, ducked and hit his microphone button, "Rock!"

Then he braced for the impact of Tim's fall, but Auger hung on, scrabbling for a foothold.

As the rock boomed down the face, a piece of it flew off like shrapnel and hit Lance on the wrist. Down below, Morton heard the cry of "rock" on the portable radio and flattened instantly against the wall with Everts and the stranded man. A chunk of rock bounced off Jay's helmet, nearly knocking him off the mountain and deflected into the greenhorn's face, breaking his nose.

"His nose was knocked clean over to one side, said Morton. "Got blood all over me before I got it taped up."

Up the mountain, where the air stank with the sulphurous smell released from the broken rocks, the other two wardens had their own problems.

"I've got a bad lead here," yelled Tim, feeling he might fall at any moment.

"I can't belay, Tim! My hand's buggered . . . " Lance called back. Tim looked down, stuck on the rotten walls. He saw the drop and Lance's small foreshortened figure on the belay stance. Then he saw the filaments of perlon trailing where the rock had struck the rope on a ledge and cut clean through most of the fibres. It would never hold a fall.

"I guess it doesn't matter much," said Tim.

Tim Auger, who has been on many difficult climbs, told me that the next ten minutes of unprotected climbing were among the worst he ever spent on a mountain.

Finally he made it to the victim, who had fallen a short distance and jammed in a chimney. There he was able to get the second rope out of his pack and belay the injured man down to Lance before rappeling off himself.

After that things went smoothly, with the four wardens belaying and lowering their charges down the mountain to safety.

The coffee room cleared, while Morton and I finished our cups, talking. We could hear the single-side band radio going down the hall. Assiniboine Provincial Park over in B.C. was calling. They seldom radioed in the middle of the day unless there was trouble. Sure enough, a few minutes later, Lance Cooper hurried in with his climbing boots on. The short, wiry Cooper and Tim Auger acted as rescue leaders in Banff.

"We have a sling job to do at Assiniboine," he told us.

"I pass," said Jay.

"Morton, your eyes look like two cherries in a snowdrift. Why don't you get married and settle down?"

"You got that right."

"I need a volunteer. Marty, you're it."

Put that way, I could hardly refuse. Besides, Morton had done his share the day before.

There were a number of ice chutes in the Assiniboine group, snowy ramps swept by falling rocks and avalanches. I hoped that the injured climber wasn't stuck on one of them. Bill Vroom and Monte Rose had spent a miserable night that summer, standing behind a rock in the middle of such a chute at Moraine Lake, tied onto the rock with rope, while tending an injured climber in an electrical storm. Monte's account of the rescue made my hair stand on end. It was an experience I could do without.

I went in and put my climbing clothes on, with that queasy feeling inside that I got whenever I had to mess with any kind of rescue machinery. I didn't trust it, any of it, because it was all designed and made by human beings; the carabiners, the ropes, the rotor blades of the helicopter. Always I suspected deep and secret flaws, built in by the same malignant spirit that sabotaged my dreams.

Ten minutes after getting the call for help we loaded the helicopter and took off, flying over the toy houses of Banff, over the power lines, the spiked forest, and one single yellow canoe floating down the Bow River like a big poplar leaf.

A steadily increasing rain beat down on the plexiglass cockpit, and lowlying layers of cloud rushed toward us, borne on a headwind. The Jet Ranger rocked and jumped in the cross winds as we turned left up the narrow thread of Brewster Creek. Davies was headed for a notch between two high peaks that would lead him out in a direct line to Og Lake below Mount Assiniboine. I tightened my seat belt and hung on to my breakfast. I hate flying. Lance grinned at my nervousness and went on talking with Jim about their mutual passion—airplanes and helicopters.

With nothing to contribute on the subject, my thoughts were occupied with present problems, such as the sling rescue technique, with which I had had limited experience, though I knew the history of it all too well.

It all started one day in 1969. Peter Fuhrmann, the Regional Alpine Specialist, had read in a German climbing magazine about a new technique known as the Helicopter Vertical Rescue Method. The method was being developed by a Swiss rescue expert. A specially made harness, designed by Ludwig Gramminger, who had previously helped to develop the cable rescue technique, was the key to the operation. Peter went to Germany on vacation that spring. Intrigued by the possibilities of the new method, Peter looked up Gramminger in the hopes of acquiring one of the new harnesses. The two men repaired to the Hofbrau House in Munich, and there, over steins of beer, Gramminger gave Peter an impromptu lecture on the helicopter rescue method, and presented him with a brand new harness to take home to Canada.

The Alpine Specialist returned to Banff, where he rushed into the office one day and told the wardens that he had the ultimate solution for rescue work. "We hang ourselves under a helicopter, and then we fly to the climbing accident and whisk the casualties away in our arms like angels!"

There was an embarrassed silence around the office. The wardens were used to Peter's poetic raptures about new pieces of deadly-looking climbing hardware, but this time it looked like he had finally popped a rivet. The men sidled away, or turned back to their desks.

Undismayed by their lack of enthusiasm, Peter assembled the double climbing rope and the special carabiners and other hardware necessary to connect man to machine. Like any explorer, he was groping in the dark, armed only with a diagram and a theory, but anxious to test them in the hard light of experience. He was soon ready to do a test flight.

There was a good pilot available in Jim Davies, a native of Banff whose father had been a warden. Jim knew the mountain passes well, and agreed to try out the new method.

In his enthusiasm, Peter forgot to inform the Superintendent of his plans to use the Banff airfield for the training flight. The Superintendent was against using the airfield for other than emergency landings. To make things worse, he was busy making his anti-airfield views known to a meeting of the local chamber of commerce, when the helicopter flew by his office window with a warden in full uniform hanging underneath it. The warden waved hello; the members waved back.

The Superintendent was furious and made it clear that there would be no more such experiments in Banff Park.

Peter kept a low profile for a while but remained determined to prove his method in the field.

That day was not long in coming.

In July of 1972, a team from the Army's Mountain Warfare School was climbing Mount Edith, west of Banff, when a falling rock struck a soldier, seriously injuring him. The news was relayed to Banff by two hikers, and Peter arranged for Davies to sling him into the scene. He saw at once that an improvised rescue, using climbing ropes, or a full cable operation, would be too time-consuming to save the man's life. The rock had demolished his hard hat and had produced a depression in the skull. Blood loss was severe and his breathing was shallow, faltering.

Peter radioed Jim and explained the situation. Jim replied that he would try to sling, but doubted if he could get enough lift to hoist both Peter and the stretcher at that altitude. Peter had to go along with the victim to apply mouth to mouth resuscitation in case he stopped breathing.

Jim brought the helicopter in and Peter hooked them up to the 'O' ring on the end of the sling rope. The Alouette rocked unstably in mid-air, unable to get enough lift.

Peter had an idea. Waving Jim off to fly a circuit, he called the officer and remaining soldiers over and explained his plan. They would move the stretcher to the edge of the precipice, then hook onto the machine. On a count of three, they would push the stretcher and Fuhrmann over the edge, thus solving the problem of lift. He called Jim on the radio and asked him what he thought.

"I think you're nuts," said Jim, "but in theory it should work."

If you ask Jim Davies, as I have, what he thinks about mountain climbers, how he feels about flying rescue missions under the kind of conditions and strains that are a normal part of emergencies, he'll probably reply with an obscenity. But when the phone rings, signalling another mission, he will put on his flight suit and go down to the helipad.

There are much easier ways to make money than flying a helicopter. Although they are well paid, helicopter pilots have a notoriously short life expectancy. If you try to pry out of Jim Davies what some of the hazards are, what makes for such high mortality rates among helicopter pilots, he clams up, as if it is bad luck to mention the subject. It is probably the only superstition he has.

What makes the helicopter so difficult to fly is the very thing that makes it different from airplanes. Warden Monte Rose, a budding helicopter pilot himself, once explained it to me.

"It's the hoovering, Marty," he said, tongue in cheek. "No wings, no tail, no stability. One mistake, and you're tits up. It just sits in the air like a vacuum cleaner, hoovering."

As the Encyclopedia Britannica says: "The helicopter in hovering flight is essentially neutrally stable and responds to the controls as would any system with inertia only, and with no damping or static stability. The pilot must therefore develop an anticipatory reaction in order to arrest the motion of the machine when it responds to the controls."

Anticipatory reaction equals lightning-fast reflexes, talented synapses, and a cold logical mind working out the factors of wind speed, updrafts, downdrafts, altitude, and what the man underneath is doing that's taking so long when the radio fails to work; while the right hand, never quite stationary, gently moves the control stick, adjusts the throttle and the pitch of the rotor. All of it worked out behind the cool and calculating eyes of Jim Davies.

When I asked him what the difficulties were of flying such a thing compared to a fixed-wing, he replied in one sentence, "The helicopter is very unforgiving."

The rest of the hazards he keeps to himself. The man sends

175

out vibrations of confidence that practically lull his passengers to sleep. Everyone but Marty, the nineteenth-century man.

By 1973, Jim had flown over 100 rescue missions in this part of the Rocky Mountains, and in 1975 the Helicopter Pilots' Association of North America voted him Pilot of the Year.

The rescue on Mount Edith was one of the earliest, though by no means the hardest, that Jim has logged but he had one or two things to consider as he came in through streamers of low-lying cloud to where Fuhrmann and the soldiers made a flower of colour on the edge of the blue-grey walls of the mountain.

The helicopter eased in over the ledge and Peter grabbed the 'O' ring on the sixty foot length of rope. Peter's voice crackled through static and engine noise in Jim's headphones.

"Radio test . . . "

"Loud and clear, Peter."

"Okay. On the count of three. Copy?"

"Ten-Four."

Peter was yelling into the radio, so the soldiers could hear him over the noise and the rotor blast. Dirt blew into his eyes, into his open mouth. Jim sat inside the glass bubble, serenely unaware of the chaos below, concentrating completely on the motions he would make four or six steps ahead of what he was doing then.

"One . . . two . . . three . . . . "

And they were going down in a long glide for the thicker air below. Peter saw the white hands of the soldiers still outstretched from the edge of the cliff, as the Alouette swung out, falling away from the earth. Far below was the highway leading east to Banff.

"Can you land us at the hospital, Jim?"

"I dunno. Never landed there before. Maybe on the front lawn."

"We better try it. This man is fading fast."

The ambulance trip across town through mid-summer traffic could take much longer than the flight from Mount Edith. Jim changed course and came in over the Administration Building, circled the hospital, taking a look, then brought down the Alouette, landing Peter and the injured man a few yards from the emergency door, where two orderlies were waiting for the patient. The sudden appearance of the helicopter created an instant traffic jam on Spray Avenue.

The Superintendent was standing outside the fence of the Administration Building, glowering at the action across the street. Then he turned and strode away, headed for his office.

The victim was in a coma for three days, but it was six months before he could remember his name, and a year before he left the hospital.

Peter had staked his life, as well as his career, on the new method but, in doing so, he had disregarded a direct order. He could have been fired for insubordination. In his favour was a life saved and a letter of commendation from the medical specialists and the Army, praising the speed of the new sling rescue method.

He sent his bosses copies of the letters before he went to see them. The administration studied the record, and began to reconsider. Although they could see that the use of the helicopter was inevitable for such emergencies, they were worried about the low-powered machines that were available in the mountains.

Jim Davies solved that problem when he mortgaged his soul to buy a much more powerful helicopter than his old machine. He offered to make it available to the government on a priority basis when there was an emergency. It was then we began to train with the new method in earnest.

The operation looks deceptively simple. The hardest part of hooking up to the helicopter is the sorting out of the harness, with its shoulder, thigh, and crotch straps that have a tendency to tangle together like a Gordian knot of twisted nylon. During training operations, there was always time to figure the thing out, but in a rescue, human anxiety, combined with the need to move quickly, can lead to serious mistakes. Like the helicopter, the sling rescue method is very unforgiving.

During one early rescue, Warden Joe Halstenson requested the helicopter to take him into Elk Lake. A hiker with a broken leg was stranded on a steep mountainside about nine miles from the highway.

Jim set down near the entrance to the Elk Lake trail, and Joe hooked up the sling rope, stepped into his harness and snapped in to the 'O' ring. He checked the hook-up. Everything looked fine, so he gave Jim the thumbs-up signal to take off.

As the helicopter began to lift, he hit the microphone button on the portable radio Jim had flown in for him. Nothing happened. The radio had chosen that moment to go out of service.

Joe wasn't too alarmed, since he trusted Davies absolutely

and he knew he could get by without radio communication. The helicopter came tight on the rope and he began to lift. As his feet left the ground, he expected his weight to transfer to the thigh straps. Instead of that, he fell backwards and found himself hanging upside down. Frantically, he grabbed at the sling rope. The crotch strap alone keeps the flight rescuer sitting comfortably in his parachute-style harness. Joe had forgotten to snap it in.

Davies flew on, unable to see Joe without leaning out of the machine or hear him yelling over noise of the rotor. The G-forces of flying through the air, at well over 70 miles per hour, tore at Joe's mouth, stifling his shouts. Blood rushed to his head as he clung to the rope. Then, realizing he wasn't going to fall out of the harness, he relaxed his grip, spinning in a tight little circle, head down, seeing the trees far below, and spots in front of his eyes.

Above Elk Lake the injured man waited, cheered to hear the sound of the approaching helicopter. As it came near, however, he was alarmed to see a man on a rope upside down underneath it. The pilot gave him a nonchalant wave. Is that how they planned on taking him out?

He watched the helicopter coming in, and as it got closer he saw a warden swaying, head down, yelling curses over the roar of the engine. The warden did a handstand right beside him, then collapsed on the ground, fumbling at the rope, releasing something.

The hiker tried to get away, dragging his injured leg pathetically behind him. Who could blame him? He had a broken leg, but he didn't want a broken neck. It took some fast talking to convince the poor guy to get onto the stretcher for the flight out.

After that, the word came down from above, loud and clear. "Personnel will not fly sling operations without a second to double check the hook-up."

There were other problems that had to be ironed out, and one of the most serious ones involved the use of the Mine Litter Basket, which Peter had brought out of dusty retirement in the basement to serve as a helicopter rescue stretcher. Peter discovered the limitations of the basket on Cascade Mountain one day, when he was flown in to pick up an unconscious hiker on a steep trail. The victim had no detectable pulse, and an empty vial of pills near the body indicated an attempted suicide. Peter bundled the victim up, and strapped him into

178

the litter basket. He called Jim in, and in a few minutes was flying high above the Bow River with the stretcher.

As they flew, Peter applied mouth to mouth resuscitation to the victim in mid-air.

Peter had a thick, black beard at the time and was wearing a shiny red helmet, headphones, antennae, and sun glasses. He looked, in his strange garb, even weirder than one normally looks dangling underneath a helicopter going 100 miles per hour.

Just what was going through the victim's mind when he took that fatal overdose is hard to say. Whether he believed in an afterlife, I don't know, but in the light of what happened next, it seems possible that the young suicide was not a complete agnostic. Perhaps there was in his mind a subconscious fear of God's wrath.

He began to respond to resuscitation. He gagged, then began to breathe more evenly, and opened his eyes. Fully awake, though still drugged, he found himself being whisked through space and clouds in the arms of some alien being. He spoke and Peter, relieved to see him conscious, leaned closer to catch his words.

"Who are you?"

"Peter," said Fuhrmann, with a smile.

A wild look came into the suicide's eyes.

"NO! NO! LET GO OF ME! I DON'T WANT TO DIE! NO, NO!" He had changed his mind.

He began to struggle and tear at his straps, a thousand feet above the ground. Peter wrestled with him, trying to get on top of the stretcher, while the man pulled one arm free and clawed at his rescuer's face. Desperately, Peter punched at him, trying to knock him out, scared that the carabiners might be jarred open by the flailing hands. He called Davies on the radio and told him to fly low and slow.

Spectators on the crowded streets of Banff were mystified to see a helicopter approach the hospital lawn, with a bizarrely-clad man half kneeling on top of another man, trading punches on a swaying stretcher hung in mid-air, while a group of white-clad orderlies waited for them with outstretched hands.

Clearly a more sophisticated stretcher was needed. After shopping around via the mails in international climbing circles, Peter found the solution in the Jenny bag, a kind of waterproof envelope which restrains and protects the victim,

179

and is at the same time small enough to be carried in a ruck-sack.

From the very start, the helicopter proved itself a miraculous craft that meant the difference between life and death to injured mountaineers, hikers, heart-attack victims, or anyone else who suffered misfortune in the mountains. Operations that had taken three days in the past, and wound up turning into a recovery of dead bodies, were done now in a matter of hours, saving human lives as well as money.

By the time of my flight with Lance Cooper, the system had been standardized to the point where it was routine. Most of the bugs had been ironed out. Certainly Cooper, who had done over two dozen sling operations, was not particularly worried about the one we were headed for.

If many accidents in the mountain parks are the result of sheer folly on the part of inexperienced hikers, the one at Assiniboine was more typical of what can happen when fate conspires with the mountain to strew its cosmic banana peels in the traveller's path.

As we flew up the thread of Brewster Creek towards the Great Divide that day, an injured woman and a strained and anxious husband waited for us on a rock slope above Lake Magog, near Mount Assiniboine. The weather was fast moving in on them.

The couple had been scrambling up a steep ridge when the woman slipped on a wet patch of grass, and skidded over a short cliff. She had tumbled down over a slope of loose rock for thirty feet before rolling to a stop. Her husband hurried down to help her and found her lying on a pile of rocks, conscious, but in extreme pain. A member of the party worked his way down to the ranger station at the foot of the mountain to get help, moving as fast as he could. It was raining. Her husband covered the woman up with blankets, and tried to comfort her, while two hours dragged by. Then he heard the sound of the helicopter and looked up, searching for the sight of it through the lowlying clouds.

We were coming up through a narrow pass known only to eagles, ravens, hawks, and Jim Davies. We flew through a door of rock and cloud. Now Og Lake winked up, then Lake Magog at the foot of the diamond peak, Assiniboine, 12,000 feet high. God was crouched up there among the rolling clouds with a handful of lightning bolts. I know he hates helicopters, but I prayed that he knew we were there to do good works. *Please, oh please; don't snuff out my little candle.*

180

Down below, groups of tiny folk were trekking their way down over Assiniboine Pass, headed for Og Lake. I could plainly see two of them shaking their little fists at us, outraged at the clamour and noise that was spoiling the serenity of it all. We were coming in through wisps of cloud and rain toward the ranger station near Sunburst.

Ranger Scot Gain was talking to Jim on the single-side band radio, directing him to the scene of the accident in a cirque on Sunburst Peak. Then we banked hard to port, levelled out, and angled up over a stand of trees.

There was a man in a yellow coat down there, waving his arm towards the cirque. Then, above a snow patch on a ramp to the right of the cirque that led up to the summit ridge, we saw a man huddled on the rocks, close to a prone figure. To my relief, I saw that this rescue was going to be on rock, not on an ice chute.

Jim flew slowly by the two and Lance held up five fingers meaning "back in five," as we sized it all up. We turned out toward the lake and descended onto the snow field below the accident.

The sling gear was in the luggage space. Cooper crawled underneath the machine and hooked the rope to the steel eyes on the frame while I laid out the working end in front of the helicopter.

We never attached onto the cargo hook because a malfunction in that mechanism could cause it to open prematurely, with fatal results. Peter had told us how some fool in B.C., claiming to be an expert in this technique, had been quick-released over a mountain top and had fallen 100 feet. The angle of the slope and twenty feet of snow broke his fall and saved his life.

I stepped into the red nylon harness, poking my awkward climbing boots through the crotch straps and pulling the shoulder straps over the bulky layers of anorak, wool shirt, and quavering, life-loving tissue and bone. Cooper joined me and strapped himself up.

It was time to go and we shouldered our packs. There was no time for conversation and the roar of the turbine would have made it impossible anyway. I strapped up my helmet, aware that both hands were trembling slightly, although I was too busy to think about danger. Lance hooked a bag with a metal scissors stretcher onto his harness. We checked each other's harnesses and snapped into the big ring. The roar of the turbine built in intensity, the rotor was a blur of noise. The rescue carabiners had locking screws to protect the gate from snapping open. I went to close mine, and Cooper grabbed my hand, motioning "no." There was no time for questions. I checked my crotch strap for the third time. Then Jim was lifting the machine and his face went up out of sight until we could see the white underbelly of the craft overhead, like the ventral surface of some huge fish.

The harness went tight on my seat, and we went up as if propelled from the snow on a gigantic spring. We were flying, trees and rocks hurtling past below, and there came the deep, calm void of the lake, rising as if to engulf us. The rain beat into our eyes and the wind rushed through the front of my anorak and roared by my ears under the helmet with messages of power, promises of doom. We were spinning.

Cooper showed me how to hold out one arm, countering the tendency to spin in the cross winds. He adjusted his harness in mid-air as we hung facing each other. He did it as coolly as if he had been sitting in an easy chair. I saw his lips moving in his blond beard, as he talked to Jim on the radio. A bone conductor microphone in the hard hat picked up his voice through the top of the head, like science fiction. I was relaxing, almost feeling exultant in the wild absurdity of it all. Men working together, doing something of value—it felt good, made for camaraderie. Lance nudged me to signal that he would unhook. He ran a hand across his throat, meaning he'd cut mine if I grabbed the ring. I grinned. The ground came up to meet us, an inhospitable shelf of jumbled rock. I touched before I knew it, found my feet had gone numb from dangling free, and had to grab on to the rocks with both hands. We were awkwardly tied together there, suddenly clumsy on the earth.

Lance unhooked in two quick motions, while I helped balance him with a hand on the back of his harness. I saw why he didn't lock the carabiners; there is no time for fumbling and fuming around, no time to get out a pair of vice grips to free any jammed-up threads.

The weighted rope went swinging away and, as the noise of the helicopter receded, the first thing we heard was the woman's moans of pain. The juxtaposition of realities confused me for a moment, then I started traversing across the rocks after Lance.

"Boy, am I glad to see you guys," her husband said with a weak smile. He sounded tired and strained as he turned to comfort his wife with a forced cheerfulness.

As we opened the first aid bag he told us how his wife had fallen.

Miraculously, there was no head injury, but whenever touched, the woman cried in pain. A stretcher carried down the rough mountainside would have caused her unbearable agony. It seemed possible that her spine was injured, a leg broken, and one shoulder dislocated. Her face was cut and bleeding, and she was soaked through to the skin from two hours of lying in the rain.

I got out the Jenny bag and shifted rocks to get a level place for it, while Lance applied heat packs and dry down coverings to warm the victim. She complained more of the cold than of pain.

We eased an air splint on the leg, inflated it and tied her arm in place, working as quickly as possible, rain starting to soak through the canvas anoraks. Then, moving a few inches at a time, we worked to ease the scissors stretcher between her bruised flesh and the sharp rocks, one man at her head, another at her feet, while her husband stood downhill, keeping her from sliding down the slope. This metal stretcher allowed us to pick up the victim without moving the spine, which it is crucial to avoid.

We picked her up at head and foot to put her in the Jenny bag. Lance called Jim on the radio and, in a moment, I heard the engine and saw the rotor slowly whirling. I held the Jenny bag balanced on the ledge while Lance hooked himself and the victim in.

In a few minutes, Davies was setting them down in the cirque, to transfer the patient inside the heated helicopter. There was nothing more for the husband or me to do but gather up the gear into my pack and descend in long gliding slides down a slope of loose scree to the helicopter. He would hike out to Banff first thing in the morning, since with Lance and me, the helicopter was full to capacity. As it turned out, although the woman was bruised so badly that she could not walk for several days, her most serious injury was a dislocated arm.

That rescue had a happy ending, but the way the next one finished left my blood cold.

It was a week or so later. I came into the office to find a harassed Area Manager standing over the radio with notebook at the ready. There was a sling rescue in progress on Rundle Ridge, above the golf course. Apparently a climber had fallen

400 feet, and his chum was stranded on a cliff, frozen into his holds. Tim Auger and Lance Cooper were climbing up to the survivor to get a rope tied on him. I went down to the golf course to help control the crowds of curious spectators that were watching the action. Jim took Monte and Joe Halstenson to where the fallen climber lay at the foot of the cliff. In a few minutes, we heard Monte's voice on the radio as he called the office.

"I'm at the scene," he said tensely. "The victim is 10-7," which meant, in radio parlance, out of service–dead.

While Monte and Joe bundled up the fatality, Tim moved on a belay up the rotten cliffs, talking to the survivor as he went, to reassure him.

Shaking visibly with shock, the young climber shouted, "How's my friend? I want to know how he is before you come up."

Tim had to do some fast thinking. The climber was too deeply affected by the fall to act rationally. He must know that his friend could never have survived such a fall, but Tim decided that he must tell the young guy what he wanted to hear, to keep him from moving.

"Your friend is fine," he lied. "Just stay where you are. Give me a chance to get to you, and we'll talk."

There was silence for a minute, then "Okay," came the faint reply.

Tim moved carefully, though the climbing was easy enough for him. He wanted to keep to the left of the survivor, in case he kicked a rock down on his would-be rescuers. In a few minutes, he reached the shaken boy, and anchored him to the mountain, while he tried to reassure him, and get him "psyched up" for the climb down to a wide ledge where the helicopter could sling him off.

While that was going on, Jim Davies went back in and Monte hooked the stretcher up. We waited on the golf course as the stretcher came in, the Jenny bag forming an ominous hood to cover the head of the dead man. Monte's face was white, strained, no trace of his usual contentious grin.

We bundled the victim into an ambulance for the trip to the hospital, where the doctor waited to fill out a death certificate. His rucksack, damaged and abandoned, lay on the ground where Monte had left it.

"Those guys were climbing unroped up there, for Chrissake," he told us, "but there's a brand new perlon rope in that bag, and brand new hardware. Never been used."

Sickened, I remembered the young guy who had registered out for Mount Rundle a few days before. Was it today that he was supposed to climb?

"What colour was the rope, Monte?"

"I dunno. Why?"

I took a look in the bag where it was coiled up. Red. Relieved, I told him, "Thought maybe it was somebody I knew."

The helicopter came back in with the survivor in a harness underneath, Lance riding with him. We snapped him out and got him over to the police car. The boy was crying now, sensing what had happened. They would tell him at the hospital, which was plenty soon enough. Meanwhile, he would have to explain to the RCMP how it was that his friend had fallen.

Lance told us that the two had been "bouldering," free climbing without the restriction of the rope. At some point they had decided to continue to the summit of the mountain, neither one of them aware, it seems, that the summit of Rundle was at least two miles away from where they were climbing on a little known face. They were headed into steepening pitches, completely enclosed by overhangs. By the time they realized they were in trouble, the distance had grown too great between them to tie into the rope. The lead climber had panicked, trembled on his holds, grown tired and made a desperate move before his friend could get up to him. Then he fell.

We were discussing the tragedy back at the office, when young Blue Rope came back to return his registration. There was some blood on his shirt and his climbing pants were torn. The Intrepid Mountaineer seemed a little subdued.

"What happened to you?" I asked him.

"I took a little fall, that's all," he said evasively.

"Solo climbing, eh?"

The boy shuffled his feet a little. Some of the snottiness had gone out of him and I decided not to push it. Whatever had happened, however close the brush had been, he seemed to have derived his own lessons from it.

"I've got a partner for next time," he offered. "One of the guides said he'd take me out on his day off."

"Fine."

The kid looked up and grinned. "I see where a guy can get hurt out there."

There are hundreds of climbers in the Rocky Mountains, from the very best to the very worst. In spite of the incidents I have related here, very few get seriously hurt, and fewer yet are killed. But looked at through the jaded sensibilities of a rescue man, they are all potential victims. We tend to see the worst ones and the unlucky ones.

Despite the accidents, I still believe nobody has the right to tell another man how to live his life or what chances he should or should not take, especially here in the mountains, the refuge of the free spirit.

I think it was John Fowles who wrote that a young man who never takes a chance in his life is a fool. I agreed with that, though I wondered if the tragedy could have been prevented. The two climbers hadn't registered out with us, hadn't asked anybody's opinion or advice, though the town of Banff is full of experienced guides and amateur climbers.

Through the office window I could see the main peak of Rundle, where a raft of cloud floated, tethered in the lee of the cruel north face. No sign of pity in the indifferent profile of that proud mountain, and nobody but a warden would describe it as a tombstone–9,000 feet high.

Another day was over.

8

The Highway Blues

"Let's not fool ourselves
The automobile is a wheelchair."

Nicanor Parra

One day that summer an old white mountain goat, his long wool tattered here and there into white flags that streamed in the wind, looked up from where he stood chewing yellow lichens off the rocks. He had heard the sound of human voices calling faintly from below, and turned to peer over the edge of the cliff, listening and scenting the wind.

"Tension!"

I felt the rope that was passed through a carabiner above me tighten on my chest harness, pressing me in to the poor holds. Tim Auger belayed me from below as I led the fourth pitch of a training climb that was pushing my ability to disconcerting limits.

My body felt sluggish that day. Life around the town, spent mostly behind the wheel, is not conducive to keeping in shape for the severe strains of mountain rescue work.

In my B.C. era (Before Centralization), I had kept in shape doing the labouring work that had been part of my job. Now, in my new role as "Technician," I was supposed to be part of a planned management program, applying my technical knowledge to planning and supervising, while others did all the work. Only there were no others to do the work when it came to emergencies such as rescues. The managers talked constantly about the "new role" of the Warden Service, but it soon became clear that the only new role was the roll of lard on many a warden's middle.

Formerly a feature only of management staff, "centralization gut" was now insidiously creeping into the field as well.

The Warden Service has always managed to do at least part of its job, despite the efforts of a bureaucracy that often seems bent on preventing it. Indeed, "despite all" could very well be the outfit's motto. Our rescue team worked very well, thanks to teamwork and a combination of good, young climbers, and stolid but solid veterans.

One of the best climbers in the service is Tim Auger, a warden who is also a licensed mountain guide. In the fall of 1977, Tim was part of the first Canadian expedition to climb a Himalayan peak, Mount Pumori, 23,000 feet high.

I glanced down at him, my face a study in consternation, feeling my arms beginning to tremble. I had to make a move. Quick.

"There's a nubbin two inches under your left boot," he called.

For a moment I almost disliked him for his serene smile, which he always wears when working on highly exposed cliffs, his favourite milieu.

I poked a booted foot in a lower direction, feeling the rubber sole sliding into space without interruption. About 900 feet of it stretched below me, tugging at my ass. I refused to look down, but in my head I could not put off a nagging voice which kept suggesting "you're getting a little bit slow for this."

"Your other left, you ass!" Tim shouted derisively.

I moved the other foot angrily, and felt the toe come to rest on a slight bulge in the limestone. The cap of it was worn off, by weather and time, into a tiny ledge about an inch square where a fragment of moss had been colonized from a single spore, who knows how many years ago. The moss made this toe hold slippery. I scraped it off with one brutal swipe of my boot and heaved a sigh of relief, as some of the terrible weight of my body was released from my left hand and transferred to my leg. But I had to work fast. Soon the weight being held on that tiny toe hold would make itself felt in my leg muscles, causing my knee to tremble uncontrollably. From the nylon sling around my shoulder I pulled out a short vertical piton, poked the blade into a crack that would have been narrow even for a butter knife and began to drive it in with short blows of the rock hammer.

As I worked, there came an eerie feeling of being watched. A few strands of gossamer spiralled past my eyes and I looked up to suddenly confront a white bearded face that peered down from 100 feet above me, as if fixed to or hung on the rock itself. Two jet black horns shone against the dull grey stone. Caught, the goat withdrew its head, and the apparition vanished as quickly as it had appeared. The sight was comforting. It indicated a ledge up there, a place where we could stop and eat lunch, perhaps even sit down.

As if in confirmation, the goat appeared again. This time I could see his side as he shuffled along his airy sidewalk, pausing to sniff at an old rusted piton. Then, deciding it was inedible, therefore worthless, he moved further to my left with unerring speed on his cupped hooves. I hoped he wouldn't decide to challenge me when I reached the lip of the ledge, with a sudden butt in my chest to prove he was the lord of the mountain.

Once, on Wiwaxy Peaks at Lake O'Hara, an old billy, jealous of his small harem of dams, chased me down some small cliff bands, with head lowered as if to butt me in the behind with his wickedly sharp horns. It was an experience I wouldn't want to repeat.

I snapped in a carabiner, threaded the rope through it, and leaned back on the rope to relax a bit as Tim applied some tension so that I could survey the route. A horn was blaring loudly, hysterically, on the highway far below. I called for slack and made three fast moves that took me to a little belay stance.

Tim climbed quickly on the belay, with an easy grace that I knew would never be mine, and I gave him a few inches of slack in deference to his skill. As I took up rope, I watched the traffic jam on the highway below, caused by a herd of bighorn sheep that was moving methodically from car to car, while begging handouts from the tourists.

Anchored to the rock by a piece of steel a few millimetres thick, I was standing on a small wrinkle on the face of a mountain. But down there on the highway was the most dangerous place in Banff National Park. Although no warden has been killed on a mountain, it was that same Trans-Canada Highway that had taken the lives of two young wardens a few winters before, in a head on collision with a semi-trailer. It is a road that kills several human beings and well over a hundred big game animals every year.

189

As I watched, apprehensively, a westbound truck came roaring around a curve toward the hidden crowd of sheep, adults, and children. I winced as the driver far below suddenly came into sight, and I heard the truck furiously gearing down. I imagined I could hear the driver cursing and yelling in the cab as he gave them a long blast on his air horn. The people scattered in all directions but closed in behind the rig again as if nothing had happened. The sheep were intent on getting their fill of peanuts and potato chips, and the people were engrossed in photographing their kids as they fed the sheep. It was a dangerous mix of high speed, commercial traffic, and dawdling, curious vacationers.

Above me, the old goat cocked a quizzical eye toward the brouhaha. He sensed a poisonous imbalance in the air drifting up from the highway, and turned to go.

Hidden from the goat by a bulge of rock, Tim didn't see the master mountaineer as he turned to climb up a ramp of crumbled rock that led out on the ridge of the mountain to the left of the face. I heard a whirring in the air above before I saw a dark object sailing by.

"Rock!" I yelled.

We flattened ourselves against the cliff. The small stone raised a puff of dust from Tim's pack and rattled off down the face.

He peered cautiously up at me. "Must be somebody on this route ahead of us."

"Yeah, there is—a goat."

"No goat is that clumsy, Marty," said Tim suspiciously.

The goat had gone out of sight, the evidence abandoning my explanation, leaving no tracks on the sharp stones of the ledge where we stopped to eat lunch.

———

I was on the 3:00 P.M. to midnight shift that week. I arrived at the office one afternoon and greeted old Timberline Jim, the dispatcher. Rick Kunelius stood behind him, his arm dangling out one of the windows that wasn't hermetically sealed. He'd been stuck in the office for a week, writing some report or other.

"What gives, Rick?"

"I'm maintaining contact with the alpine environment," said Rick, sarcastically. He gave me a wicked grin, the wickedness accentuated by a black handlebar moustache that a number of young ladies found irresistably attractive, and which the Chief Warden found repulsive.

"Shee-it," said Jim. "I thought you were airing out your armpits."

Rick's shift was over for the day, but he followed me into the main office anyway, searching for some way to aggravate me, as usual. It was one of his most endearing traits and he was very good at it.

"Look at this, Sidney!" he crowed triumphantly.

"No."

"Ah, c'mon. Be a sport."

I took a look. On the bulletin board, next to the latest memos from "Fantasyland" (one of the nicer epithets we used to describe the Park Administration Building), there was a picture from a recent edition of a city paper showing a pretty little girl holding out a potato chip to a bighorn ram. I bit my lip.

"C'mon, Marty, let yourself go," Rick urged. "Give me a primal scream."

Irritated, I swore violently and threw my hat across the room. Rick chortled and left to go home, while I studied the picture.

The ram had a beautiful, massive set of horns, curving in a sweeping arc from behind his ears to a point in front of his eyes. I counted the seven annuli on his horns, each one representing a year's growth. The tip of the left horn was broomed off, possibly from a fight during the winter rut.

I was looking at a brood sire, a well-formed animal that fought off lesser males every winter for the right to breed the ewes, ensuring that the best seed was sown to perpetuate the species. Now this magnificent animal, dominant among its own kind, was reduced, by its craving for salt, to begging handouts of human garbage food. It was as good as dead. Sooner or later it would be run over by a semi-trailer or crippled by a speeding car, as it became habituated to hanging around the highway. The newspaper, by using this shot of beauty and the beast for a human interest fillip, was glamourizing the feeding of animals, undermining all the work we are doing to discourage the practice.

Disgusted, I left Rick to his own devices and went back to my locker where I pawed through the climbing gear and riding clothes to piece together a uniform for the day.

There would be two of us on duty this shift. Since I might be many miles from the office, I made sure that I had a rifle, tranquillizing kit, fire-fighting tools, and some climbing equipment in the plywood box behind the cab. With close to 100 miles of road and four campgrounds to patrol, it didn't really matter which direction I took.

The weather was clear and hot, with a drying wind blowing from the west, the kind of a day that makes a forester's nostrils flare, expecting a whiff of smoke at any moment. The fire hazard was extreme, so I decided to concentrate on putting out illegal campfires for the first few hours. Benny, the Tunnel Mountain lookout, directed me in to several illegal camps that were set well back from the road.

Law enforcement in the national parks is tempered with a public education angle, since some newcomers are blissfully ignorant of the park regulations. A warden spends considerable time explaining how driving through the bush and building fires at random destroys scenery for other visitors. North Americans, by and large, still suffer from "frontier hangover," though the age of the pioneer is long since over. This cherished myth, with its exploitative outlook toward the environment, is too prevalent to be ignored in the islands of wilderness that are the parks. But most people see the light of sweet reason, if approached in a friendly manner. There are a few, however, even in this late day on spaceship earth, who believe they have a god-given right to destroy the landscape. Then Smokey the Bear must become Smokey the Pig, with full police powers, and I had occasion that day to issue several appearance notices for Banff court the next morning.

Two of the fires Benny called in had been started by barbeque briquets thrown away on the thick duff of the forest near Two Jack Lake. I radioed John Wackerle, my partner on the shift, and together we worked at digging the fire out of the roots of two ancient spruce trees, roots that had been killed by the intense heat of the fire.

An hour later, with my nice, clean uniform reduced to a sweaty, crumpled sack, I threw the fire-fighting tools back in the truck, and drove down to the Trans-Canada Highway, Highway Number One–the Meatmaker.

I nosed the truck out into the slipstream behind a semi and headed west. As I drove, I wondered about the kind of people that would throw red hot coals on top of a compacted layer of dead needles, roughly akin to throwing a match on a pool of kerosene. Whoever had done that had taken his body on vacation but left his brains at home. It disturbed me that people could come to the mountains and regard the place as if it was somehow unreal, as if no action of theirs could have an effect

192

on the landscape. I shook the notion aside, in no mood for abstractions, figuring these prune-pickers, whoever they were, were just too damn lazy to throw some water on the live coals. I found that explanation much more reassuring than the other.

Speeding along the highway, one leaves the world behind. Geography is reduced to miles per hour and a hill is sensed, if at all, in the changing purr of the engine, a slight slowing down in speed. Men climb mountains in their machines without even knowing what a mountain is, except if they get out for a minute to tend to some errand, like snapping a picture, or taking a leak. Suddenly one is astounded, moving a few feet uphill on natural power, to discover the amazing force of gravity, the strain on flaccid muscles. No wonder most people prefer to drive.

Park wardens, too, have a helluva time trying to figure out what's going on in the great outdoors, while jockeying a half-ton through the landscape at sixty miles per hour, dodging the insane trajectories of confused tourists and semi-trailers. But there are a few obvious shifts in the balance of energies that can be seen from the windshield of a truck, like the flock of ravens I saw that day circling the slopes of Inglismaldie Peak. The black scavengers were setting down in some big spruce over a creek bed, a few hundred feet above the road. Wondering what held their morbid interest, I slowed down, and found the answer as I pulled over to the shoulder; skid marks, burnt into the grey hardtop for sixty feet, showed that a car had been moving thirty or forty miles over the posted speed limit.

At the end of the tracks, was a long streak of blood, ending in a patch about five feet square, mottled with chunks of fur. There was nothing else in sight on the road or in the ditch. No report of a crippled animal had been lodged with the office. The speeding driver had reasons for not wanting to call the authorities.

I checked the hair in the pool of blood to make sure it was not an injured bear I was up against. It was ungulate hair. Whatever the species, the animal was mortally wounded and I hoped for very good reasons that it was already dead. But the sight of the ravens wheeling and rising again, restless, impatient, meant the animal was still alive.

Out of luck again. I loaded the .308 Browning with a clip of bullets, and began to climb quickly up the creek bed, wanting to get out of sight of the drivers who would soon start pulling in with their endless questions, questions I was in no mood to answer.

There was a bright trail of arterial blood beaded on the green leaves and, in the wet sand of the creek bed, I saw what I had expected to find; the cloven print of a bighorn sheep, a ram by the size of it, and a big one. The animal was close. I could smell it, though it was not visible in the shadowy spruce above the purling creek. Swearing savagely at the prospect of this dirty work, I levered a round into the chamber and slid the hammer forward with my thumb. Having to kill the very animals you are hired to protect is a distasteful duty of the warden. It is a job to be done as quickly and as mercifully as possible. Still, there is a sense of schizophrenia in that moment of lining the steel bar of the foresight on an imaginary cross drawn between the eyes and ears of an animal that watches each movement with unwavering, limpid eyes, and a mute but terrible pain.

Each time this happens, I have to will myself to make that leap between emotion and logic and to let logic, which I distrust above all, control my feelings. Always a part of me, the boy part that was raised with guns and taught to shoot straight at an early age, marvels at the ease with which I handle a rifle, the ease with which the human finger fits a trigger. It is so very much harder, for instance, to learn how to hold a pen or a guitar than it is to hold a gun. And while part of me notes the perfect logic that is completed by the expansion of gas in a chamber, the killing line of intention, the other, earth-loving, part shrinks at the chaos in bone and flesh that results from all that twisted efficiency of rifling and jacketed slug—from that sound of blood spilling from a wound.

The ram was kneeling in the shadow of two fallen trees to hide from the nosy birds and their jubilant cries. As I approached, it tried to stand, as if it would move toward me. But one hind leg was smashed and bloody and a bright pink froth rasped from its mouth at every breath. It collapsed.

I saw the massive horns, outlined against the bright edge of the stream. There were at least seven annuli on them and one horn, the left one, was broomed off near the tip. It was the ram of the photograph, the ram that had fed from a child's hand. Something glinted, oddly, in the animal's rump. Apparently it was a strip of chrome paint that had flaked off and pierced its flesh on the impact of the bumper. It seemed the ram would die by itself without any further help from man. But the ram tried to stand again, with a low, almost imperceptible cry from deep within itself, like the sound of a big tree groaning in a high wind.

I raised the rifle, took aim, drew a breath and exhaled slowly, the way the Navy taught me long ago, to keep my hands from shaking. "Squeeze, don't pull the trigger, son," the gunnery instructors used to say. Still, I had time to be regarded by those eyes before the bullet in the brain put out the light behind them.

The report of the high powered rifle, louder even than the roar of the traffic, echoed and rolled like a brief thunder clap from crag to crag over the valley, and the black birds squacked, lifting in a cloud, fleeing out toward the river.

Dead, its nerves still trembling, the ram's mouth gaped open and the heavy, beautiful head slumped sideways into the creek, dissolving the crystal water into a pool of blood that billowed out, flowing out to the highway. Sickened, I jacked the round out of the chamber and put the clip away in a pocket.

The ram was heavy, too heavy for one man, really. But I didn't want any coyotes or black bears killed on the road on the way to feed on the carcass, and the temper I was in gave me strength enough, so I grabbed it by the hocks and started dragging it down the creek bed to the highway.

With a cum-a-long bar, I hauled the ram up onto the tailgate. Traffic whizzed by, some faces registering shock at the bloody sight of this animal lying dead. They were pained to see the needless waste. But to the rest, the whole affair, though gruesome, was only a momentary titillation along the road of summer pleasures.

People love to feed wild animals along the park roads, as if they were in some huge drive-in zoo, and until recently the practice was legal. North Americans are used to manipulating the environment and feeding wild animals puts them in a familiar and therefore secure position. This need to control and order the natural world mitigates against the very idea of wilderness. Perhaps that day, when the last grizzly bear shambles down the road to oblivion, will mark the transition of man into quite another being, one cut off from its kinship with the rough beasts from which we once sprang in some long forgotten instant of time. Maybe that new and future man will resemble more the inventions made by his own hand, than the image created by an omnipresent god.

But I am bent not on metaphysics, but butchery.

At the Banff dump, I hauled the ram out onto the ground and went to work on it with my knife and a bone saw. The proud head would wind up a dusty specimen in some museum, and as I worked, the eyes, brown as the muddy origins of man, regarded me from a spray of yellow daisies on the stony earth.

I cut open the powerful chest and pulled out the lungs to dissect them, checking for parasites. The result would be recorded on wildlife cards for the benefit of scientific researchers who might want to check them. Thus libraries and museums are eventually stuffed with knowledge of animals who have ceased to exist on the hoof. If the information helped in any way to protect the dwindling herds of bighorns in North America, the effort would be worth while, though it offered little consolation.

I finished dissecting the lungs and cleaned my tools with a rag. My hands were bloody, a souvenir of the Meatmaker.

In the Park Administration Building in Banff, and in the Regional Office in Calgary, there were engineers pondering and considering at that very moment plans to twin the Trans-Canada Highway and the CPR rail line through Banff Park. Soon there may be two more bowling alleys of flying steel that game animals will have to thread through to get from their food supply to their mineral licks and water.

The demands of the nation—that the major transportation corridor of the country must be upgraded and developed—collide head-on with the ideals of the parksman.

But King Automobile does not always prevail over Mother Nature. I remember one autumn morning when I drove out to the scene of an accident, east of town, where a herd of cow elk had been feeding along the road, jealously guarded by a magnificent bull with a seven-point rack. The bull had answered the bugled call of several young challengers and had driven them away from his harem. Then a semi came down the highway. The trucker sounded his air horn, sounded the cry of progress at the dumb beasts that blocked his path. The bull elk responded by charging the truck head-on. When I got there, the truck was lying on its side in the westbound ditch, the driver pinned in his cab, dazed, but otherwise uninjured. In the westbound lane lay what was left of the mighty bull elk.

Engraved in my consciousness is the picture not of the bull lying mangled in the ditch, but of the front wheel of that truck, the wheel of man spinning idly in the mountain wind.

It was hot driving around in the half-ton. Up above the valley of the Cascade River to the north was the Stoney Creek backcountry area where I would spend my shift away from town in a few more weeks. There would be cool winds blowing among the big pines and the splash of cold water under the horse's hooves as we forded the Panther River. That was where I belonged, where people are few and far between and of a different breed, with mountains shining in their eyes.

Still, most problems occur where the people are, which is usually within a short distance of where tires can take them. And with all the people that roll through Banff Park in the course of a summer, it's inevitable that the odd one has a nut or screw loose. One such person would cross my path that afternoon.

The dispatcher radioed in a complaint that some partying youths were building a fire near the Bow River Bridge, which is in the middle of town. No town in the country tolerates bonfires and drunks in such a location, and Banff is no exception.

"Call the police," I advised the dispatcher, politely.

"Nice try," he said drily. "RCMP advise that this is clearly a matter of an illegal campfire, which is warden business, not police."

"Catch-22," I signalled.

"Come again?"

The dispatcher had never heard of Joseph Heller, and from his perch in the Boredom Office, he figured that my job was a lot more attractive than his, so why should I complain? I had to agree. But although empowered as police constables, wardens are neither trained nor armed for dealing with drunks who are notoriously disinclined to obey the park fire regulations or any other kind of regulation.

It was 5:00 by my stomach, which reminded me that I hadn't found time to eat. I parked the truck near the museum, noting a thick cloud of smoke rolling from under the arch of the Bow Bridge, enveloping pedestrians on the sidewalk above in choking fumes. The sound of drunken laughter and breaking glass echoed over the river. I took a fire shovel with me to put a damper on the fun and walked down to the party, expecting to find some young campers who were too lazy to walk up to the main campground or to the youth hostel outside of town. There were four young guys and two girls under the bridge, and they were well into their second gallon of wine. They had built a roaring fire in the middle of the hiking trail that leads under the bridge, and littered the ground with broken glass, tin foil, and half-empty cans of food.

The sun was still up on the river, but under the shadow of

the bridge it was dark as a cave. Nobody noticed me at first and I stood quietly for a minute, letting my eyes adjust to the dimness.

"Hey, man. Who the fuck are you . . . Smokey the Bear or something?"

I looked toward the voice. The kid had a buffalo hairdo and all I could make out through the electrified frizz were two beady eyes and a little pink tongue. But the way he was weaving around he appeared more drunk than dangerous, and more like a puker than a drinker. The people were quiet, wary. I wasn't much of a policeman; I smiled too much.

"Look, this isn't too good a place for a party. I'd like you to put out the fire and clean up the mess."

What I was asking was more than reasonable. The fire was good for a fine of about $100, the littering worth from twenty-five to fifty, and judging by the amount of booze lying around, the police would have a field day writing up drunk and disorderly charges. The kids were all roadies, hitchhikers. I doubted if they had five bucks between them, and if they couldn't pay a fine, it would mean a jail sentence.

"Hey, man," said the Buffalo, "we're here for a good time not a long time, so why don't you just get lost?"

I had heard that "good time" line a hundred times before. Somebody should write it into a rock song, and call it the "Banff Park Boogie."

"Look, fellah," I said, trying to keep a civil tongue in my civil servant head, "I was here a *long time* before you got here, and I'll be here a helluva lot *longer* after you're gone. And it ain't no *good time* cleanin' up your mess. Dig?"

"Hey, man. Fuck off, man, hey?"

Well, I was still willing to ride with it, put up with a little abuse and arguing, figuring they would go along with me in the end, to avoid the heaviness of The Law. That was how it usually went. You went in easy, you tried being pleasant first; you could always get tough later. But this time it was going to be different.

One young guy stood up then and stepped towards me. He was well set-up, about five foot eleven, and moved with the easy confidence of a street fighter. The guy was smiling and it was my mistake to take that as a sign of co-operation. I handed him the shovel, asked him to put out the fire; one step at a time.

"No sweat, man."

He took the handle and I saw his eyes glitter as he looked at the others sitting around the fire in the dim light. Their laughter, as they watched him, had an ugly tone to it, little fingers of violence prodding at the nerves. One of the two girls, sensing trouble, got up and left.

"Hey, Jack. Put out the fire like a good Boy Scout," said the Buffalo, with a laugh.

Jack held a little gravel over the fire, seeing how slowly he could let the pebbles drift off the end of the shovel, making little titters of delight, noises of anticipation.

Behind me was the safety of the light, the voices of children in the park near the museum. But the day had been one long cloud. I had wanted to salvage something out of the murk and the chaos, though right then I wasn't sure what it was I wanted to hold on to. What held me there? I wondered, standing rooted to the spot, unable to run for help, not even *wanting* help. I was going to defend, I realized then what it was, my integrity, for God's sake, under the absurd bridge, in the absurd town, in front of these absurd folks. My integrity was at stake. I had lost it, somehow, when I blew away the ram.

Smokey the Pig was making his stand. P.I.G.—an abbreviation, someone once wrote, for "pride, integrity, guts." Now I had a fairly good-sized gut, some pride, and too much integrity. So there I was—stuck.

"Is that fast enough for you, asshole?" said Jack with a sneer. And the others laughed, passing around the second bottle of wine.

He was the bullgoose deadbeat for sure, and I had given him the shovel. "Tell you what. You put out your fire right now 'cause this little marshmallow roast is over. I'll give you five minutes. You can put it out and walk away, laughing, or you can refuse and spend the night in the slammer. That's my last word."

"Heyah, heyah! Me big chief. I have spoken."

"Go get 'im, Jack."

My eyes met his. Something remote and cold glittered there, something that warned, and I stepped back just as he threw the shovel down at my feet. That was a relief.

"Fuck you, man. You put it out."

So there it was. No more cards up my sleeve, no aces. Just a cosy little game, one against four.

We stepped towards each other; violence was inevitable. I

found myself wishing to get on with it, felt the sweat pouring down my back under the green serge. He had to swing first. He had the right to try it; I, the peace officer, did not. Where to hit him—in the scarred face, like the bottom of an ashtray, or in the gut? *Come on mother. Make your move.*

"You're under arrest."

"Bullshit!"

"For maintaining an illegal fire . . . " The words sounded ludicrous, even to me. "You have the right to remain silent . . . " I began, but he bent quickly, and came up with a half-empty bottle. I ducked as it sailed over my head, heard it smash on the abutment, and splash into the water. Mr. Jack Flash followed with a drop kick that dusted my shoulder. He was one of those fools who figured he could learn karate by watching it on TV. Then he turned and took a club from the Buffalo, who shouted behind him. It was a green limb of poplar, about four feet long and three inches thick. The other two were circling me, trying to push me toward the river.

A wise man would have turned and run. But it is difficult to do when wearing the green uniform. It would draw too much attention and create such a lasting impression. I decided to back away like a bull elk, its antlers extended toward the foe.

I bent and grabbed the fire shovel; couldn't leave government property lying around like that, especially when forced to exit through a rain of blows. The wicked edge of the metal glinted in the light that filtered in from under the arches.

The remaining girl got up and fled, smarter than the men—as usual. They were picking up rocks and circling, still screaming.

"We'll kill you, you sonofabitch!"

"We'll bash your fucking head in!"

If their mothers could only have seen them then! A rock winged by my ear as I backed up toward the light, figuring to yell at the people near the museum to send the police, still reluctant to run and give my playmates a chance to escape.

Jack swung the club at my head and I warded off the blow, holding the shovel like a stave. "Drop the shovel and fight, you sonofabitch!"

Jack had underestimated me. I was rash, it's true, but I wasn't crazy. Besides, I figured the shovel would come in handy for hitting home runs on the rocks that his friends were picking up to throw at me.

I dodged around him, keeping his body between me and the others.

"I'll kill you!" he screamed, and attacked, swinging his club. I fended off a half dozen blows that struck the shovel handle and fenced away two directed at my eyes from the splintered end of the club. Fear had sharpened my reflexes.

Startled by the noise, tourists on the bridge leaned over and watched while two grown men, one of them clad in green, emerged from under the arches. Robin Hood and Little John were at the bridge.

"I'm gonna getcha, man!"

"The only thing you'll get is time in the joint."

"Yeah, bullshit, man."

"You'll love it in there, *man*. They have regular beatings for morons like you."

We circled each other. A portly gentleman of about sixty-five approached and asked if I needed help. I told him to call the Mounties and he hurried off. Other tourists were fiddling around with their cameras, waiting for the light to change so they could get a good shot. It was embarrassing, surreal.

Jack pressed forward again, some invisible volcano of hatred was ebbing and boiling inside him. The club struck a glancing blow on my fingers. Yelling with pain and rage, I moved forward and feinted twice at his head, backing him up. I would have dearly loved to clout him with the shovel, but the thought of what that sharpened blade might do to a man's skull stopped me just short of hitting him. He hesitated, and I feinted twice at his knees, and made him jump.

"Hey man, we're splitting," cried the Buffalo.

Jack dropped the club, and turned to run after them. I raced back to the truck, planning to head them off. There were some pretty big men standing around watching the action, but none of them would lift a finger to help a minion of the law. In a few minutes, I caught sight of a blue jacket flying down an alley and there they were. Jack's three cohorts turned and ran to the right, leaving him to his own devices. He vaulted a fence and took off back toward the river, so I slammed on the brakes and went out after him, doing a straddle jump I hadn't tried since high school track days, the wicked iron spikes on top of the fence inspiring in me a gazelle-like grace. I came down over the hedge and into the middle of a tea party. Three old ladies, still shocked at Jack's uninvited entrance, sat under an umbrella on a manicured lawn, mouths open and cups poised.

"Afternoon, ladies," and I sprinted after Jack. He was tiring rapidly, but he made a comfortable tumbling mat when I tackled him on the gravel. Faced with equal odds, Jack seemed strangely subdued.

Poor Jack. I'm sure he was the victim of a troubled home and an uncaring society. No doubt I represented to him an oppressive authority figure, which some social scientists might claim gave him the right to try and cave in my skull. Jack was just doing his thing, man. The Mounties came and took him away.

They captured the other three desperadoes the next day.

"You pigs are just pushing me around 'cause I'm a long-hair," Jack protested.

"Not true," said the constable. "To me, you're just another pretty face."

My thumb was throbbing painfully and I fumbled through the first aid kit for some tape, wondering if I should go to the hospital and get it examined. I was still feeling shaky and tense, a result of the rush of adrenalin that takes over the body when it is threatened. There was a taste of bile in my mouth. It had been a frustrating day and it wasn't over by a long shot. The radio was buzzing away at the edge of my concentration. I ignored it and opened the kit. The dispatcher kept calling my number. Irritated, I picked up the microphone, still taping my thumb, and called in.

"Fifty-eight."

"Ten-four. Go down to the golf course right away, please. Some lady down there has been nipped by a coyote. Wackerle needs the tranquillizer kit."

Startled, I laughed aloud, wondering who needed the tranquillizing, the lady, the coyote, or my partner, John Wackerle. I wouldn't have minded a tranquillizer myself at that moment, say, a triple shot of Johnnie Walker.

I radioed my assent, though it seemed to me there were more important things to do than hassle poor old Spalding, the golf course coyote. It was true, though, that biting lady golfers was a new wrinkle in Spalding's repertoire of tricks and was bound to get him in serious trouble. For the past month the coyote had taken to sneaking out on the fairways and stealing golf balls before they rolled to a stop, which infuriated the golfers. As I saw it, the coyote's antics were about the only contact many of these people would ever have with the national park; indeed, for some of them, the first indication they would have that they were even *in* a national park. Mark Twain said that "golf is a good walk spoiled," and with the advent of the electric golf cart, many golfers choose to ride instead of walk. Chasing Spalding through the trees might be about the only exercise these golfers would get.

Spalding must have had several dozen golf balls cached somewhere back in the bush. Why he was into golf balls was his business and none of mine. Still, his motives were intriguing. Maybe he liked the shape of the balls. Maybe he liked to bat them around with his paws or maybe, because of their dark fluid centres, he regarded them as some kind of exotic éclair. It was just possible that he was stealing golf balls for the sheer hell of it, for fun. Not for nothing has Indian mythology all over North America assigned to the coyote the role of the trickster, because the most impressive thing about the yellow dog is his mischievous cunning.

He is the only animal I've seen that actually looks both ways before stepping out on the Meatmaker, and as a result, the coyote, despite its abundance in the park, is not often represented on road kill records. On rare occasions, an individual is flattened. Then, we make special efforts to remove the corpse, because the coyote's mate will muzzle and whine at the remains until it, too, is eventually struck down.

The coyote has a symbiotic relationship with the park grizzly bears, on occasion, like that of a court jester to an emperor. Several times that summer I had seen a big silvertip stalking majestically along near the airport, preceded by a grinning coyote and followed by another. Although the tricksters, in deference to Ursus Arctos, were careful not to get within range of his massive claws, it soon became clear that they were actually using the bear as a beater to flush game for them. While the bear dug furiously into a ground-squirrel colony, the coyotes sat nearby guarding some of the emergency exit holes that range out from the main burrows. While old Mustahyah dug, the fat ground-squirrels popped out of their holes directly into the jaws of the cunning coyotes who hadn't strained a muscle to collect their meal. Then the bear, catching on at last, would let out a terrible roar and chase the tricksters away, his dinner dangling from their jaws.

The Banff Springs Golf Course is a beautiful, cultivated garden in the mountains, a world away from the plebian tumult of the town itself. The heavy traffic and the crowds of people are left behind. Here, there is the murmur of wind in the spruce trees, the whack of club on ball, and the gentle purr of electric golf carts on the well-groomed fairways. The famous hotel overlooks the golf course, its graceful walls of natural stone rising high over the meeting of the Spray River and the Bow. I could almost hear the clink of cocktail glasses in the hotel's elegant bars, the placid roar of knitting needles in its spacious sitting rooms.

I got out of the truck, blinking my eyes in disbelief at the unreal tranquillity of it all, which had now been spoiled by one dotty coyote with a golf ball fetish.

Wackerle was waiting for me and noticed the bandage. "What happened to that?" he demanded. "Did you catch it in a door or something?"

I told him about the fight. John had been too far out of town to get there in time to help. "Why didn't you nail the bastard with the shovel?" he demanded.

"I was afraid of braining him."

John scoffed. "What brains?" He looked at me and shook his head. "Marty, Marty—how are you going to play the guitar with that thumb buggered up? How would you feel if that hand was crippled for the rest of your life, so you couldn't earn a· decent living anymore for your family? Do you think· maybe the public would give you a medal or something for being a nice guy?" He shook his head, disgusted. "Your own skin is closest to your back."

I looked up and grinned at him. "You're absolutely right, John," But I knew that the good-natured Wackerle would never hurt anyone, despite all his tough talk.

We walked over to talk to one of the greenskeepers, a wiry old Scot. The lady in question was being treated by the hotel doctor for slight lacerations caused by the coyote's teeth, but the Scot had witnessed the horrifying event and had all the details. Wackerle got out his notebook as we listened to the story, delivered in a full Highland burr.

"She had jest driven off the neenth tee, and made a poor lay doon the fairway."

John looked up, puzzled at the mixture of golfing terms and rolling r's.

"She was short of a hundred yard drive by aboot fifty," the Scot explained.

"Oh, I see what you're driving at," said John slyly.

"Yes," said the Scot, who was not amused. "Well, as she was walkin' up to the ball, yon coyote came trottin' outta the rough, and picked it up with his teeth, neat as you please, and turned to make off with it. Well the lady was furious and she chased after him with the cloob . . . "

"The what?" John interrupted.

"The cloob. I think 'twas a five iron."

"Oh, I see," said John, with a wink at me. "Harassing the wildlife, eh? Highly illegal."

"Well, she was pretty angry, you see." The Scot looked around and lowered his voice. "To be quite honest, she dinna seem to grasp the game too well, if you know what I mean."

"I'm hip."

The Scot gave me a suspicious glance and went on.

"Anyway, on the next tee, she'd pretty well forgotten it, but I guess your coyote haddna, because when she bent over to address the ball, he came trottin' out of the trees with a mean look on his face, and he bit her."

"He bit her? Where?"

"Right below the breeks."

It was my turn to be puzzled.

"On the ARSE, mon," said the Scot impatiently.

I turned away, choking back a laugh.

"Go on, please," said John, poker-faced.

"Well, she screeched jest like a banshee, and swung at the coyote with her driver. But he kinda feinted a wee, then grabbed on to the shaft with his teeth.

"The lady was holdin' herself with one hand and pullin' at the driver with the other, and her friends were laughin' too hard to help. So the coyote got her driver away. That's when I phoned you. The coyote's over there somewhere," he pointed to the trees on the far side of the fairway, then, dropping his voice, "Confidentially lads, I can't say as I blame the wee wolfie too much. I wouldna have minded bitin' her myself. She had a bonnie . . . she was a bonnie lass."

Spalding had retreated to the safety of the woods to gnaw, no doubt, on his new driver. He was too clever to show his face on the course for a few days but when he did, Bill Vroom bagged him with a shot in the behind out of the tranquillizer gun. The coyote, slightly doped, was moved well out of town and released far from the sound of an indignant "Fore." Unfortunately, he soon worked his way back to the highway, where he exhibited a further kink: stealing toys or stuffed animals from the arms of little kids who had climbed out of their cars to feed him illegal sweets. Fortunately, no kids were nipped by the crazy dog, who eventually disappeared. He probably died of old age.

I looked for his cache of golf balls several times, but to no avail. All I ever found was one ball lying on the dirt pile in front of a ground-squirrel burrow, too far away from the course to have been hit there by a golfer. A wild notion of why Spalding wanted golf balls entered my head. With no grizzlies handy to spook the ground-squirrels out of hiding, I imagined him flushing them out by dropping a golf ball through their front doors. To a dozing squirrel, the sound of a ball rumbling through its subterranean halls, caroming off the odd pebble, was perhaps equivalent, on a human scale, to an approaching subway train, disconcerting enough to scare it out into Spalding's grinning jaws. This theory, for which I have no empirical evidence, pleased me no end for some reason.

Once in a while, the animals like to strike back at their tormentors and Spalding's case was only one example of many. Even the most diminutive critters get fed up with man's continual insistence on interfering with their lives. In Banff Park it's possible for the foolish to get charged by an angry bison in the buffalo paddock, butted by a mountain goat, punted by a mule deer, forked by a bull elk, speared by a porcupine, or swatted by a bear, this last being the most familiar threat, though not as common as newspapers would have us believe. The animals usually suffer fools gladly enough, if they come bearing gifts, but there comes a point when the visitor imposes too much on the territorial instinct of the wild creature, as in the case of one unfortunate man, who insisted on not only feeding a grizzly bear, but following it into the forest. The bear chased him a few feet, not really in earnest, but the terrified tourist ran out into the highway without looking, where he was ironically run down by a truck.

The report on Spalding completed, the shift was nearly over. With any luck, by the look of the clouds, there would be a rain after midnight that would drown out the parties at Tunnel Mountain Campground that got going after the Cascade Hotel closed for the night. That meant that I'd be able to get a good night's sleep instead of wrestling with drunken teenagers into the morning hours.

Time to call it a night. Wackerle and I put our equipment away and left, he to drive outside the park to Canmore, where he had bought a house "outside this looney bin," as he called the park, and I to take the short, winding road to Bankhead where the saw-whet owl in a big tree near the house sang me to sleep before the rain began.

9

"Killing Bears so They Won't Die"

"True conservation is the effort of the
artist and the private man to keep things true."

Jack Spicer

The next day was a day off. In the morning, my family and I got up to find the rain of the night before had turned to light snow during the early morning, and the mountain crests were etched like engravings against a sky so blue it made you ache to look at it. We were going on a short camping trip, outside the park, away from the mobs, and we were hurrying, trying to get away before the phone rang with bad news. We had just about got everything loaded, sleeping bags, tent, Coleman stove, too much grub, not enough beer, mosquito repellant, first aid kit, and baby's plastic pee-pot with blue elephants painted on the side, when there was a knock at the door. I swore, vehemently.

"All hands to abandon ship," I yelled.

But Myrna had foolishly answered the door. "You'd better come out front for a minute," she said, and I knew by the resigned sound of her voice that we wouldn't be going on any trips that day.

A young man stood on the front steps panting for breath, as if he'd just completed a long run. He had three others with him, dressed in T-shirts and hiking boots. They were bathed in sweat. Little wisps of steam trailed up from their armpits in the chill air.

I regarded the leader hopefully. Maybe they were just

health fanatics, out for a little jog in the country and they'd lost their way.

"What's up?"

"Bears!" gasped the leader. "Big bear, three all together . . . ."

I thought "not again." It was the second time a group of hikers had come running out of the Cascade Valley that summer.

"How big was this bear?" I asked, wanting to establish whether it had been a black bear or a grizzly.

"*Big*, man. Tall enough to play centre for the Boston Celtics."

The leader described how the bear had reached nearly eight feet up into a tree to try and get their packs down. That was too high for a black bear, which would have climbed the tree anyway.

Myrna got the fellows a sealer jar of water. They drank it down, then told me the story.

They had been camped the night before at Stoney Creek, about nine miles north of our place on the Cascade Fire Road, up which they'd hiked the night before. The four had read our park bear pamphlet, which is handed out to visitors when they enter the park. They had kept their camp clean, had the cook pots set up a good distance from the tents, and their garbage and food, along with packs, had been tied up in a tree, about nine feet off the ground.

During the night they were sleeping the sleep of the righteous when the sound of a large animal walking about the camp woke them up. Then they heard something raising hell with their cook pots. There was the sound of metal being crumpled, as if in a press. It was the kind of sound that, heard on a pitch black night from inside a tent, could make one break out in little beads of icy sweat that run with excruciating slowness from vertebra to vertebra.

There had to be a bear out there.

The young men did the wisest thing they could have done under the circumstances—nothing. They listened while the animal prowled around their camp until morning, and lay still when it brushed against the nylon tent cloth.

Near dawn the camp grew quiet and one fellow eased open the flaps of his tent. By the light filtering through the walls, he thought it must be bright enough to see but when he peered outside it was ominously dark. There was a strong, musky smell out there. Then the dark stepped backward and growled and the camper saw he was nose to nose with the biggest bear he had ever seen. It had long, yellowish claws, and a head as big around as a beer keg. They never made black bears like that in Ontario.

"What the hell is it?" one camper whispered.

"I think it's a grizzly."

As if to acknowledge the announcement of its title, the big bear gave a disdainful sniff. When a grizzly sniffs at close range, it sounds to the human ear like the warning note of a locomotive bearing down on a level crossing, where one has inadvertently stalled the car, only to find that the seat belt will not open.

The campers lay still. There was no food around them so the bear left their tents alone and concentrated on trying to get at their packs.

They heard the scrape of claws on bark and watched as the grizzly stood up on its hind legs to try and reach the food. Their eyes widened as the bear stretched up and up on its hind legs until it had reached to within a foot of their packs. But it could get no higher. Frustrated, it dropped to all fours, and chewed on an aluminum canteen for a minute before dropping it to the ground. The bear moved slowly away.

The campers didn't wait to see if it was coming back. They tied on their boots, abandoned camp, and lit out for the warden cabin a half mile away. The poor fools thought they would find a warden there who would offer a little moral support. There should have been a warden at Stoney Creek. If there had been, he would have known there were bears in the area, and he could have helped the hikers to find a better place to camp. But the warden had been centralized into Banff to take part in a "planned management process" to run the backcountry more efficiently–by remote control.

Unfortunately, grizzlies have never heard of planned management, and roam anywhere they damn well please, regardless of human plans for them.

On the way to the warden cabin, the campers sighted a small, dark-coloured bear on a ridge above the trail, an immature grizzly. They didn't bother to question its motives, age, or experience, but climbed a tree immediately. Intent on other business, the bear came down from its ridge, stood up to regard the four with near-sighted eyes for a moment, then hurried off towards the Cascade River. They watched its bum recede, then scrambled down from the tree and ran up the road to the cabin where disappointment awaited.

209

They found a shutter ripped off, windows broken, and the rank stink of bear coming from inside the place. One of the bears had broken into the cabin the night before, searching for food. On the siding under the window were the unmistakable gouges of bear claws, lined starkly into the painted wood. The man-smell around the cabin should have kept the bear away, but bears have gradually learned to associate human smell with human food, having gotten their education in the garbage dumps, and woe to the cabin they find unguarded out in the sticks.

Discouraged at not finding a warden, the campers considered what they should do next to retrieve their food and equipment, which was a mile and two bears away. A crackling and popping noise from the forest near the woodpile made them jump.

"Quick! Up on the roof!"

They boosted each other up to the eaves and two of them hauled the last man up by the arms.

Then out of the woods, with rack held high, came a bull elk, his nose pointed out to sound the wind. He was breathing hard but stopped, nostrils flaring at the human scent around the cabin, then circled the place, trying to figure out where the people were.

The boys were just beginning to relax when they heard the woods erupt again with the sound of crackling branches. It was another young grizzly, moving with all the subtlety of a bulldozer. The elk was gone before the grizzly even saw it. The bear circled the cabin twice, ignoring the men perched on the peak of the roof and left on the trail of the elk like a gigantic blood hound. The bear's ambition was astounding; it was not fast enough to run down a bull elk.

The campers were not interested in the bear's capabilities or hobbies, however. They'd had enough of the ecosystem. They slithered down off the roof and ran and staggered for nine miles until they got to our place.

After they told me the story, I loaded them in the truck and we drove up the fire road to their camp. Everything was as they had left it. There were tracks of grizzly bear around the camp and in the yard of the Stoney Creek Station.

I cleaned up the cabin and nailed the shutters back in place, then scouted around a bit more. The signs seemed to indicate that the bears were passing through the area, heading deeper into the backcountry. A mile or so north of the campground, there were tracks of two bears on the road and mounds of crap, full of undigested soapberries, streaked north in a dotted line pointing away from town.

Maybe the earlier frost that year had made the bears anxious to find a winter den before the snow began to fly, or maybe wads of compacted polyethylene, which sometimes forms in the stomachs of bears that live on garbage, had given them a gut ache and they were in search of soapberries, their natural laxative; perhaps they were just out for a stroll in the woods, tired of the old rat race in the town garbage dump.

We loaded the camp gear into the truck and I drove the four campers into Banff. They were relieved to get their gear back and they sat marvelling at an aluminum canteen that the bear had punctured with its teeth and bent into a mangled U.

It was all over, and a little distance and time lay between them and the camp; the night with the grizzly seemed destined to be a highlight of their trip.

The men were in a pretty good mood by the time I dropped them off at their car. My good mood lasted until I got into the warden office. There was a note on the desk from the manager, instructing me to close the Cascade Fire Road, due to bear activity, and to put up the regulation warning sign. That was reasonable enough, but a memo on the bulletin board informed me that all signs erected, including temporary ones, had to be in French as well as English, and that before being posted, these signs had to be approved by the official interpreter in the Calgary Regional Office, about seventy-five miles due east of where I was. There were, of course, no such signs available in the park as yet and the Regional Office had shut down for the day. Legally speaking, the Cascade Fire Road couldn't be closed to the public because of this requirement. Any francophone who hiked up the road would be in serious trouble, unless he happened to run into a bilingual bear with a sense of humour.

I went in to raise hell about the memo with my boss. The Area Manager was a kind of flak catcher for the Chief Warden or, to borrow a nautical image, a breakwater that we hurled our energies against in an attempt to rock the boats of the administrators, bobbing at anchor in their tranquil backwaters.

The Manager was out for the day. Determined to run him to earth, I tracked him up to the Administration Building, but lost his spoor at the closed door of the Superintendent's office. A meeting was going on, the Secretary informed me, and the Soup had left word they were not to be disturbed.

211

I went back out through the peaceful halls. On one wall was a copy of *Desiderata*, a placebo for the troubled bureaucrat, forced to deal with disruptive folk like me. "Go placidly amid the noise and haste, / And remember what peace there is in silence." On another wall someone had pinned up the career bureaucrat's favourite poster to show what a good-humoured, regular guy he is, though terribly overworked. Set in Gothic print, the last lines read, "When you're up to your ass in crocodiles, it's hard to remember that your initial objective was to drain the swamp."

I was up to my ass in grizzly bears, yet helpless to do much that would improve the situation.

The root cause of the problem can be found within that galvanized steel container which sits in a yard behind most houses in North America—garbage.

To a bear, garbage represents raw energy in the form of easily obtained food. Nature designed the bear to be an efficient utilizer of energy and as a result the bear always seeks to find the maximum amount of food with the least expenditure of effort, hence the preference for garbage over natural foods like ground-squirrels, which can only be obtained by strenuous excavating work.

Thousands of pounds of potential bear energizer (garbage) can be found around the park on any given day, and when a human being gets between the bear and this food supply, the resulting altercation is known as a "bear problem." In a very real sense there are no bear problems in the national parks, but there is the very real problem of garbage management. Until it is solved, the conflict between people and bears will probably increase.

An ideal solution might be to install a pollution-free incinerator, or to transport the garbage out of the park by truck or rail. So far these ideas have been discarded as economically unfeasible.

The situation has improved since the days when bears used to congregate in the town dump, and a sign near the entrance encouraged tourists to come in to photograph the action. A new dump, or "sanitary landfill," as it is called, was built a few miles from town, kept closed to the public, and surrounded by a frost fence which was supposed to keep out both bears and tourists. In two weeks the bears had all followed their noses to the new site. They dug under the fence to get in and, later, when cement pads were laid down to discourage digging, the grizzlies simply tore the wire fence apart with their claws, making an opening for themselves and their black cousins. The tourists, however, had trouble scaling the fence so it was a partial success.

Another problem is that of containers. Bear-proof garbage containers had been in use in Jasper Park for many years. Made of cement, with a letter drop lid and a sliding bar to hold the barrel in place, these had proven effective in discouraging bears from raiding people's camps late at night.

For some reason Banff has never implemented that kind of bin. Instead, to centralize garbage pick-ups at apartment buildings, campgrounds, and restaurants, it was decided to use the sani-van system; large, 4 x 6 foot bins. Unfortunately, not everybody went along with the idea and the department seemed reluctant to interfere with free enterprise by coercing the local burghers into renting the bins. So those dissenting citizens continued to use plywood bins and old metal garbage cans, well-known and loved by generations of bears who destroyed them at will.

However, the locking bins were useless, since nobody bothered to lock them. The bears appreciated them because it made garbage collecting more convenient and ensured that large quantities were available in central locations. The bins became gathering places for black bears, sort of late night ursine supermarkets. They were mounted on wheels and a bear was observed, one moonlit night, pushing a bin down Banff Avenue in an attempt to knock it over.

Soon there were new bear trails beaten through the forest that rings the town, connecting bins. If the bins happened to be closed, a black bear would move on to the next one. Campers occasionally got a nasty surprise when they went to drop a bag of garbage into a bin, only to find a black bear inside, ready to receive it with open jaws and an ungrateful snarl.

At Lake Louise the grizzlies simply turned the bins over to jar the lids open. One grizzly, which habitually turned over these red painted boxes, got into considerable trouble when it mistook a red Volkswagen, smelling of Kentucky Fried Chicken, for a garbage bin, and turned it over on its roof.

Not all bears in the park are habituated to human food, but those that are constitute a menace to the public. Normally, both black and grizzly bears avoid encounters with man. Some scientists believe that bears can live within smelling distance of a campground, without venturing into it to steal food because of the presence of people. The factor that breaks down their natural fear of humans is the presence of accessible garbage. Conditioned to the smell of man, the bear enters the campgrounds or town, where it makes the first attempts to forage in the presence of humans. People now make the mistake of thinking the animal is tame; nothing could be further from the truth. It is still absolutely wild, but twice as dangerous as the unspoiled bear of the wilderness who moves away at the first sign of man.

With these thoughts in mind, I left the Administration Building and went back to the warden office. The least I could do for the public was to cut through the official nonsense devised by a bureaucrat sitting in an ivory tower somewhere east of the mountains. A sign was needed. The existing ones were in the patrol room and read:

Danger
Grizzly Bears
Area Closed

I got out a sheet of plywood and a grease pencil and, drawing on my limited French, composed a warning for our Quebec brethren, to be hung on the gate near my house. It read:

FERME
Ours Grizzly
Plus Fort
Tres gros
Tres, Tres Horriblement!

Crude, but effective. Pleased with my handiwork, I lit my pipe; one small victory for the forces of sanity.

Above my desk I had put up my own little poster, a nasty little epithet ripped off from the park naturalist, another undervalued employee. It read, "I feel like a mushroom. They keep me in the dark and feed me horseshit."

I finished my report on the Stoney Creek incident, one of many bear reports logged that summer, then went home to salvage what was left of my day off.

Even at home I would find no respite from the bears. The Bankhead house, along with the garbage dump that lay a few miles downwind, was located right on the ancestral trail of migrating black and grizzly bears, travelling down from the Cascade Valley to get to the dump or the campgrounds. The bears came and went through our yard like commuters.

214

As I drove up to the house, I saw Myrna rushing up to the back steps with the baby while our yellow mongrel dog, which was a refugee from the local pound, chased a little black bear runt around the back yard. The bear had scrambled under the haywire fence to raid our garden, and now it couldn't find its way back out.

The dog, Lion, was a spayed bitch with a tendency to crawl on her belly when threatened. We had bought her to sound the alarm whenever a bear came into the yard, but this day she had fallen asleep on the job and when Myrna looked out the window the baby was in the act of stalking a bear in the lettuce patch. Once awakened by yells from my wife, the dog wasn't that keen on getting too close to the bear and, sensing that, the runt finally stopped running in circles, turned around and cuffed the bitch alongside the ear, sending her flying ass over tea kettle. That was enough for Myrna. She grabbed a broom and went after the runt as the dog crawled back into its kennel.

"Hey!" I yelled, piling out of the truck, but it was too late.

"He ate all my lettuce!" Myrna yelled over her shoulder and whacked him a good one right on the nose. "Scat!"

The bear had had it. He turned and, climbing a tree, sat in a fork pouting down at her.

"Go on, beat it!"

"You've got more guts than brains," I said.

"I don't care. Look at my garden, he's ruined it. Trampled all my flowers, ruined everything." Suddenly she turned. "Paul! Leave that alone!"

The kid had found a bear dropping and was just digging in for a sampler. He was at the age when everything he found went into his mouth for existential analysis; leaves, bugs, stones, and especially elk pellets, perfectly round and aromatically enticing. Myrna grabbed him and took him into the house, muttering something under her breath.

The bear looked at me. I shrugged. "If I were you, I'd make like the birds."

After a minute, he swarmed down the tree, which was close to the fence, and gained his freedom. He ran off into the woods and the dog elected to stay in its kennel for the rest of the day. She wasn't hurt but I could tell that she was bugged but good. I went into the house, cracked myself a beer, and tried to unwind.

"Well, if that was our day off, I guess we've had it," said Myrna.

"Better luck next week," I told her.

As the summer drew to a close, the bears began to raise hell in town, fattening up for the coming season. Most of the trouble involved blacks, fortunately, which are somewhat easier to intimidate than grizzlies. Every day there were complaints from Tunnel Mountain Campground. A bear had raided somebody's tent, or a sow and cubs had moved in on somebody's picnic and had stolen the lunch.

Once we got a call from the Banff School of Fine Arts. A sow with two cubs had climbed a fire escape to the second floor of the women's residence, and gained entry to the building via an open fire door. She took the cubs on a tour of the building, looking for food. Girls exited, screaming, from windows and doors, some of them only half clad. Could we please send a warden up right away? The entire office emptied in about ten seconds, and trucks wheeled out of the parking lot, burning rubber to get up there. There were wardens everywhere, interviewing the girls. In the confusion, the bears got away.

I had a theory. Outside the park, bears aren't so bold about coming around human settlements in broad daylight, since they might be subject to receiving a blast from a twelve gauge shotgun wielded by an angry farmer. Animal behaviourists call this "negative conditioning"; conservationists call it murder.

Teleshot, a kind of clay firecracker you shoot out of a twelve gauge shotgun, might scare the sow and her cubs away from town, I reasoned. Farmers use it to scare ducks out of their grain crops and we had tried it, with limited success, to scare the bighorns off the highway. I talked it over with Wackerle.

"It'll never work on bears," said Wackerle, glumly.

"It's worth a try," I told him, and decided to do the experiment that afternoon. I found an old single shot Cooey in the basement that some canny Chief Warden had refused to condemn many years before—just the thing.

Wackerle took one look at it and warned me, "That thing will kill at both ends."

Undeterred, I took a young seasonal warden with me and we went up to Tunnel Mountain Campground. The sow was in loop G and she had been working sites 24 and 23. The people in 23 had left for the day, leaving behind them a pile of leftover food, a full dog dish and a bag of garbage. The sow went in and cleaned it all up but left their tent undisturbed. Then she went over to number 24 and, ripping a hole in the side of a tent trailer, demolished a wooden box inside of which was a rucksack, which she similarly ruined. She then carved a hole in the other wall to get out. The cubs trailed along behind her, getting their education in how to forage for food in Banff Park.

The owners of the trailer were there and they were very upset. The sloppiness of the other campers had drawn the bear to their camp. I told them I would be laying charges against those campers for setting out food for bears. That cheered them up a little.

"I can't understand what made her rip into our tent like that," the woman said.

"What was in the rucksack?"

"Just a tuna sandwich—left over from our hike yesterday."

I told her how the Russians used to keep a tame bear on a chain and use it to sniff out truffles, a fungoid delicacy that grows three feet underground near the base of oak trees. A tuna sandwich inside a wooden box wasn't even a fair test of the olfactory skill of a black bear.

The seasonal spotted our bear then, and I loaded the old Cooey. We walked into the woods and moved towards her, the kid to one side trying to get ahead of me all the time. I waved him back. It was his first season in the parks and he was keen.

He stopped when the sow stood up and barked at us; she was a real live one all right, used to humans and used to pushing them around. A complete bum, prosperously fat on stolen grub and garbage, she would have weighed in at about 200 pounds, big for a black bear sow in the mountains. The cubs were right behind her. I waited until she dropped to all fours, then I drew a bead on her ass.

Since it was the first time I had ever used that stuff, I didn't know that it always goes off at a pre-set range of about forty yards; we were about thirty-five yards away. In addition, the muzzle velocity is just about nil. I pulled the trigger. There was a "poop" sound and I could actually see the clay pellet tumble through the air, bounce off her rump and continue on behind her. It went off with a hell of a bang and it scared her plenty, causing her to run hard and fast—straight at us, which definitely wasn't in the script.

217

"Run for it!" I yelled, but the kid was already gone, sprinting back to the truck, little puffs of dust trailing behind each stride.

The sow veered off when I shouted, about ten yards in front of me, and the cubs were hard on her heels. If anything, she ran faster than a grizzly. They disappeared, heading east, while I walked stiffly back to the campsite.

"Do they always run at you when you do that?" asked the woman, who had been watching from her car.

"Invariably."

We got back into our truck and the kid gave me a nervous smile.

"That's a nice hop you've got there, Larry," I told him. The boy was no fool, that's for sure, and I knew he would go far.

"Sorry. Guess I got kind of scared. Weren't you?"

"I'll tell you after I've checked my underwear."

Clearly I would have to rethink my little theory. Back at the office John told me he knew it wouldn't work.

Actually, as it turned out, it does work some of the time on some black bears, but, like everything else, they get used to it after a few incidents, so you have to practically boost one right up the rectum to get any kind of response. As for grizzly bears, I wouldn't want to annoy one with a firecracker. Along with the lion and the African water buffalo, the grizzly bear is an animal that, when wounded, will turn and hunt the man who injured it. Such a beast commands respect.

Old-time Banff guide, Jim Boyce, once told me about three men who were hunting grizzly back in the thirties, near Whiteman Pass, south of Banff. One of them wounded a big boar with a .30-.30 rifle, a very underpowered weapon, and the bear ran into the woods. The men were trailing it, single file, not realizing that the bear had backtracked and was hunting them. The man who had wounded it was in the centre when the bear suddenly reared up from the bush and killed its tormentor with one swipe of its paw before making off into the forest again.

If old Mustahyah would attack a man with a rifle, I can only speculate at what he would do to a man harassing him with firecrackers. In the meantime, there is the culvert trap and the tranquillizer gun, standard equipment to deal with bears who hang around town. Since we couldn't cure the garbage problem, we had to treat the symptoms and move the bears back out into the bush, either by towing the trap out behind a truck,

218

or slinging the doped bruin in a cargo net suspended under a helicopter.

Of the two methods of capturing bears, the culvert trap is preferable, at least when dealing with adults, and works well on both species. It has a spring-loaded door at the entrance connected to a lever at the far end on which the bait is hung. This is usually a sack of rotten meat, rubbed with fish oil and smelling strong enough to draw flies off a gut wagon. When the bear pulls the lever, the door slams shut behind it. The trap is dangerous to use with a sow and cubs, however, because if a cub gets caught and the sow doesn't, there will be one highly irritated fang-monger racing around the trap.

Bears who are too smart to go in the trap, usually from prior experience with it, have to be tranquillized, though the tranquillizer gun can present serious danger to both the bear and the operator due to the lethal nature of the drug used. Until recently the only drug available to us, under the legal requirements of the Food and Drug Act, was Anectine, which works on the muscular system. The dosage can only be determined by guessing the weight of the bear on the hoof, and evaluating its general state of health. The drug is administered by means of a jab stick if the bear is in a trap and by a dart fired from a tranquillizer gun if the animal is running free.

Once the bear goes down, it has to be watched closely as occasionally a bear is overdosed and dies. The diaphragm will seize up, and the bear may start choking to death. An overdosed bear must be placed on its brisket and given artificial respiration, an awe-inspiring feat to perform on a 600 pound flesh eater. It takes good judgement to decide when the bear is revived enough to breathe but not revived enough to buck the first aider off and claw hell out of him. While one warden works on the bear to try and save it, his partner stands by with a .308 rifle prepared to shoot it dead, a situation that is as dangerous as it is macabre.

A dose of Anectine could be lethal to humans also, and there are horror stories told about vets who have accidentally injected themselves and died.

I dislike the drug intensely because the animal under it is aware of every move you make, though it can do nothing to prevent it. What kind of stress this puts on a dominant creature like a grizzly bear, who has never been made helpless before, can only be imagined. On top of that, the equipment we have to use has been described by one zoologist, an expert in this field, as the worst that money can buy.

The dart syringes have a tendency to expand on impact and the next time they are used they may stick in the barrel of the tranquillizer gun. The large dose of drug and distilled water, injected under pressure, causes a haemorrhage in the bear's tissues.

Clearly, there is too much guesswork and crudity involved in the tranquillizing method, yet, faced with no alternative except the destruction of bears by shooting, we have captured many black and grizzly bears with the device over the years. No tourists have ever been injured by the procedure, though it often has to be done in crowded campgrounds. The knowledge of what a mistake could mean hangs over our heads like a hammer. Tranquillizing bears is something to be done only as a last resort, and then only by highly experienced wardens. A Canadian Wildlife Service technician was killed in 1973 because of an error in judgement made while observing a tranquillized bear.

Once the bear is captured, there is the problem of what to do with it. Bears, like humans, have a highly developed territorial imperative. Each bear has its own territory, defined by its position in the bear hierarchy and that position, as well as the territorial boundaries, are known only to it and other bears.

Generally speaking, black bears are easier to relocate than grizzlies because they don't require quite as much country and they are usually less potentially dangerous to the visitor than a "garbage" grizzly bear. Blacks are transported out of town by truck, their ears tagged for future identification, or behinds marked with spray paint in order to identify the repeaters who work their way back to town. Incurable garbage bears that show aggressiveness to the public have no future in the national parks that are supposed to preserve them. Occasionally they are donated to a zoo or a game farm, where they go slowly insane pacing the confines of a cage. As a last resort, they are shot to death.

Relocating a grizzly is never done easily. The bear needs from five to twenty-five square miles in which to roam, preferably free of any humans. There are very few places like those in Banff Park, where hiking trails and primitive campsites are found in every major valley. Bears are usually dropped off into the north end of the park where rough trails and lack of bridges discourage all but the toughest hikers from travelling. Since so little of a warden's time is allocated to the backcountry in Banff Park, current information on grizzly bear movements is sporadic and there is always a chance of dropping a bear into another grizzly's territory. This often means a fight between bears to re-establish the limits. How many are injured or killed by their own kind, due to this kind of manipulation, is unknown.

Perhaps the gravest danger to the grizzly lies in the attitude of the growing number of people who would be quite happy to see all bears removed from the parks. This point of view was expressed recently by one writer to an Edmonton newspaper. The gist of his argument was that bears frightened him, therefore they should be removed from the national parks. The park boundaries should be fenced to keep them out and, failing that, people should be allowed to carry tranquillizer guns around in the backcountry.

"Bears," he said, "serve no useful purpose."

I would have dismissed this as the narrow point of view of a crank, except for the number of letters the paper received praising this man for his courage in speaking out, and agreeing completely with his stand.

Clearly, the fight to protect the grizzly bear is just beginning.

I don't intend to argue the usefulness or redundancy of any creature on the earth, since I don't happen to believe that the human race has the right to extinguish an entire species just because we find it inconvenient to share the earth with it. Fear is a point of view that changes with experience.

Destroying the grizzly bear is one more step in the destruction of the wilderness, because without the predators, such as the wolf, the bear, and the mountain lion, there is no wilderness. The grizzly bear, guardian of the backcountry, is also an indicator pointing to the state of man's biological integrity—our ability to live and let live. It is frightening, unpredictable, gentle, intelligent, awe-inspiring, dangerous, and beautiful—like God. Maybe it is God, or one expression of Him.

When I try to imagine the mountain parks without the presence of the grizzly, I am left with a depressing picture of a rather large lawn cluttered with stage scenery mountains here and there, a tame, safe, unmysterious, dead landscape.

It's true that the bear is dangerous. It is a fool killer whose existence makes it impossible to take the natural order for granted. It reminds us of our place within the chain of life and with that knowledge comes humility, for evolution teaches us that no species is safe from extinction, including our own.

As far as I've been able to determine, based on all the relevant data, as well as the bruises and scars on my hide, about the only species that serves no useful purpose in the national parks, and actually does untold harm by its presence there, is *homo sapiens*.

Those of us who want to become useful in the battle to protect our national parks will have to, sooner or later, butt heads with those that don't.

To its lasting credit Parks Canada has done an admirable job of preserving the grizzly bear, considering what happens to the big bear outside park boundaries. But with an increasing number of visitors (over 2,000,000 a year enter Banff Park alone), will come increased conflict between man and bear.

A partial solution to the problem is public education. But the danger of placing too much emphasis on this approach lies in the tendency to blame the tourist or the hiker for the conflict as, in nearly every case, it is his food or garbage that attracts the bear. This may be true, but it is also true that people have to eat every day, which means they have to carry food. The question to be asked in each case, is why did that particular bear lose its natural fear of man, which may lead us back to that image of the garbage can, and into pondering on whose responsibility it is to supervise what happens to the contents of it.

One day that summer a grizzly sow and three cubs were foraging around in a backcountry campground when the sow came upon a man lying in his sleeping bag in the middle of a game trail. The sow, cantankerous and thin from the strain of nourishing three cubs, was disinclined to change her route to avoid him. Instead, she grabbed the sleeping bag and shook the camper awake. Frightened, he began to struggle, and the bear bit him in several places. The man's friend, sleeping nearby, distracted the bear by beating some cooking pots together, and she moved away, taking her cubs with her. The friend went to get help and the injured man wound up in hospital, briefly, where his wounds were treated.

Our Chief Warden studied the report of the incident. It was his unenviable job to decide the fate of the sow and her three cubs. The department had taken away his control over the handling and storage of garbage in the park, so he was powerless to break the chain of behaviour in park bears that led from garbage to conflict with man. But the responsibility to protect the public from bear attacks still rested squarely on his shoulders, and on those of each warden in the field. He could not take chances with people's safety, faced with the history of that particular sow, nor did he have the political power to close down a portion of the park long enough for the sow to raise her cubs free from human interference.

His alternatives were clear cut. He could have the sow killed now, or run the risk of more human injuries, in which case other bears might be sacrificed in an attempt to find the one bear "responsible." There was no choice at all.

He picked up the phone and called the duty warden at Lake Louise. The bear was still in the area, feeding with its cubs high on a slide path above the campground. With the helicopter it would be over very fast.

"I've got nowhere for them to go," he said.

"That's what I figured," said the voice at the other end.

And they hung up.

One afternoon, as I passed the wildlife lab, I saw a collection of warden vehicles in the lot and pulled in to see what was going on. I walked to the big back door and saw a sight I never want to see again. A grizzly sow and her three small cubs lay in a row on the bloody cement floor. A spreading stain of blood widened from beneath their bodies and trickled into the drain.

The wardens stood around, completely silent. I could sense the anger and frustration in the air, the sense of futility in following a policy that one friend of mine describes as "killing bears so they won't die."

Two Canadian Wildlife Service researchers readied their tools to examine the sow, but I didn't have the stomach to examine the evidence or to hear the reasons, logical as they might be, why the sow attacked her human victim; I had heard them all before, and the knowledge didn't seem to help anyone very much.

I walked away, my faith in the ability of Parks Canada to save the park grizzly from extinction was shaken to the roots, along with my personal integrity as a conservationist. Later that day, I drove what was left of the grizzly sow and her three young cubs in the back of the truck to the sanitary landfill. The road, littered with sheets of plastic, tin cans, and old boards, leads up from the main valley of the Cascade River. I drove through the gate and up onto a set of weigh scales while the attendant weighed my load, 400 pounds of bear meat. A terrible stink emanated from the edge of the "sanitary" landfill. There was a pool of water down there, brown as a sewer from the contaminated earth.

A horde of seagulls and ravens lifted in clouds from the garbage as I backed to the section of the dump where the carcasses are thrown. There were two new holes in the frost fence, torn by grizzlies to whom the bear-proof fence offered about as much challenge as a volley ball net.

I rolled the small bodies of the cubs out over the tail gate, one at a time, then slid the body of the sow out after them. They tumbled and rolled down into the maw of the pit, down with the soup cans, cigar butts, the broken TV sets, K-Tel vegetable choppers, and a rusty baby carriage–all the thrown away artifacts of our disposable civilization.

The operator brought the big yellow loader around and covered them with earth. Outside the fence, coyotes, well fed on roadkills and garbage, howled from the edge of the trees and, from the opposite side of the fence two others took up the plaintive lament. The coyotes, unlike man and the grizzly bear, are natural-born survivors. If the holocaust ever comes, the coyote will adapt to it. He will sit on the graves of man and sing his funeral dirge.

Sheets of paper and plastic garbage bags blew across the grey earth and flattened against the frost fence like lost souls in the coming light of evening.

I turned the truck around and headed home. My wife and child were waiting for me there. I hadn't spent a day off with them for three weeks, and my obsession with park problems made me a difficult man to live with. Maybe it was time to forget about the problems of the grizzly bear and start paying attention to my young family.

In spite of the frustrations and dangers to life and limb, I have a pretty good job, one that a lot of people might envy, and I've worked at enough menial jobs for enough small-minded bosses to appreciate it. The job has security, which is something, though not everything, and the pay, though very poor in relation to the risks a warden has to take, is enough to get by on.

Why rock the boat? Why make trouble?

There was a time when it was hard to find recruits for the Warden Service. That was just a few years ago, when people were still throwing beer bottles on the road, when farmers were "hayseeds" and everybody wanted a slice of the Big Apple, before the Beatles and Flower Power.

224

Times have changed. The universities are full of zoologists, and graduates are out driving taxicabs. Jobs are scarce, and with an increasing number of people becoming interested in the great outdoors, a warden's job looks pretty attractive. There are a thousand applicants for every opening.

"Don't ever think you're not expendable," a Superintendent told me once. Maybe it's time to make peace with the bureaucracy, instead of constantly banging your head against the government's brick walls–this only produces scar tissue and more headaches.

Maybe. But I doubt it.

10

A Drumming
in the Earth

"I will make something else
out of meat in the snow
to raise the failing argument
we wage with death ..."

Headwaters

One day in September John Wackerle drove the stock truck
up the long winding road from Banff and pulled up in our
driveway at Bankhead. Peering over the top of the rack were
two brown mares, Dove and Camille, jets of steam wafting
from their muzzles in the chill morning air. Behind them, just
setting on the peak of Cascade, was the faint sickle of the
hunter's moon.

The big game season was under way in the forestry reserves
along the park boundary, and John and I would be patrolling
the backcountry to watch for poachers.

Big game, the wapiti and bighorns, were hanging well back
in the park and, despite the early hunting season, hunting
would be poor until winter snows drove the game to leave the
high passes and migrate down to the Alberta foothills, and the
waiting guns.

Nothing else held the game in the park except the instinc-
tual knowledge that these valleys seemed safer from the incur-
sions of men than those on the other side of the passes. There
was no fence to separate them from their ranges and the only
division between safe and dangerous ground was a line drawn
on a map and a metal sign in a cairn reading, NATIONAL
PARK BOUNDARY. NO HUNTING ALLOWED.

I kissed my wife and son goodbye. We wouldn't be seeing

much of each other until the horses were sent back to the ranch in November, when the snows got too deep for travelling.

John and I headed up the fire road, bound for Windy Cabin on the Panther River twenty-five miles away. According to a report at the office, two poachers from Edmonton were headed our way. We didn't know what pass they might try, or what day they planned to slip into the park. Given the number of possible routes, and the number of wardens on patrol, the chances of catching the two were about one in fifty.

In deep-snow country the long winters that last well into May or early June exact a heavy toll on all the ungulates and they have only a few months to fatten up, unharassed by man, before the hunting season opens about the middle of August. Without the extra grazing time they get in the sanctuary of the national parks, it seems likely that the hunting in this part of the country would be very poor indeed. Nevertheless, the odd hunter gets exasperated when the sheep won't step across the boundary to be gunned down and comes into the park after them.

This year's crop of deer and sheep was in prime condition, fat from a bountiful summer of lush grass.

In an hour's time we drove down the steep hill to Windy amid the growl of shifting gears and the clumping of shifting hooves in the stock box behind, and pulled into the station, one of the prettiest spots in the country. John shut the engine off and I began to rave about the peace and quiet.

"You can hear a pin drop, John."

He looked at me enquiringly, saddle in hand. "Quiet? You should have your ears checked, boy. There's sound everywhere. Why, there's a river running, wind blowing, horses farting. If you listen hard enough, you'll hear a coyote licking its nuts. And by the sound of your guts rumbling, it must be lunch time."

John was right, I'd been around the tourist trap and highway too long. I was beginning to talk like a tourist myself.

John threw his saddle on Camille, buckled it up, and got out his makings for a cigarette. "You bring any lunch?"

"No. You?"

"This is my lunch," he said, and lit up the roll-your-own. It was a sixteen mile trip to Dormer Cabin, and we'd had to leave the packhorse in Banff to get re-shod, so we were travelling light, fortified with a bottle of vodka and a few cans of meat.

We mounted the horses and headed them down the Panther River to the notch in the Bare Range that opens onto the wide meadows of the Sulphur Springs, where we expected to see plenty of bull elk. A few miles away was the park boundary, and beyond was provincial land where it was open season on anything that moved.

We stepped the horses into the Panther River, a pellucid dazzle of a stream, startlingly cold, troubled only by riffles and floating poplar leaves. A small school of bull trout flashed out into the current and disappeared under the opposite bank. The smell of autumn rose from the wet leaves that lay in yellow reefs along the river bank or crackled and rustled beneath the horses' feet.

The wind came up and shuffled through the trees, blowing the dead leaves down in clouds along the trail. They floated onto our hat brims, and into our open parka fronts. We crossed and recrossed the river, water splashing over the horses' manes, striking our foreheads with a cold that made the skin tingle.

The valley opened up into a wide meadow with low, open hills. The grass was cured and thick, the trees aspen parkland. After half an hour we stopped on a knoll and glassed the slopes with my binoculars. The grass was good enough to keep a herd of cattle fat, yet there was no sign of big game anywhere, except for the tracks of a few migrating sheep and two ewes on a mountain to the south.

John shook his head. "I can't understand it. It's been like this for a couple of years now. I used to ride up here and see sixty or seventy head of elk in this big meadow alone."

The land was quiet. Only the wind stirred among the low bushes of cinquefoil and dwarf birch, as we rode down to the river again and forded to where a steep trail goes over the mountain to Dormer Cabin.

The horses were sweated up and panting by the time we gained the high meadows between the Panther and Dormer Rivers. The grass was dotted here and there with cast-off antlers of the elk, some a few years old, and some that had been chewed on for their mineral nourishment by squirrels and porcupines for a decade. It was prime elk country, but there were no elk to be seen.

"There should be bulls bugling all over the place," said John. "Looks like the last couple of winters really killed off the females."

228

Then, as we sat our horses, glassing the nearby mountainside, a solitary bull, an imperial stag with a seven-point rack, appeared at the meadow edge a half mile to the west. He trotted stiffly out into the open, his broad-beamed antlers pushed back along his dark, swollen neck, and bugled a deep, brassy rutting call.

We waited to hear an answering call but none came. He called and called again, trying to locate a harem-master with cows that he might fight for, but there was no answer from the quiet forests.

The bugle faded behind us as we worked our way down to the Dormer River. The trails in this part of the park are little more than game trails, steep sections of hardscrabble and narrow passages through the trees, half blocked with overhanging limbs; wild country, country for those who don't mind losing a little hide now and again, or taking a chance on running into something large and dangerous, like a horny bull elk or a grizzly bear.

We were just about down to the river when the mare stopped abruptly, snorting and eyeing something through the timber below. I stood up in the stirrups to look around and saw the toe prints of a bear in the mud. The mare's ears swivelled forward like antennae, tuned to something I couldn't hear over the roar of the Dormer River. I sighted along one hairy tip and saw the grizzly, a sow, fording the river with two dark cubs in tow. Well behind, dawdling over some item on the bank, was a little cinnamon cub. In a moment he splashed across after the others as they disappeared into the thickets below an old slide path.

We sat our horses, letting them blow. Plumes of steam jetted out into the cold blue of snow and sky. A hawk went over, followed by the thin contrail of a jet, so high it couldn't be heard, for which miracle I gave thanks. I dismissed it as an illusion. Right here, sitting on this worn leather and the animal heat, the smell of horseflesh and Neats Foot Oil, with a whiff of grizzly thrown in, joined to the centre of the spirit's lusty energies, was the only reality I cared to believe in.

We waited for a few minutes until we could see the sow moving up an avalanche slope well above the trail, a case of "withdrawal with honour." Then we took the ford and rode on, ducking limbs, riding up the narrow valley with steep mountains rising straight up like a race of giants on either hand.

A few hours later the horses turned abruptly onto an unmarked path and in a few moments we crossed the ford, and there, on a bench above the river, were the brown walls of Dormer Cabin, the shutters studded with long nails and a welcome mat of spikes lying in front of the door, to discourage bears from breaking in.

It was 7:00 P.M.. We kicked the horses out to graze and I started a fire in the big Enterprise stove to make tea. We drank it down, scalding hot, thinking of supper. Even John was hungry, constantly rolling smokes while he drank his tea. There was canned food in the cupboards, but nothing much to eat. I decided to catch some fish for supper from the flowing fish cooler just below the cabin. I got out my poacher's rod, kept in the saddle bags for emergencies like this, and looked around for some no-nonsense bait, something with red in it. Bull trout are cannibals, they go for blood.

John took some canned meat out of his saddle bag to make a sandwich.

"That'll do just right for bait, John." I held out my hand for it.

"Bool-shit! That's all we got to eat."

The meat had been canned by a plant where I'd worked one summer in my student days. I watched as John took out his knife to cut the meat, wondering how I was going to get it away from him. Somehow I had to ruin his appetite. Then it came to me; I would tell him about how the stuff was made.

"I used to make that meat, John. I'd fill this hopper with pink swill in a slop bucket . . . "

"Enough!" John interrupted. He pushed the abominable mess away from him.

I grinned and got out my belt knife, cutting some pieces for bait. "I'll be back in five minutes with five fish for supper. You're the big eater, so you can have three. How big you want 'em?"

John spread his hands about three feet apart and then showed me how he'd like them about ten inches thick.

"You got it."

His voice followed me out the door. "I hope you got lot'sa pipe tobacco, because you'll need it for your pipe dreams."

I ignored him, bent on serious business.

The Dormer brawled down over black sand and slides of polished limestone through little gardens of rock and moss, by stands of overhanging willow. Beneath the banks there were deep pools. Downstream, the mountains stepped away into the north, shadowy, fading out as night drew on.

I put a piece of meat on a number ten hook and, sitting with my shadow away from the water, tossed it upstream and let it float over a riffle behind a rock. A small torpedo, about ten inches long, came out from under the bank and hit the bait so hard it nearly knocked it out of the water.

In half an hour, with five pan-size fish lying on the bank, I telescoped the rod and went back up to the cabin.

I cleaned the fish on the front steps, setting the guts aside to burn in the stove, and marched in to the cabin, ready for congratulations.

Yeats' wandering aengus at least had a good-looking wood nymph beckoning him on as he stoked the fire to fry his little silver trout. All I had was John, collapsed on his bunk like a dirty accordian, snoring.

I treated him to a tintinnabulation of cascading pots and pans rolling out of the stove warmer. John geared down into low range, prepared for an uphill struggle. It was obvious that if I didn't want to starve to death I was going to have to do the pot wrangling as well as the fish rustling. I found a can of bacon grease in the cupboard and used some to fry the fish in. My mistake was to complain that a guy shouldn't have to catch, clean, and cook the fish, too. That's what John had been waiting for. An unpleasant smile curled around his thin lips and he jumped out of bed, rubbing his eyes, then pulled on his boots.

"Why didn't you say you wanted me to cook? Nobody *ever* asks *me* to cook."

This sounded ominous. "Now just a moment, John. Don't go to any trouble."

"No trouble at all. Not at all. Chust step aside."

I watched with growing uneasiness as he stoked the stove until the air was chugging through the draft and black smoke was curling out the pipe joints. When the pan was smoking hot, he tossed the cold fish irreverently in. They began to buckle and crack in the hot grease.

I swallowed. "Aren't you going to flour them?"

"Oh, yah. We must have flour."

There was no flour in the cupboard, but John found an old bag of pancake mix and, before I could stop him, poured half a cupful over the greasy mess in the pan. He snickered at the sick look on my face. "Isn't that the way you'd do it?"

231

I could see the trap he had so neatly constructed, but there are some outrages that can't be tolerated. I shouldered him aside while there was still time to salvage the once beautiful fish.

"Okay, you win."

His face was cherubic with innocence. "I win?"

"Yeah, from now on I do the cooking. And stop trying to pretend your feelings are hurt, you sonofabitch."

"Well," he drawled, "I was only trying to help. But if that's the way you feel, that's okay."

The stars came out as we finished the meal, the fish tasting miraculously good under their matted coat of Aunt Jemima. The wind was wailing in the chimney pipe when we laid out our bedrolls.

We stayed at Dormer, climbing into some of the tributary valleys to take stock of the game, or patrolling to the head of Stoney Creek to sit on the cold rocks near the boundary, watching and listening. There were goats high on the cliffs above the cabin, and by watching their movements we could tell when something was coming in the valley below. In the high basins there were bighorn sheep and everywhere there were reminders of elk, narrow bones, scapula, old antlers, and the red vertebrae of an old bull killed the winter before by the small band of wolves that live tenuously in the Dormer Valley. But the elk themselves were mysteriously absent.

The bighorn sheep stayed well in the park. "You can only poach game if you can find it," said John, who disdained hiding behind a rock on the boundary to wait for a hunter to cross the line, preferring instead to travel off the beaten track, following the game.

Once we rounded a corner and confronted eight bighorn rams lying down under an overhang to chew the cud. They got up and moved slowly uphill. I made a rifle out of my hands and said "bang bang, you're dead." Three of the rams were legal-size heads, horns sweeping down and over the eyes. A hunter could have taken them with a .22 at that range with little noise.

The rams watched us going down, the metal shoes of the horses clattering and ringing against the stones.

It had taken several days just to rid my head of the muted thump of motors running and still I imagined I heard the heartbeat of twentieth-century man. What most people refer to as the real world, was not many miles away.

The real quiet usually set in about midnight and lasted until 4:00 A.M., when John would get up to build a fire in the stove, banging stove lids and swearing at the bite of the bare boards on his naked feet. He would get the fire roaring and then jump back in his bunk, waiting patiently for the place to heat up.

By 4:30 he'd be wondering aloud why someone couldn't get up and keep a fire going so a man wouldn't freeze to death. I'd open one eye and say two words, one of which was a verb, and go back to sleep, only to be jarred awake by the sound of lids rattling again.

John was the breakfast cook—his joke. He boiled the coffee and burnt the tobacco, then went out to capture the horses, using a tin of oats in lieu of a lassoo. As soon as they heard the tin rattle they came running. As long as we had oats, the ponies would forego any trick stuff, like jumping out of the corral and buggering off to Banff at high speed, leaving us with a forty mile walk to get home.

John came in while I was drinking my coffee. I was trying to psych myself up to get on the mare, Dove, who was a cold starter. She had a tendency to pull back, buck, and generally dance around on frosty mornings. I had brought her bit and saddle blanket in to warm up in front of the stove, though I secretly regarded this as candy-assed. John had won me over with his patient logic. "How would you feel, Marty, if someone woke you up, stuck a cold spoon in your mouth, then jumped up on top and dug his spurs into your ass? You'd buck. So do the horses."

John put the oat pail down. "I was down talking to Dove. And she's not too happy."

"That old slut! What did she have to say?"

John began in a mournful tone of voice. "She says, 'Did you see the way he jerked me back and forth yesterday morning? Just 'cause I crowhop a little. Then he wonders why I tried to throw him the other day. Why should I work like a slave packing that hulk around when he treats me like that? If he treated his wife like that, she'd buck him off too. At least she gets some pleasure outta the sonofagun. All I get is hard work.'"

"Huh. Most long winded-horse I've ever heard of."

Chastened, I went down to the corral and gave Black Beauty another can of oats, which she accepted rather ungratefully, I thought, considering her attempts to buck me off every morning.

While I was bribing my horse, John radioed Banff on the

single-side band. They told him that the two outlaws from Edmonton were expected in the area and we should concentrate our patrols in areas accessible by four wheel drive. That meant a ride toward the Ya-Ha-Tinda Ranch, west of Sundre, Alberta. A road from there connected with seismic roads that led up to the park boundary. It was going to be a rib tickler of a day, all deep purple, sunlight and flaming colours, and maybe later there would be the flaring of tempers and violence, the thud of fist on skull. Terrific.

We lit up the killer weed, inhaling frost, river, fermenting leaves, spruce gum, and horseflesh smells, trapped in the tobacco-thick air, drawn into the lungs and heart. It was our sacrament, our protection against the haemorrhoidal bite of the saddle, cold as iron in winter as we creaked on.

Dove crowhopped a couple of licks, just to keep me honest, then settled down and plodded after Camille.

We rode through a Group of Seven landscape of lush, burning colours, out of the shadow of the Dormer Range, and into the sun. The sudden heat fanned into our eyes and caressed our cold faces.

In a few hours we passed the rock cairn with the Banff Park boundary sign. John glanced back over his shoulder. "Well now, it's open season on us, so if I get shot, I hope it's a clean kill."

I pictured my head, with stetson set rakishly over one ear, mounted on some hunter's rumpus room wall, teeth showing in a snarl, as admiring guests sipped drinks and one commented, "Sure is a mean looking beast," unaware of what a beautiful and sensitive creature—a poet, even—they had wantonly destroyed.

I patted the butt of Lady Browning which projected from the scabbard under my left stirrup, and ran my hands down to the cold, wicked steel of the receiver. "If any sonofabitch shoots at me, John, he better get me on the first shot, 'cause I'll be shooting back."

John nodded his head. "Yah. Well just don't shoot me, 'cause I'll be galloping back the other way."

We splashed across a turbulent ford, the exit being a narrow, high-sided rut worn in the far bank, a likely spot for an ambush. I squinted into the dazzle of sun in the conifers, knowing that the forces of evil, hunters, could be lurking nearby, and I remembered the story about the two hunters caught skinning a moose, which turned out to be a horse. Should any-

234

one shoot my horse out from under me, I was resolved to draw Lady Browning and fire a salvo before sinking.

Sure enough, I no sooner reached the bank when the enemy attacked. I had my head down, watching for bull trout, when there was a low snarl from overhead, and I looked up to confront the bared fangs and little black eyes of a marten, which had run out onto a limb over the trail.

The mare spooked sideways, rearing to lift her knees above the confining walls of the bank, making a sharp left turn, pivoting on her hind legs. She hit a tree and kept going up, wild-eyed.

Time to eject.

I bailed off backwards, just a tad too late, as 1,100 pounds of horse toppled over on me. We hit with a splash in the three foot deep water. I got a mouthful, as she came down on the left leg and pinned it between two large rocks, which fortunately took most of her weight.

John was already in action, grabbing for the reins in case my foot was caught in the rigging. The mare got up, shook herself like a dog. The marten, victorious defender of its territory, had scampered off.

That left me in the creek, water merrily churning down my neck. I tried to get up, not sure yet if I was hurt, couldn't quite do it, so crawled up the bank like a salamander, swearing. Water streamed through my jacket and underwear, down my pants and into my riding boots, which had filled to the tops, and now overflowed onto the ground. The temperature that day was about twenty degrees fahrenheit.

"Are you okay?" John asked.

I tried the leg. It worked, but painfully.

"I think so," I said, eyeing the horse who was studiously looking the other way. She had a few vices, but this one could prove fatal. "They should fox that hammerhead and make some dog sick."

"Now, Marty. It's not the horse's fault."

"Well, Jesus H. Christ on a crutch!" I was deeply hurt. I had lost my hat badge, which I imagined was even now being modelled in the depths by some eager beaver who likely had in its mouth my favourite Peterson, also gone. My leg felt like a soggy pretzel. But what really hurt was knowing John was right.

I took off my boots and emptied a new tributary of the Panther River on the bank. Then, shivering in the twenty-degree air I slithered back on the horse into the spongy wetness of the saddle.

We went on, still three hours from the ranch. John waited as I stopped to wring a few gallons of water out of my down parka. I told him that a man might as well be dead if he couldn't get a drink of something or have a pipe to smoke. He fished into his saddle bag, and gestured hypnotically. Something flashed like Excalibur in the light; the twenty-sixer of Smirnoff Vodka. I took a long, grateful drink of it and felt fire going on again in the boiler room below.

The sun came out from behind a cloud while I steamed away blue handed and wet headed. I took another shot of the Smirnoff; highly illegal, which made the vodka taste even better. Things were definitely looking up, I allowed, and one thing about cold weather, it sure helped to numb the pain of a bruised shin bone.

Afternoon drew on and with it a change in the weather. Dark clouds were moving up the valley and a few tentative flakes of white soon thickened to a full-scale snowfall. We stopped and put on our slickers, then rode on.

"Hungry, Marty?" said John.

My stomach was complaining bitterly, but I wouldn't give him the satisfaction. "You know I never eat, John."

"Well I think I'll have a little bite of something." Then he rolled another cigarette.

The snow soon stopped, leaving a dazzling layer of white on the fallen leaves. Life stirred again in the wet forest. We passed a male spruce grouse, dusky black with a barred tail and a flaming red patch over its eye. It landed on a log beside the trail. Puffing out its chest with male vanity and cockiness, it strutted up and down on the log, tail feathers held out in a little fan, plumed feet mincing up and down in the snow.

"Why, you vain little slut!" said John, delighted with him.

The valley opened up into a wide meadow. In another mile we rode by the old Corner's Cabin. Formerly a warden cabin, it had been opened up to the public, who had converted it into a pig sty. The valley could be reached by four wheel drive and as a result the sign and scent of man were everywhere, the meadows tracked by his favourite toy, and the cabin strewn with his leavings, plastic garbage bags, half full of tin cans and other smelly crap.

There were no elk in sight, which didn't surprise me. It would be hard country in which to survive with a Bronco,

Land Cruiser, Travel-all, or whatever, hard on your frightened ass. I clasped my hands right there and said a little prayer that the good Lord might grant us a gasoline shortage. John looked on, bemused.

God answered my prayer, at least temporarily, since no motorized cavalry appeared that day. Discouraged by the shortage of elk in this Wildlife Management Unit, they were tearing through the wilderness somewhere else in the forestry reserve, aided and abetted by the oil companies that bulldozed the roads, and the Alberta government, which licensed the mayhem that was tightening the noose around Banff Park.

In a few more hours, we hit the Red Deer River, and rode across the flats to the ranch. Slim Hogan walked out of the barn and watched us riding up, puzzled at the look of my wet clothes. We hadn't seen each other since a rainy night several years before.

"Well, I'll be go-to-hell, Marty. Here you come again. The last time I seen you, you was soakin' wet. Ain't you dried off yet?"

"Slim, all I can say is, when do we eat?"

We put the horses up in the barn for the night and went into the bunkhouse for supper.

Slim told us that the two Edmonton desperadoes we had been watching for had been caught by two wardens that afternoon. Uncommonly stupid, arrogant, or both, the poachers had driven by the ranch to the east gate of the Cascade Fire Road and had winched a cement hub post out of the ground to get into the park. They had driven up the road about twelve miles and stopped when they saw a lone bull out in a meadow. They shot him, dressed him out, and were just driving away with the evidence, when two wardens came along in a horse truck and forced them to a halt. They had everything confiscated, truck, rifles, elk, knives, even their blood-stained pants. When they arrived at the warden office, under arrest, they had to wait in their shorts while Monte dug out some old coveralls for them to wear.

We finished supper.

John and I headed for Banff the next day to pick up the packhorses and some groceries. Snow was falling that morning as we drove up the road. It was going to be another hard winter for the elk.

_____

It was January when I returned to the ranch, this time to protect the property as well as the winter herd of saddle and packhorses from being shot as fair game during the January elk hunt, and to issue snowmobile permits to the hunters so they could haul out the elk carcasses. The January elk hunt would open at 8:00 the next morning.

I drove north on the forestry road that leads from Cochrane, Alberta, to the turn off at the Mountainaire Lodge, taking the eighteen mile long stretch of ruts that leads west to the ranch gate.

The night was a bell jar, the stars towering up into space in sidereal splendour as I pulled up in front of the bunkhouse.

I woke up the next morning to the sound of Slim's voice, as he sat on his bunk patting the ranch dog.

"Morning, Slim."

"Morning, young fellah."

Out of bed, not feeling too young, I scraped a thick layer of frost off the window with the back of my belt knife and looked outside. Plumes of smoke stood straight up from the main house, where the hired man and his family lived. The mountains hurt my eyes. It looked like a real snotwelder out there, about thirty-five below.

I finished dressing and started breakfast. Slim shuffled around, setting the table, his long back stooped and his legs bent like callipers from forty years in the saddle. The dog watched him closely, licking its chops with an audible flourish.

"What kinda dog is that, Slim?"

Slim considered a minute, scratching his head. "I don't really know. But he must be part setter and part pointer, 'cause all he does is set on his ass and point his nose at the table."

The dog thumped his tail on the floor and grinned up happily at this account of his lineage.

We sat down to breakfast, plenty of fresh eggs from the hen house, farm cream from the one cow that wanders the yard, toast, and hot coffee.

The conversation centred on the weather. Slim told me he had never seen the snow so deep on Forty Mile, the high country to the north that led down to the Clearwater River.

The ranges of the Ya-Ha-Tinda were drifted deep in every hollow and creek, but the rolling hills were still bare. The mountains that shelter the range on three sides and the open valley of the Red Deer River, which funnels the warm west

238

winds over the range, make the ranch a hospitable place for elk and bighorns, many of which spend their summers in the park, and winters on the ranch or adjacent lands. The management of this winter range is absolutely crucial to the big game animals, since winter range is in such short supply.

Elk had become nearly extinct in Banff before 1900. The old timers believed that a plague of some kind attacked them and wiped them out. They were reduced to a few isolated herds in the Kootenays of B.C. and in the Kananaskis forest to the east of Banff Park. A few individuals wandered into the park from time to time over the high passes.

A plague there may well have been. But rather than some exotic and heretofore unknown disease, arising to reduce the mighty herds, a malady of more understandable origin was the probable cause—an influx of white men brought in by the construction of the Canadian Pacific Railway in the 1880s. They dynamited the streams, shot everything in sight for the hides or the stew pot, logged off the timber for CPR road construction, and burned off what they didn't use with fires started by blasting operations, campfires, and the sparks from the locomotives.

As early as 1886, W.F. Whitcher, who was sent out by the federal government to make the first report on the condition of game and fish in Canada's first national park, wrote:

> Large game and fish, once various and plenty in this mountainous region, are now scattered and comparatively scarce. Skin hunters, dynamiters and netters, with Indians, wolves and foxes, have committed sad havoc. The rapid settlement now progressing in that vicinity will add other elements of destruction. . . . How to avert irreparable disaster to the remnants of game and fish, to restore partial exhaustion, to restock the mountain uplands, valleys and plains, and to replenish the waters, is worthy of immediate and serious consideration.

It has been suggested that if things had run their course, the surviving herds just outside the park boundaries would have gradually moved into the park habitat, where they would be protected after the Warden Service was formed. In 1917, however, steps were taken by the park which would dramatically speed up the process.

Two herds of elk, thirty-two animals from Manitoba and 100 from Yellowstone Park, were relocated to Rocky Mountains Park, now Banff. With few natural enemies to limit their growth, the elk expanded their numbers so quickly that by 1942 they were seriously overgrazing the range and threatening to starve out the bighorns and mule deer with whom they competed for grazing land.

There were not enough wolves, the traditional enemy of the elk, left in the park to keep the elk in balance, thanks to a policy of exterminating predators in the national parks that had been in effect since 1886. As a result, the balance of nature was disrupted. A later generation of park wardens had to harvest the elk every few years to ensure they didn't starve out other ungulates, such as mule deer and bighorn sheep. To this day, there are very few wolves in the park, though they have been protected for many years.

In the forestry reserve in Alberta, elk began to compete not only with the other ungulates, but with domestic livestock on the grazing leases. The wolves that might have controlled the elk had been trapped or shot here also, and the normal hunting season didn't appreciably decimate the numbers to what was considered desirable for the range.

To reduce the number of elk a special hunting season was inaugurated in 1969 to open in January and run into February. Females, juveniles, and bulls, were all to be fair game, and the hunters were selected by lottery from those who had not shot an elk during the regular season, ending November 30. By shooting the young bulls and the pregnant females, the reproductive rate would be reduced over the entire range.

Historically, the elk that winter in this part of the forestry reserve spend part of the year in the park on the drainages of the Dormer, Panther, Red Deer, and Clearwater Rivers. The elk were numerous and the park meadows resounded with the bugle of the bulls in autumn. Then came the severe winters of 1970-1973, with unusually low temperatures and deep snow, and with them a dramatic decline in the numbers of elk within the park drainage.

The most worrying aspect of the decrease was the low ratio of new-born calves to adult females. The deep snow, combined with harassment of females during the hunting season, seemed to be causing a high abortion rate, or the birth of calves too weak to survive into the summer—or so went the theory. One thing was certain: the elk were declining, fast.

The elk on the Ya-Ha-Tinda had a month of grace after the close of the regular season. By December, they had filtered back down to the meadows by the Red Deer River and found the hunters gone. Slowly, the small herds from the Clearwater and the Panther regrouped into one large herd of about two hundred, feeding quietly among the stands of pine and aspen, bedding down at the forest edge in gregarious security.

Together their strength was pooled against the snow. The herd packed trails through the forests that led from one upland meadow to another, saving its stores of energy for the long winter.

On this morning, January 10, the main herd, females, juvenile bulls, and young-of-the-year, were grazing a few miles east of the ranch buildings, as we ate our breakfast. The horse herd grazed a half mile to the west of the elk.

On the cat road below, out of sight of the elk, the hunters loaded their guns and moved up the slope, taking positions on the edge of the herd, closing in. They waited, fingers on the triggers, for 8:00. Down below, latecomers were still arriving, having driven in early that morning from various towns in Alberta.

At 7:30, Slim and I went down and took a load of hay to the brood mares. Then I drove east, alone, toward the Big Horn Campground. I pulled out my Timex. Five minutes to the hour and the thin edge of the sun was breasting the hills to the east. I topped the hill. It was 8:00.

From the north came a ragged thunder of gun shots, as the main body of about seventy hunters opened up on the encircled elk. The shots died down to a brief flurry.

Then I saw the main horse herd coming down a draw straight for the truck, their manes flying out behind them, their breath steaming back in a cloud as they ran past, snorting and bucking with fear. They went on past and headed west toward the ranch buildings. I stood in the cold, listening.

There were one or two more shots, then silence for a moment. Quietly, rising and growing near, there came the sound of leaves blowing across a field of crusted snow. There was a drumming in the earth. Then the herd, or what was left of it, came over the brow of the hill, the females barking for their young to follow. They streamed down through the aspen and went out over the flats toward the Red Deer River and the forest. Some hunters around the corner opened up on them.

I hit the ground. Looking out from behind the truck, I saw a cow drop. The rest had nearly made it to the trees when a juvenile bull with two spike antlers came floundering, shambling desperately after the herd, trailing a length of entrail be-

241

hind him. The white rumps had nearly vanished among the far trees. He struggled through a drift, catching the guts on a branch, ripping himself open, dying.

The cow elk lay in a ditch, breathing her last. The opponent pulled into view, a shiny new four wheel drive truck. The elk had four feet, an excellent nose, superb hearing, good eyes and a top speed of about thirty-five miles per hour. The truck had four wheel drive, a 302 motor, automatic transmission, mag wheels, 8,000 pound winch, eight track stereo, a CB radio and cruised at about sixty-five.

Two men jumped out of the truck with a happy shout. One went around the hill on foot to finish the bull as I got up from behind the truck. The other was fumbling with his rifle, which was pointed my way.

"Hey! I got one," he shouted to somebody down the road.

I got back in the truck, dodging the rifle, which he seemed to have jammed. The damn thing was following me around like it had a life of its own. I drove up alongside and rolled down the window.

"Say, mister, watch where you point that thing."

"Hey?"

"Look, it's loaded, and you had it pointed at my head."

"Yeah?"

"Yeah."

The hunter scowled, "Look, buddy, I know the regulations. This ain't exactly a numbered highway, ya know."

Then I saw the cow was still alive, thrashing in the snow, trying to get up. Its movements propelled it out onto the road. It lay trembling in front of me.

"Hey, that's still alive."

"Naw, it's finished."

I got out of the truck and faced him. About thirty-five, lumpy, dressed in a new red coverall outfit, this specimen was over-gunned and under-brained. He had a shiny new rifle under his arm and a new skinning knife on his belt, the best that money can buy.

The cow thrashed some more. The hunter's lower lip quivered slightly as he glanced at it, trying not to look too closely. I got the picture then. He had never shot anything before, he hadn't imagined the violence of it, the ugliness, the pain. You don't kill a 500 pound beast without the gaping wound and the stink of hot blood, the agony you have caused more acute if you do the job poorly. I had no sympathy for the hunter even though he lacked imagination and didn't know himself well enough to handle a dangerous weapon.

"Finish it."

"Huh?"

"You got a friggin' knife on your belt worth about fifty bucks. Take it out and cut that animal's throat."

He looked at me sullenly. "You got no legal authority out here, pal," he said.

I stepped toward him then, on the verge of striking out. His partner was still out of sight, so it was his word against mine. As it was, there would no doubt be a complaint. "The warden swore at me," a civil servant most uncivil, a clear violation of the citizen's right to maim and torture at will.

I took out my knife, went over and stuck the elk in the jugular. Blood spurted out over my hand and steamed into the snow. The cow grew still.

"Jesus," the guy muttered, sounding sick.

I got back into the truck and got to hell out of there.

A mile to the west, the rear-view mirror showed the horse herd on a knoll, a cloud of steam rising from their collected heat. They stayed where they could watch for any fresh threat of hunters.

There was a battered pick-up on the road. A man and his young son were struggling to drag a young bull down through the drifts towards it. The man was carrying an old .303 Enfield that had seen service in at least two wars, but he had dropped the bull with one shot through the neck. I got out to give them a hand. He told me they were glad to get the venison but it was a terrible massacre up above. They were heading back to the "stump ranch," their little farm west of Sundre at the edge of the forest reserve. He wasn't too happy about the boy seeing the slaughter up on the hill.

The boy was very quiet, wide-eyed. He had a brand new .270 his old man had bought for him, but I wondered if the feel of that deer rifle had been spoiled forever by the slaughter of the innocents he had witnessed up above. I'm sure I would never want a son of mine to form his first impression of the sport of hunting on the basis of the January hunt.

"There's cripples all over the bush up above there," the settler told me, "the damndest mess you ever saw. Half of 'em are gutshot. Nobody knows who shot what. They just opened up on the whole herd.

"Some of us picked our targets and finished 'em off. Hell,

you couldn't miss the poor buggers. They kept circlin' around, confused by all the noise. But the others just kept firin' into the herd until they'd see somethin' drop. Then they'd rush out there, yellin' bloody murder, bullets whistlin' around their ears, and try and beat some other so and so who was runnin' out from the other side of the clearing to claim the same animal. It's a wonder them fools didn't shoot each other."

We hefted the carcass up to the tailgate. The rancher rigged a pulley rope onto the cum-a-long bar mounted across his truck box. I wrapped the end around the elk's hock, and we skidded the carcass up into the box.

He got out his makings.

"Go start the truck up if yer cold, Donald," he told the boy.

The boy got in and the settler looked at me. He had a beaten, stubborn face, a fighter with easy crinkles of humour visible around the eyes.

"Who's that dipstick that was ridin' around on a horse up there?" he asked.

"Don't know. Might have been the scientist that's collecting elk foetuses for the Fish and Wildlife Branch."

"Well, there you go then. I figured it must have been somebody like that."

"Why do you say that?"

"Well, cristamighty. You say he's there to collect the elk's bags? He was lucky somebody didn't collect his. Ridin' around in the middle of the herd on opening day!" The rancher grinned. "Jeez, when those guys opened fire he went out of the saddle like shit from a goose. He was that slick. By God, didn't he make the snow fly! He went down like a submarine. Damn good thing, too."

"Did you see the Fish and Wildlife guys up there?"

The rancher pointed up a draw that led up on to the meadows a quarter of a mile to the east. "They should be up there somewheres. Like I say, they're still arguin' over who shot what. Some of that stuff ain't worth claimin' either. One soft-nosed bullet is bad enough, but two and three . . .

"The Fish and Wildlife guy, he's runnin' around tryin' to make them that has no elk follow the blood trails and finish the cripples. But nobody wants to admit they missed their animal. They just kinda weasel out of it sayin' that wasn't the one they shot.

"'Let the guys that can't shoot straight go get their cripples,' they say. 'This one's mine.' 'Like hell it is,' says somebody else. And while they're arguin', the cripples crawl away."

The rancher got out his thermos and poured us a cup of coffee.

"That snow's pretty deep in the trees," I remarked.

"Yeah. But hell, there's a Ski-doo for every second guy here. Snow won't stop them."

We finished the coffee, pursuing our separate thoughts.

"I'll tell you one thing," the rancher said, as he climbed into his truck, "anybody who'd leave that good meat lyin' in the bush for the crows—don't let him tell you he's huntin' for meat. Them kind of people haven't missed too many meals."

He headed off down the road.

I drove around, issuing snowmobile permits to hunters who had bagged an elk. I didn't envy the job that Wildlife Officers Bert Freeman and Ken Davidge had this day. There were some seventy hunters in the area and the officers had to try and be everywhere at once. The only way to make sure every cripple was accounted for would be to have an officer accompany every hunter. There were only seventy officers in the entire Province of Alberta.

I met up with Ken and Bert at the Big Horn Bridge. They were unloading their snowmobiles and I offered to help them with skidding some of the cripples out of the bush.

Bert, a stocky, tough outdoorsman, usually has a smile and a quip on his tongue for anyone he meets. But that day, he and his tall sidekick, Ken Davidge, were positively funereal, nodding curtly at the hunters driving past.

A truck stopped.

"Hey officer, are there still some elk around here?"

Bert looked up at the latecomers. There were three in the truck. His face brightened.

"There sure are. I can lead you to three of them right now."

The driver laughed, "You must have them trained, eh?"

"Well, they're kinda weighted down with lead, and nobody has claimed them."

"Oh, I see," the driver said, and shifted into gear. "Well, we've come a long way, and we'd like to kill our own meat, you see."

"Yeah, I see all right," said Bert unhappily as the hunters drove off.

Bert told me he estimated thirty elk had been taken so far by the hunters in the area. He figured there were an additional twenty head crippled and laying up in the timber.

"With any luck most of those will be dead by now. The

245

weather forecast is for thirty below tonight. That will sure as hell finish the job."

Bert and Ken had made sure that every hunter in the upper meadows who didn't have an elk had followed the blood trails. To those that showed a reluctance to exhibit the ordinary rules of a good hunter, they quoted chapter and verse of the game laws of Alberta. It's an offence to "allow the edible meat of any big game animal . . . to be wasted, destroyed or spoiled." They were running a bluff on the hunters, really, as they didn't have any proof of who was responsible for shooting which animal. Bert and Ken, however, had a pretty convincing way about them. Trouble was, there weren't enough hunters to follow the crippled animals, after the downed animals were claimed, proof that some of the hunters were "flock shooting" the elk, without picking out a single animal to bring down and finish.

We worked until dark tracking elk through the snow. The blood trails ran out in rays of crimson from the bloody circle of snow where most of the slaughter had taken place. Some of the animals had run for several miles and these had to be left on the chance that they might survive.

The temperature that night dropped to forty below zero. In the morning, we would find three more animals lying in the timber, curled into pathetic balls, and lying in a pool of their frozen blood. Weak from bleeding, they were unable to maintain enough body heat to survive. Slowly, and in mute agony, they had frozen to death in the snow. The snow that had driven them down to the guns had taken them home in ironic refuge and now coated their stiff bodies with a thin winding sheet of shimmering crystals. At least twenty head of elk died that way after the January hunt. The ranch hands still found the occasional cripple or carcass in the forest for a month afterwards. How many cow elk aborted due to being run through the snow is unknown. Elk, like all deer, live on a very thin margin of energy through the winter. Being run through the deep snow can be enough to put their metabolism in "negative balance." If they can't feed undisturbed it may take only a 17 per cent loss of body fat before a pregnant cow re-absorbs the foetus in biological self-defence. Perhaps this accounted for the scarcity of young elk that I would notice the next summer on the east boundary of the park.

For me the hunt was over. I loaded my gear and the snowmobile in the truck and drove back to Banff. Bert and Ken remained to salvage what they could of the elk meat that lay for the ravens and coyotes in that bitter winter. There were two more "go rounds" of the hunt left in case any elk were foolish enough to try and make a living around the Ya-Ha-Tinda Ranch. It would be well into February before the harassment stopped for the year.

Back in Banff, I wrote an angry report on the January hunt for my employers. There was no acknowledgement.

I wrote an article about the hunt, which was broadcast over CJCA radio in Edmonton, which is where the head offices of the Fish and Wildlife Branch are. Nothing. I guess maybe people had other things on their minds, such as the rising cost of beef.

Another January hunt was held the next year, in 1975, this time restricted to bulls. Apparently, some concern was beginning to register about the declining elk population in the vicinity of the Ya-Ha-Tinda.

In 1976, I was handed a report on the hunt prepared by the Fish and Wildlife Branch. I opened it, hoping to see some recommendation that the late season elk hunt be discontinued on the grounds that it was inhumane. Instead, what I found was a financial statement on the economics of the hunt, which read like a shareholder's report.

I learned that successful hunters tend to be in the middle or upper income bracket because they can better outfit themselves with high-class rifles, snowmobiles and four wheel drive vehicles.

I also learned that between 1969 and 1976, hunters spent a total of $630,332.60 on this late season hunt (good for the economy), that the cost of shooting an elk in 1976 was about $155 when you figured in all expenses and equipment. The Fish and Wildlife Branch not only knew how much the hunters spent on oil and gas, but the amounts they spent on liquor and accommodation as well.

I had hoped to at least find a recommendation that no hunter be allowed on this, or any other hunt, if he was unable to shoot straight. We have long since gone past the time in our history when any moron who can buy a hunting licence should be free to maim and cripple game at will. Hunting should be the privilege of the competent, and, indeed, the best kind of hunter shows concern for the management of game, as evidenced in the Fish and Wildlife report: "The majority of the hunters expressed the opinion that there were not enough bull elk in the area to warrant a season." But the authors of that report comment: "As hunters become accustomed to hunting bulls only, complaints of this nature should be reduced."

Perhaps when the brood sires are eliminated, the herd can be propagated by artificial insemination.

What right does an insignificant federal officer (albeit a citizen of Alberta all his life) have to poke his nose into provincial game management? Let me answer with an illustration.

Once I crept up on a boundary ridge in Jasper Park with a veteran Jasper warden. We took out our binoculars and peered across the pass to land administered by the provincial government. On the other side we recognized a guide of dubious reputation, who was sitting as close to the boundary with his dude as he could get without being illegal. They were waiting for a herd of rams to come up out of the park and cross the boundary, and we could see the rams just below us.

The guide had recently been remanded for trial on charges of shooting a grizzly bear out of season. He was later convicted. The bear he shot spent most of its time in Jasper Park, but had wandered into his hunting camp, which was a fatal mistake.

Ordinarily, it would have been unethical for us to disturb the rams and, in dealing with honest hunters, we would not do it. But this was different.

My partner said, "Why should we protect these animals all year long so that sonofabitch can collect on them?"

So we stood up on the skyline, and casually sat down on a rock to eat our lunch. Startled, the sheep ran back into the park and stayed there for the rest of the hunting season.

The game belongs to everyone. Wild animals don't recognize boundaries, they wander in and out of preserves and hunting lands at will. No one government can claim the exclusive right of ownership of this resource, and neither provincial nor federal authorities can afford to operate independently of one another, as though what happens on the other fellow's side of the line is of no concern. Without joint management, there is no management.

I hope communication between these two levels of government will at least be better than it is between the management and field staff in Parks Canada. Like most wardens, I read the newspapers every night to find out what the latest management schemes are, having long since realized that the media are far better informed about what my job will be from day to day than I am. Last summer, I read that my employers had hired an expert to try and discover where the elk were hiding, which had once been so numerous in the drainages of the Dormer and Panther Rivers.

I read the account with interest, cheered to see management sharing my concerns for the welfare of the big game. Then I drove out onto the Meatmaker and picked up two young bull elk that had just been creamed by a semi.

Meanwhile, the late season elk hunt, still restricted to bulls, for now, is scheduled for January of this year.

11

Snow, Gravity, and the Smell of Money

"Soon the avalanche must roll
down its accustomed paths
where only alder bushes grow

long forecast
by the shifting view
of rocks, of wars

that all must end
with gravity and power
here in this wintry hour
and without, in the flowering cold ..."

Headwaters

The north wind rolled hosts of black cumulus into the cloud traps that form the tributary valleys of the Bow River. It was a bear of a wind, a boasting brawler that blew a strident tune in the branches of the stark poplar trees. It sent the chicadees and the snowbirds scattering for shelter in the arms of the spruce forest. Then came a lull in the wind and the hushed valley waited. The first snow flakes fell, ticking on the dead leaves of the forest floor, then quieter and heavier inevitably the hand of winter covered the earth, outlining branch and leaf before burying them deep in the new, the longest season.

Overnight, the mountains are translated into a white language. The country is opened up to the skier's foot, closed to the bear deep in his den.

The white hills are seductive, inviting. But gravity and the heavy snow have shaped their own rough beasts to catch the reckless: the avalanche; a white bear sleeping lightly on the mountainsides. It will suddenly awaken at the touch of a skier's foot or be roused by the warm rays of the sun—even a sudden, sharp noise can send the white bear sweeping downhill with a force that could knock a freight train off its tracks with an accompanying air blast that could blow down a whole forest. Any living thing in the way will be mauled by tons of compacted snow, broken trees, and rocks.

250

The greatest hazard occurs where the greatest number of skiers congregate, at the ski resorts of Mount Norquay, Lake Louise or Sunshine Village, a resort southwest of Banff in a natural snow trap near the Great Divide. It was at Sunshine that I first began to work on avalanche control.

The phone rang at 3:30 A.M. and I piled out of bed in the dark to catch it before the baby woke up. On the way, I managed to step on a painfully sharp plastic building block with which my son had booby-trapped the doorway.

A yelp of pain, a curse of rage.

Sometimes I think that the designers of children's toys get their inspirations while reading *Marquis de Sade*.

I grabbed the phone by the throat in mid-jangle.

"Yeah?" I intoned in the interrogative.

There was a pregnant pause, while Old Timberline Jim, the warden dispatcher, savoured for just a moment the fun of getting a young buck out of bed in the middle of the night, something that had happened often enough to him in his own career. But when he spoke, Jim's voice had an edge of urgency.

He had called me out for a search at first light with ski mountaineering and avalanche rescue gear. A young American skier had been missing for a day and a half from his motel room. Because he had been travelling alone, it had taken that long for his disappearance to be reported. The last seen point, a crucial factor in organizing a search, had been on the Great Divide ski run on Lookout Mountain above Sunshine Village.

I hung up the phone and layered on clothing, starting with long johns and knee socks, finishing with woollen knickers and a wool shirt.

There were three ways to get down off of Lookout Mountain. One was to climb down a short cliff to reach the top of the suicidal Delerium Dive run, frequented only by madmen and park wardens. Another was the usual ski run that led to Sunshine Village, and the last was straight over an 800 foot high cliff that formed the north face of the mountain. There is a rope fence, set up by the resort, and warning signs stretching from the top of the run to a point down the mountain where bare rock, blown free of snow by the wind, makes a natural barrier to the skier.

Despite the warning fence, skiers sometimes like to play cat and mouse with death by skiing just outside the fence, or working their way over the rocks toward the edge of the mountain to admire the view—at least what they think is the edge of the mountain. The point of solid ground is difficult to find because the entire ridge is a cornice, a platform of snow plastered against the rock and held in place only by a thin layer of icy weld. The strength of that platform varies from day to day depending on the weather. Sometimes it is as solid as cement, sometimes no more substantial than a cloud, needing only a puff of wind, or a man's foot, to send it hurtling down the face.

A piece of that cornice had collapsed recently and had touched off a number of avalanches in the snow bowl below the cliffs of Lookout Mountain. It was in this bowl that the search would begin.

The baby, who was a notoriously light sleeper in our house, was now in full cry. I peered into the nursery and found my wife at bay, with a distinctly feline glint in her eye.

"Can't you be a little more quiet, dear?" she hissed.

"I'm sorry, dear" (we always called each other "dear" when things got tense), "but I've got to go out in the freezing cold and save somebody's ass."

"Oh you poor, dear *man*," she said, managing to assign a ludicrous inefficacy to the whole male sex by her tone of voice.

I waded out in the cold to the frigid half-ton, started it up, and drove through a blizzard to Sunshine Village ski resort, in the early morning darkness.

There I found the others sorting rescue equipment. We loaded the packs with avalanche probes, shovels, blankets, and the rest, stepped into our ski bindings and started up the hill in Indian file in the dark. Earle Skjonsberg, the dog master, brought up the rear with the German Shepherd search dog, Ruff. We packed a firm trail for him so he wouldn't waste his strength floundering through the deep snow. Once the search began, the dog would do most of the leg work.

The wind dropped as morning sun touched the top of the moody face, outlining in vermilion a half-dozen fresh avalanche tracks, each one a few hundred feet wide, that led from where water courses broke the cliff walls and stretched 200 yards down the forty-five degree slopes to a stand of larch trees below.

It was silent except for our laboured breathing. There was no sign of any living thing anywhere in the bowl, except for the single track of a snowshoe hare, like a long line of apostrophes on a blank page.

252

Down below, we could see the bright anoraks of John Wackerle and Keith Everts. Keith, who co-ordinated the snow research and avalanche rescue program in Banff, was a seven-year veteran of the Warden Service.

Acting as rescue leader, Keith had gone ahead to plan the search. John, armed with a metal avalanche whistle, moved back into the trees where he could see the cornices hidden to us by the dark wall of the cliffs. He would sound an alarm if anything fell from above.

Once buried in a slide, a man has perhaps an hour to survive, at the most. Unless he remains close to the surface, he will not be able to move so much as a finger after the snow begins to harden. He is in a straitjacket of snow, hugged in the fierce embrace of the white bear.

"Gentlemen," Keith called on the portable radio, "do you realize what day it is today?"

Earle and I exchanged looks. It was April 1–April Fool's Day. If there was a joke, it was on us.

The tawny Shepherd watched his handler with eager eyes, anxious to begin the game he lived to play.

Earle cautioned us in his soft-spoken voice to leave no scent in the slide area that would distract the dog. No spitting, no food, no urinating. The dog's nose is so sensitive that he can find a ten-cent piece buried under three feet of snow.

In Europe, where hundreds of thousands of dollars have been spent to develop a more sophisticated method of avalanche rescue, no man-made electronic gadget has ever been found that is more efficient than a trained avalanche dog. Willi Pfisterer, Jasper Alpine Specialist, likes to sum up the whole expensive exercise in a few heavily Austrian-flavoured words: "They can put a man on the moon, they can make un armpit schmell like a lilac boosh, but ven it comes to finding a skier in an awalunch, it all boils down to a dok's nose."

Earle pulled his toque down over his ears and rubbed his weatherbeaten cheeks with a mittened hand to restore some warmth. He called the dog to him and slipped his skis over the ridge to glide down into the shadow of the avalanche. The dog ran behind in the ski track.

We watched as he reached the first slide and took off his skis. The surface was hard enough to walk on, compacted into a jumbled sweep of slabs.

"Search 'em out, Ruff," came his faint call.

The powerful dog began working its way up the steep mountainside in a zig-zag pattern, head low to the ground.

253

Keith, watching from below, was worried and his state of mind was shown in the heavy cloud of pipe smoke that fanned up from his chunky figure. He was still debating with himself whether, as rescue leader, he should have blasted the cornices down with dynamite to make the area safe to work in. He had no evidence that the skier had even been buried, only a last-seen point—the ski run far above us— and a hunch. But what if a warden was injured on the strength of his hunch alone? What if the skier was not even in this area? These questions worked at his resolve. The minutes went slowly by.

We were watching the dog when the shrill note of the whistle echoed through the bowl. All eyes turned toward Earle, but instead of running downhill, he called the dog, which was high above him. He wouldn't go without the dog. There was an ominous rumble from the cliffs.

"Run, Earle!" we shouted. "Goddamn it! Run!"

The dog was racing back down the slope, but still Earle hesitated. The old timer was thinking, as usual, not wanting to run out of what should be a safe spot into a fresh avalanche track. The dog reached him, and he retreated down the hill. A couple of big chunks splattered down and burst on the hard snow. Faint voices drifted up from the toe of the slide.

"Damn it, Earle, we should blast those cornices."

Earle's steady, quiet voice, "Well, I don't think so yet, Keith. The dog looked like he was on a scent. Let's hold off for a while. Search 'em out, Ruff."

The dog went high up the slope, whined, and began to paw frantically at the hard snow, plumed tail wig-wagging back and forth.

"Shovel!" Earle yelled.

Keith's voice boomed in the radio at my belt as he passed the message on, but Randy Chisholm had already jumped his skis over the edge to fly across Earle's track to the dog.

Randy dug at the place near the edge of the slide, went down three feet, and hit something. Earle bent over it, letting the dog sniff and tug it from the snow, making a fuss over it to reward the dog, then taking it away. Earle held it up, glinting in the morning sun of April Fool's Day.

A ski pole, a blue-coloured, K-2 ski pole—brand new. The victim had bought a pair of them at the ski shop on the day he disappeared. And now we were sure that Keith was right, that the missing man was lying in the snow under one of the avalanche paths. The original cornice that had broken loose from above had separated and poured down several different snow chutes. The dog was no longer interested in the first slide, a good sign that nothing else was buried there. Earle took him across to the next one, skiing over the unbroken snow between the slides.

We skied down to the toe of the slide, and assembled the twenty foot steel avalanche probes. For the first time I could see the force of the avalanche that contained the pole. Several hundred tons of snow, packed on the cliff by the eddying winds during the winter, had dropped off in a banana-shaped wedge and had fallen into the snowfield a hundred feet below. This had triggered a secondary avalanche that swept the slope clear down to the rocks, before funnelling down the chutes to start yet another avalanche roaring down to the jumble of snow on which we stood.

The barking of dogs on the ridge above us signalled the arrival of Wardens Alf Burstrom and Jack Woledge with search dogs Ginger and Neshan. In another half-hour, the dogs had indicated a total of five spots on the slide that would have to be shovelled out. In each place, there would be a scent of the lost man; a ski glove, a camera, a ski pole or a ski. In one of them was the man himself.

The hard-packed snow was sealing off the scent of the buried man, and the shifting wind direction made it difficult for the dogs to pinpoint his location.

We split up into teams and began digging at each site, one man probing the hard-packed snow with a twenty foot long avalanche probe, while the other dug. The dogs, meanwhile, lost interest, a sure sign that every spot that held a scent had been indicated. Two of them got into a brief scrap and were taken down to go to sleep in the warm sunlight at the base of the slides. They had done their work; now it was up to us.

The mountain was waking up. Tendrils of snow spilled over the cliffs from time to time, a prelude to catastrophe. A rock clattered down the face and rolled down the avalanche slope, melted loose by the sun, making us nervous and giving us a crick in the neck from looking up.

The snow was too hard to shovel. We had to chop and quarry our way through it. The day dragged on, the search reduced now to an endurance test. I was wet, cold, and hungry. The icy sandwiches we had for lunch didn't seem to offer much energy. The skin on my fingers was cracking painfully from being wet, dried, and wet again as I kept changing gloves, and the shovel handles were caked with ice. It was tempting to doubt the dogs, when all we had for our efforts was one ski pole. Tempting, but not enough to make us stop and debate the point.

As I chopped away at the snow, I felt my resentment toward the missing man deepen with each motion of the shovel blade. Because of his stupidity, I thought, I have to risk my neck digging a hole right under a cornice. It was disturbing to think I'd changed enough over the years to feel that way about a fellow human caught in such a fearful place. But the feeling wouldn't go away.

The sheer walls of the cliff towered above my head, implacable, dangerous. I was in the bottom of the pit when I felt a heavy shower of snow go down my neck, a cold hand pushing me to my knees, and I thought of the cornice above me and the grave I was digging.

In one leap I went up out of the pit for the sky, sliding back and lunging for the edge, on all fours, as I heard the whistle blowing. I went tripping, rolling, got up, and was flying down the hill in giant strides, slowing to hear laughter down below.

"Laugh, you sons of bitches!"

It had just been a sluff of powder from last night's snowfall, started perhaps by a pebble falling from the cornices above.

Hot tea from a thermos helped to still my trembling fingers. Then I went back to the digging.

The afternoon shadows were lengthening down the bowl. The dogs were out on the slide and I wondered, "Ginger, why do you always come back here? Is it perhaps my fascinating body odour?"

The dog whined at me and cocked its head to one side, the wide-set, intelligent eyes following my motions.

"That dog is trying to tell us something," said Alf Burstrom.

Under Alf's direction we moved off the slide. He felt our digging and probing might have released more scent of the buried man. Jack's dog, Neshan, went up the slide, then hesitated, turning downhill, as if someone was calling him. He ran back to one of the spots that Ginger had indicated and started pawing the snow a few yards east of the pit.

Joe Halstenson went out with a shovel. Two feet under the surface he struck a plastic ski boot. We hurried out with him and began digging the snow away. The young skier lay on his side, head down, making the thinnest of targets in the snow; that's why we had missed him with the probes.

The white bear had embraced the skier, and it was reluctant to let him go. At length we freed him and I saw the broken camera strap on his wrist, and the watch that had stopped forever at 2:10 P.M.

The dogs whined anxiously around the still form in the snow. We covered the face and readied him in the stretcher as the helicopter came in to take him to Banff.

Nobody made any reference to the dead man as we packed up our gear to ski out. Each man has his own way of dealing with such things and the best way is to try and talk about something else, to keep it impersonal, especially if you have a son of your own, especially if you have any imagination.

In each man's head there are deaths that he can never forget, for life in the Warden Service is a little bit like a war, with the inevitable body counts. Each man carries his ghosts inside and, after a while, they begin to tell on the heart in ways that can never be compensated for by Parks Canada or anybody else. I remember the dead more clearly than the ones we saved; they are the frustrating failures that couldn't be prevented, the hard luck stories of my seasons.

Back in the locker room, I sat dully on the wooden bench, feeling like a beaten jock without talent, feeling old. Death had made me cynical at last. I wondered what had happened to the young man who had mourned over the body of a drowned stranger and felt a kinship with him that death had aroused. That powerful admonition had once been burned into my heart; would I have to learn it all over again in some more personal and bitter lesson?

After about five minutes, I gave up on changing clothes and drove home soaking wet. The dog rushed out, snarling and barking as always, but I couldn't even summon up the energy to give her her usual swat on the ass. She whined fitfully, concerned at this breach of habit.

Inside the house Myrna had the fire going. The baby reached out and I felt his warm fingers on my cold skin. Myrna's arms were around me; I was safely home in the centre of my universe.

"Did you find him?"

"Yeah."

Too tired to eat, I sat on the edge of the bed. Myrna pulled off the wet clothes, I sank backwards and fell into sleep.

―――――

Each morning at 6:30 Keith Everts and I pick up the early

weather reports and set out for Sunshine Village. Keith had taken his training in avalanche control at Glacier National Park, where thirty feet of snow falls annually on the slopes, threatening travellers on the Trans-Canada Highway and the Canadian Pacific main line. At Roger's Pass, avalanches are shot down by army gunners while the highway and railroad are temporarily closed.

At Sunshine, the valley is too narrow to use artillery. Instead, we bomb the slidepaths with charges dropped from a helicopter. Then, a government catskinner clears the road of snow and debris between the highway and a main parking lot a few miles above it. On the ski hill itself we ski-test the dangerous areas for stability or blast them with dynamite to make them slide. Avalanche control, a combination of snow physics, intuition, and loud explosions, is more of an art than a science, a dubious and dangerous art, though a necessary one.

In the national parks there are a few skiers and snowshoers stranded or killed by slides each year. Aside from controlling slides on the road and ski hill, one of our main duties is to maintain an outdoor laboratory to try and predict dangerous conditions for backcountry visitors.

We bulled our way up the twisting road, battling the drifts, and dodging ski busses for a few miles, and pulled up in front of the snow research office at Sunshine Village.

Our office, a Panabode hut, is the most unpretentious of places, despite the importance of the work done there to ensure the safe operating of the ski hill. But the hut, though prone to vibrate like a tuning fork when the bulldozer starts up in the cat shed next door, is still classier than the office at Mount Norquay ski hill, which is located in the back room of the public rest rooms, an indication of the outfit's prestige at that resort. Through its thin walls there oft resounds a cacaphony of cloacal concussions, distracting a warden as he enters figures on a chart labelled "Abstract of the Wind," from readings taken on a more esoteric anemometer.

At our office, Keith and I pulled on our stiff ski mountaineering boots and went out to get skied up. Boards on, we headed up the lift, then carved our way downhill through a stretch of deep powder snow that had fallen the night before, headed for the snow research plot, set in a wind-free meadow.

On most days, Sunshine's name commends itself mainly in irony, for the sun is more longed for than present, as it peers through chinks in dark clouds, driven by the lash of a cold wind.

But that morning was clear and calm, and glancing skyward, I congratulated myself once again for my shrewd choice of occupation. Looking at the sweep of powder snow, I reminded myself that most people have to pay dearly for the privilege of riding a lift up to slide down an untracked hill like that, while for me it was part of my daily work.

Nothing is more seductive to a mountain warden than twenty centimetres of angel's down, causing him to drool slightly and gaze at it with glazed eyeballs, eyeballs that no longer seem to notice the ugly steel cables and lift towers scarring the mountain horizon. There is a terrible lust in the heart to put a track in that virgin white. A ski in such powder is a planing wing, floating, half-buried, in the white surf, with the rushing hiss of pinions cleaving the sky.

Keith danced and floated down through the larch, yipping and yahooing. But your reporter is a rather unpretty sight in the deep snow, a troll in wonderland. I tend to run silent and run deep like a U-boat, just the ski goggles protruding. I leaned back slightly to keep the tips from crash diving under a submerged log as I carved my abominable S-turns. I felt like a bird, ungainly and long-winged like a buzzard, but a bird nonetheless. The spray flew up in our faces, melting in the corners of our eyes as we came down through the trees to the fenced-off enclosure of the snow research plot.

Inside the fence, a narrow pathway leads between the snow measurement stakes to the precipitation gauge and the thermometers, protected in their screened housings.

This is Keith's element. Not only does he relish the feel of skis in snow, but the medium itself seems to hold a powerful fascination for him. On his rounds of the hill, he constantly pokes into the depths, probing for weaknesses in the pack or, bending over, he will examine the crust with his bare fingers. By the instruments, the wind gauge, the storm stake, and the thermometers, he can tell some of the secrets of what the snow pack is doing, for the pack is never as static or immovable as it looks. It's an elastic, stretching, contracting, hardening or softening, beast of white. The cells, the snow crystals, that make it up, are constantly aging, packing down under the weight of the new crystals of fresh snow.

In a snow pit dug in an undisturbed part of the enclosure, we autopsied, bisected, and examined the beast, taking its pulse, trying to predict where and when it might move.

We graded the crystals with a metal grid and a magnifying

259

glass, seeing at first hand the metamorphosis that changes stellar crystals into round forms. The ball-bearing shape of these crystals, formed in a layer, makes a natural escalator down which a whole mountainside of snow can slide.

Keith located the different layers in the pack, taking a sample to measure it for density, and would measure the resistance of the layer by poking it with either his fist, his knuckles, his finger or a pencil.

In the blue-walled pit an avalanche man can find the different layers of snow that radiate out for miles on the valley sides. The pit is the nerve centre, the ganglion of the sleeping beast. The researcher watches the layers, deciding when the weakness is critical enough to justify stabilizing with high explosives, and tests his theories in the field by ski stabilizing parts of the hill, watching to see how the snow behaves under the cutting edge of the ski, his long scalpel.

We poled down over the flats, headed for a ski lift that would take us up to check out one of the avalanche slopes. Halfway there the bright mood of the morning was soured by an acrid, soul-searing stink that drifted up from the bed of Sunshine Creek, below the sewage treatment plant whose effluent enters the creek at the point.

"Sooooooo-eee! Must be a big weekend at Sunshine."

"Wow," I agreed. "That stink would gag a maggot."

I don't intend here to burden the reader with a blow by blow account of the controversy surrounding the alleged pollution of Sunshine Creek. Being a layman, I can't endorse the data of scientists and health inspectors, or refute the claims of Sunshine executives without consigning the reader to a fever swamp of polemic, and possibly floundering, myself, in the quicksand of a libel suit. Being a layman, I can only be led by my own nose.

Sunshine had plans in the works for a multi-million-dollar development and it soon became obvious that the Minister of Indian Affairs and Northern Development, whose ministry runs Parks Canada, was in favour of approving the proposals. This despite the protests of thousands of conservationists, and the opposition of park conservation staff, including the Warden Service. What particularly galls the conservationists is the fact that the resort is being expanded, despite a promise made in 1970 that there would be no further ski lifts built in the fragile alpine meadows around the resort.

As I write this deathless prose, the development proposals have been approved by the Minister.

To wildly understate the case, the duplicity in high places has seriously undermined Parks Canada's credibility as a defender of the environment, while the politicians responsible have been transferred to new portfolios, leaving civil servants holding a rather smelly looking bag.

I wrinkled my nose at Sunshine Creek. We had a less flattering name for it, bestowed by a cursing catskinner who had the misfortune of bogging his bulldozer in the creek bed one winter, and if I had my way, that's the name that would appear on the map today.

Keith disagreed. "I think they should call it Progress Creek. You can't stop progress."

"You're right, Keith. All you can do is try."

A hundred or so skiers were lined up at the lift. The volunteer ski patrol was hard at work, skidding the first casualties of the day down to the first aid shack in their rescue toboggans.

We got in line, unnoticed by the locals who were familiar with the Warden Service, but eyed by the tourists that come from far and wide to ski at the famous resort.

A warden in full mountaineering garb is an unglamorous thing to see, looking good only to another warden, who knows that his partner is a man he can depend on to save his ass, should he place it temporarily in hock to God. Particularly on a ski hill, wardens clash violently with the fluorescent colours and hotdog demeanour of the young downhill skier.

"What the hell is that?" asked one young pilgrim, pointing to my skis.

"That's a touring binding."

"Really? Looks pretty weird, man."

It's true the binding isn't the greatest thing for downhill skiing. Keith, who works full time on the hill, had brought his own skis with step-in bindings. I explained to the skier that my boots and cable bindings were issued mainly for ski mountaineering. The department wouldn't supply us with step-in bindings. The touring bindings allowed heel movement for climbing on the skis.

"Climbing! Jeez. Whyuncha stay on the lifts like a white man?"

The poor fellow's range of vision was limited only to a horizon punctured by lift towers. Rising over his puzzled brow were many more ranges of mountains, the home of ski mountaineers, all of whom are prayerfully thankful for the above buffoon's limited vision.

My bindings were attached to a pair of fairly soft-nosed fibreglass skis, which heavyweights like me need to plane upward, out of the bottomless crud encountered on wild mountainsides, unpacked, ungroomed, and uncontrolled, except by howling winds, snowslides, ptarmigan, and the odd cougar.

On the ski hill, you could get by with a pair of those plastic snow skates that K-Tel supplies for $1.49, provided they are equipped with razor-sharp edges to help you turn them on the glare ice of the ski hill. The hill is packed hard by the expensively tailored boards of your 2,500 ski buddies, into whom you are bound to collide at intervals, if you're not careful. And the hill is polished to a high gloss by the way-out-of-control, nylon-jumpsuited novice—whose nylon suit, as he/she slides downhill on the ass at fifty miles per hour, headed for compound fractures, offers no friction to slow down the terrifying descent.

The hotdogger was right about the bindings, though. On a ski hill, step-in safety bindings are absolutely essential, as all downhill skiers know. That way, when some maniac blasts across the slope and inadvertently cross checks you, he will merely knock you off of your skis, instead of knocking you out of your boots.

Still, I remembered the last ski school I'd attended, when an instructor laboured at teaching us how to ski pretty, trying to undo the damage done by Peter Fuhrmann, who teaches you to ski like a rock in an ugly Austrian crouch, the mountaineer's belligerent, unwavering, balls-out approach to the horribly crusted crud. The instructor had thrown up his poles in despair watching Warden Monrad Kjorlien, a former cross-country ski champion, who out-skied all of us riding an ancient pair of Head 220s with twenty-year-old, lace-up leather boots. He skied in antique bear-trap bindings, the heels of his boots elegantly un-anchored, lifted casually up and down as he poled along on the flats, while the rest of us, clad in orange anoraks, shuffled along like a conga line of spastic pumpkins in our stiff plastic ski-mountaineering boots.

On the descent, Monrad had switched at random from the modern parallel turn to the obscure Tellemark used by a generation of thirty years ago. That generation learned to ski the hard way, in leather boots, which made for strong balance and a vestige of caution. The new skier starts out in mid-calf, rock-hard plastic boots, which encourages him to ski too fast too early, producing, if he should fall too hard, a boot-top fracture instead of the occasional turned ankle or broken fibula of more leisurely years, when there was less hustle and less hype in the sport of downhill skiing.

The young skier and I rode up the lift, a study in contrasts, he in his jet-set getup, I in my green woollen knickers, which allow lots of knee movement when pumping up steep grades on the climbing skins. Wool is the fabric for mountain wear because it keeps you warm when it's wet. But my ensemble, canvas anorak, knickers, wool knee socks, was ugly in the extreme on the ski hill, where sex appeal is often more important than the skiing.

We got off the lift. Noticing a Day-glo darling eyeballing my outfit, I turned to show her a bit of well-muscled calf. She was not impressed and skied off with the hotdogger, whose skin-tight red pants, adorned with a yellow police-type stripe down the leg, were gathered into a blatant codpiece at the loins. Speed boys, speed's the thing, combined with out front brazen bravado.

Keith and I skied over to the powder caches and picked hand charges and blasting caps before continuing on to the top of the avalanche slopes that threaten a main ski run. We stopped by a warning sign that reads AVALANCHE DANGER. AREA CLOSED.

The untracked surface made the slope tempting to skiers in the area, and one or two tracks showed where people had ignored the signs and gotten down without having been caught in a slide.

But the day was warm and bright. The upper layer of snow oozed water when I squeezed a handful in my fist, and down in the pack was a weakness in the snow, a layer of hoar frost that had formed one cold morning and had then been covered by a fall of fresh crystals. The wind had built a long cornice above the steep avalanche slopes, a potential trigger of a major spring slide.

Down below, safe from the outrun, the ski patrol was guarding the approach to the valley to keep skiers out of the way while we blasted. I reached into my bag of tricks and handed Keith a half-pound charge, watching while he rigged a blasting cap and a two-minute, thirty-second fuse. He slipped on a fuse igniter and pulled the wire. There was a spluttering noise and smoke trailed up the fuse. As usual, a spark flared out and burned yet another hole in my anorak. Keith checked his watch and lobbed the charge down into the snow.

Two minutes later there was a muffled boom. We peered over the cornice and beheld a dark crater on the white field. Nothing had slid.

"I guess that means it's safe," I said.

"Think so? Let's try something else first. I got an uneasy feeling about this slope."

I peered at him suspiciously. Although the man is trained in engineering and is scrupulous in recording his data and charting his snow profiles, I secretly believe that he relies more on intuition than physics half the time, when it comes to gauging what is dangerous and what is safe.

We dug three shot holes in the cornice, put four pounds of explosive in each one and connected them to a long length of prima cord, armed with a cap and safety fuse. The prima cord, exploding at a speed of 22,000 feet per second, would detonate the charges almost simultaneously, driving a gigantic knife of energy into the cornice.

I slipped the igniter onto the fuse and checked my watch.

"There's only one thing to remember about government explosives, Marty."

"Yeah? What's that?" I pulled the igniter and looked up.

"It's supplied by the lowest bidder. And now, I suggest we make like the birds."

We got out of there and took cover over the ridge. Three thunderous explosions ripped the air in a ragged burst. A cloud of snow washed over us and the sound of the shot echoed and rolled from peak to peak. We skied back down to the cornice. There were three black holes in the snow, but the cornice, though weakened, was still intact.

We decided to place another shot closer to the edge of the cornice. I tied into a climbing rope and began to work my way out toward the edge, belayed by Keith.

The day was turning hot, the sky a bright blue plate. A palpable wave of heat reflected up into my face from the glazed surface. The late April weather was more like June. Frozen waves of mountains rolled away as far as the eye could see.

I took another step toward the edge, already a little farther out than I needed to be, testing the strength of it with one ski. Across the valley was the blue wall of Lookout, the ridge where a skier had fallen to his death earlier that month.

An image came into my mind of the camera strap on the dead man's wrist. He had been travelling alone, and the blue day was more beautiful than he had ever imagined back in the

States. He had wanted a picture to show someone at home, to share that day with. He had worked his way around the end of the fence, perhaps, over the rocks. There were no doubt flakes of rock and dirt blown out onto that lip which, to a greenhorn, would make it look solid and secure. The prospect of a fine view had lured him out into thin air. But it was life, I realized then, that he was bent on capturing.

I stopped, not really sure of my own ground, probing the snow with a ski pole. Suddenly, it went right through, as if the snow was merely a white mist, and made a perfect tube leading into space. I knew then that I had found the western edge, that final frontier here on a great divide, between being and nothingness, entered through the pan of this celestial trap of snow. I knew that I would fall.

There was a muted crack of sound behind me. I half turned and saw a jagged blue line widening between me and the solid ground, saw Keith already bracing himself in the sitting belay, teeth clenched on the stem of his pipe. Then the snow and I were riding the wind.

I felt a terrifying exhilaration, the sense of being swept up in immense gravity's powerful arms, of being caressed by a huge and irresistible hand. Then my teeth jarred together, and I was sitting in my harness, watching the cornice hit the snow face with the force of a pile driver.

A hollow boom resounded in the pack and a crack opened across the slope. The whole thing began to move with a squeaking, creaking, hiss of sound, gathering speed, throwing up slabs of snow, two feet thick, as it entered a narrow neck between rocks, then went bursting out onto the flats below like a gigantic surf.

In a few minutes it had stopped. The clouds of snow settled, and the jagged shapes of the enjambed slabs were frozen, immobile, as if to deny their previous motion.

Swaying in the air, I worked my skis off, letting the poles dangle from my wrist straps. With a ski in each hand for a dagger, I kicked steps up the wall of snow, helped by Keith, who I could hear breathing hard up above.

"I think you owe me a beer," he said, as I worked my way over the top, encumbered by several pounds of snow that had been jammed down my neck.

"At least." I looked back over the edge.

The pack had been undermined by streams of meltwater and it had slid right to the ground. Nobody would be skiing it again this season.

There were glimpses of green heather through the white smear, a sign of coming spring.

"Seen enough?" said Keith.

"I think so."

We packed it up and skied back down to the road.

Epilogue

"The woods are lovely, dark and deep,
But I have promises to keep,
And miles to go before I sleep,
And miles to go before I sleep."

Robert Frost

The days lengthened toward spring, the snows were melting in
wide swaths along the road, and the first green blades of grass
made a tentative showing here and there in our yard. Then the
weather turned cold again, as if denying its promise, and a
few inches of powder snow fell on the bare spots.

All day I had been restless. Myrna and Paul had gone into
the city on a shopping trip, and without them there, I found
the empty house depressing. Finally, I closed the book I was
reading and put on my ski clothes. Something was calling me
into the backcountry and there would be a moon that night to
light my way. It would be the last trip of the season, before the
bottom dropped out of the snow and the sun turned it to slush.

I went out into the back yard, waxed the bottoms of my
scarred cross-country skis, stepped into the bindings, and
poled off through the poplar woods to where I struck the trail
leading north.

I loved the lightness of the short leather boots, the willowy
suppleness of the hickory touring skis, and the freedom to
move the body, unhampered by heavy alpine equipment. I
glided along the downhill stretches, and moved at a short dog
trot up the easier grades.

As I went, I read the calligraphy that the game had left in
the snow, noting the tracks of elk, and stopping to examine the

remains of a young mule deer taken a few days before by a cougar. With a rap of my heavy knife I broke open the femur and saw the unhealthy grey marrow of an animal too weak to survive. It had been a rough winter for the big game, with the snow deep and crusted by the wind. The predators moved easily over that surface, but the deer would break through and flounder, unable to escape. The bighorns and goats had fared best, staying close to the margin of snow near the tree line, where the wind blows patches of the range clear, and where the steep terrain offers safety from wolves and cougars.

"Yip, yip owoooo," the coyotes sang. I could hear them madly chortling, throwing their voices back and forth across the valley, making musical howls that ended in a succession of screaming yaps.

I came to the trail and broke into a long, sliding stride. The shadows lengthened and the spruce grew faint against the darkening sky. The alpen glow of coming night shone on the ridge of Cascade. In two miles, no sound but my hard breathing, and the swish of snow as a silver flood cascaded down from a spruce. The coming night was full of a hostile cold.

I stopped to rest on a bridge and immediately felt the need to change my sweaty shirt. The barometer had been steady when I left home, with a sixteen mile trip ahead of me. Time to take off my skis, make tea, and eat.

In my pack I carried a billy tin and a primus stove. I trampled a flat place in the snow and started the stove, which was soon roaring like a blow torch. With a string, I lowered the tin into an opening in the ice and drew water for boiling. Scalding tea laced with rum would provide some anti-freeze for the chill. The can was as cold as dry ice. I could feel the bite of it through my wool mitts. I wouldn't stay long where there was nothing but silence and the precise beauty of snow and black water.

There was a movement down the creek, which caught my attention; a flutter of wings and a splash in the water. Then a dark bird popped out of the stream, penguin-style, and landed on the ice with an alacrity that made me laugh aloud. It moved up the bank towards where I sat on my pack. I was ignored, I did not exist.

The water ouzel, or dipper, as it's called, bobbed anxiously up and down on the edge of the ice, its whole being trained on something I couldn't see in the darkening water. It was as if the thousands of miles of winter, stretching north to the pole, were meaningless, the towering mountains that hemmed the sky, the rolling sweep of the night cloud, and the hushed reach of the forest, were irrelevant to this one spark of life, which measures time on a flowing fulcrum, close to night, and the end of a long day's struggle to survive. The universe zoomed down to the eye of the bird, and passed through it in a beam of single intention, on a swimming insect in the dark stream. The ouzel dove in, and I saw it moving quickly over the bottom, as if swimming, but it was actually running over the rocks below, using its wings as flippers to push it forward. It popped out again on the bank, to swallow the meal, and it bobbed up and down silently in the snow, saluting its own ingeniousness. Then it flew downstream, following the faint light that shone on an open stretch of water below.

I toasted its departure with a cup of hot tea flavoured with overproof, and ate a cold sandwich while I waited for the moon to come up. *Can you see the red coal of my pipe, you stars a-way up there, lighting your own spinning fires in the black?*

The moon came up slowly, taking its own sweet time, and sent a silent rush of silver light across the water, over the black poplar limbs, and onto the antlers of one lonesome moose, which I was startled to discover watching me from the shadowy woods.

I shouldered my pack, stepped into the bindings, and slid back out onto the track. A great, horned owl followed me through the moonlight, gliding from tree to tree, watching to see what small creatures I might scare from cover.

In an hour I saw the peaked roof of a line shack shining up from the meadow below the trail but kept on going, missing the track at times, and falling through the snow to my knees. Something was drawing me on, across the steep slidepaths above the river, further into the backcountry.

Around midnight, I reached the narrow bridge over the creek and left the trail behind, breaking my way through deep snow for a few more minutes until I reached the cabin. I was not surprised, somehow, to see a pale crimson light flickering behind the frosted panes of the window. I had company. A spray of bright sparks flared out the black chimney pipe and faded out against the spruce that leaned over the snow-covered roof.

I stuck my skis upright in the snow and, taking off my pack, opened the door, feeling a rush of warm air steaming out to meet me, with the odour of buckskin and wet wool.

269

It was dark inside, but I could make out their faces, lit by the fire shining in the open door of the heater.

I took off my jacket and hung it on a hook, then sat down on the empty chair near the fire, feeling the heat on my face melting the ice out of my moustache. We sat for a moment, looking into the flames.

I handed Busby my bottle of rum.

"Well, it took you long enough to get here," he said, and took a drink.

"Hmmm. The travelling got pretty rough in spots. Nearly lost the trail in a few places. Slowed me down a tad."

The bottle went around the circle again. I took a long drink, and felt the sweet, slow burn of the spirits after hard work in the bite of a mountain night.

"So, young feller," he said at length. "Did you remember our bargain? And be careful how you answer."

They were quiet, watching, while I gazed into the fire, considering the reply.

"Yes. I had to change a lot of things around, places and dates, but it's all true. As much as I could tell without being sued into penury; as much of it as can be believed. I learned one thing, though, and it's a sad paradox. To tell the whole truth you have to write fiction."

"Uh huh," said Busby, "that's the trouble with life. Nobody believes in it until it's gone."

He took a pinch of snoose, mouthed it for a moment, and spat into the fire. "In the meantime, there's still mountains."

"Thank God for that."

"Best not leave it all up to God, pilgrim," said Pcyto softly.

The others nodded their assent.

"You said once that you wanted to hear more about us," said Busby.

"Yes."

He leaned forward then and held his gnarled hands out to the firelight, and the flames threw his shadow, magnified, onto the thick logs of the cabin wall. Then he began to weave a tale of high mountains and of proud men that rode among them, like princes surveying their estates, like lords high up in their strongholds, where only the wind could touch them, and where the world was free of pain and sorrow, and we were always young.

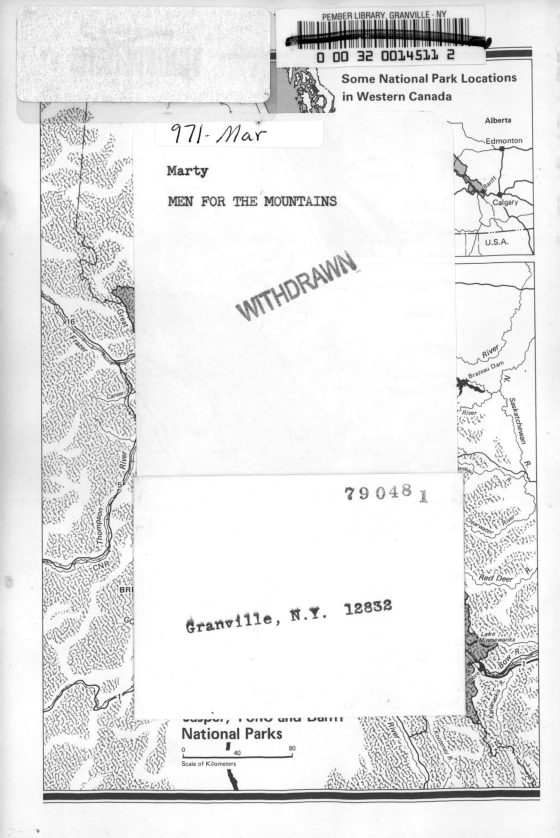

**Some National Park Locations
in Western Canada**

Alberta

Edmonton

Banff

Calgary

U.S.A.

Marty

MEN FOR THE MOUNTAINS

Jasper, Yoho and Banff
National Parks

0   40   80

Scale of Kilometers